Natural Resource Information for Economic Development

Natural Resource Information for Economic Development

by ORRIS C. HERFINDAHL

A STUDY SPONSORED BY THE LATIN AMERICAN INSTITUTE
FOR ECONOMIC AND SOCIAL PLANNING
AND RESOURCES FOR THE FUTURE, INC.

GA
51
H47

Published for **Resources for the Future, Inc.**
by **The Johns Hopkins Press, Baltimore, Maryland**

111705

Orris C. Herfindahl is a senior research associate with Resources for the Future.
Charts were drawn by Clare and Frank J. Ford.
The index was prepared by Rachel M. Johnson.

RFF staff editors: Henry Jarrett, Vera W. Dodds, Nora E. Roots,
Sheila M. Ekers.

Standard Book Number 8018-1026-4

Copyright © 1969 by The Johns Hopkins Press
Baltimore, Maryland 21218

All rights reserved

Manufactured in the United States of America

Library of Congress Catalog Card Number 69-15762

Preface

In nearly all countries development of natural resources plays a large part in general economic development, and this in turn depends to a large extent upon the quality and quantity of information upon which plans and programs can be based. Yet the provision of such information—such as maps and forest and mineral surveys—can be extremely costly in money and manpower; indeed, in nearly all instances the assembling of complete information, regardless of cost, would be an impossible task. Still, governments cannot proceed by guesswork. Large investments of money and time must be made in information.

Consequently, the strategy of collecting resources information is a matter of first importance, especially in developing countries. What kinds of data should be gathered, in what amounts, in what order of priority, and by what methods? When is it advantageous to delay development programs until more information is available, and when is it not?

Orris Herfindahl's study is concerned with this many-sided problem. It analyzes the effectiveness of various information-gathering programs under various circumstances, discusses current techniques, and offers some guidelines which governments may find useful in developing and executing programs suited to their particular needs. Although the study deals primarily with situations in Latin America, especially in Chile and Peru, it is designed also to be of interest and value in other parts of the world to both developing countries and more economically advanced countries interested in encouraging economic development.

The work was sponsored jointly by the Latin American Institute for Economic and Social Planning (ILPES) and Resources for the Future, Inc. Mr. Herfindahl, of the Resources for the Future staff, did most of his research while based for more than a year in Santiago at the offices of the Institute. Members of the Institute staff and government officials and university scholars in a number of Latin American countries collaborated in the study. Especially valuable contributions were made by Estevam Strauss and Carlos Plaza V. of the Institute.

The present study is one of several co-operative endeavors undertaken by ILPES and RFF. The English version of a book resulting from one of them—*The Water Resources of Chile*, by Nathaniel Wollman—was published recently for the two organizations by The Johns Hopkins Press. The Spanish version of this book will be published by ILPES in Chile.

We believe that the study of natural resource information requirements and opportunities presented in this book is a long step forward in a critically important area, and we hope that governments and private organizations will find it helpful in advancing national and international well-being.

CRISTÓBAL LARA BEAUTELL   JOSEPH L. FISHER
Latin American Institute for   *Resources for*
Economic and Social Planning   *the Future, Inc.*

Acknowledgments

The origin of this study dates back to 1964 when Irving K. Fox, then vice president of Resources for the Future, Inc., and the late Julio Melnick took some preliminary steps to map out a study of investment in natural resource information. I welcomed the opportunity to continue this exploration and to devote all of my time to the topic for a period of sixteen months in 1965 and 1966 with the Instituto Latinoamericano de Planificación Económica y Social as my host.

My thinking about the subject of this study dates back to my first effort to develop a view of the process of finding and developing mineral deposits. I was fortunate to be able to examine this process in India several years ago in a context very different from that to which my thinking was geared. My assignment in that country was to consider the very same problems as those studied in Latin America, but with reference only to the mineral industries. I hope that my Indian hosts will regard this study as a belated but more finished version of the tentative observations I made while there.

The subject of this study is at once very extensive and very narrow. It is narrow in that natural resource information and the development of the natural resource industries are only a small part of the problem of production and growth. But it is extensive because nature is very complex, and its study, even if oriented only to economic purposes, involves many specialties. This situation is reflected in my reliance on specialists of many types whose advice and aid have been indispensable for gaining some understanding of the problems facing natural resource information agencies in Latin America.

In Bolivia, Toni Hagen, Ian Hutchinson, and Henry Meyer, were helpful in the fields of petroleum and mineral exploration and forest products. João Paulo Velloso, of the Ministry of Planning in Brazil, provided an opportunity to examine its resource information problems. I am especially indebted to Newton Velloso Cordeiro for sharing his knowledge of Brazil's problems in the field of water resources.

Nilson A. Espino E. has kindly discussed the work of the Panama resources survey project with me. In Nicaragua, Fernando J. Montiel gave me an account of the survey recently started there.

Enrique Beltrán, head of the Instituto Mexicano de Recursos Naturales

Renovables, and Carlos Quintana, now Director General of the Economic Commission for Latin America, gave generously of their knowledge of Mexican problems, as did also Fausto García Castañeda of the Consejo de Recursos Naturales no Renovables.

Two agencies that have activities in a number of Latin American countries in the field of natural resource surveys are the Natural Resources Division of the Inter American Geodetic Survey (U.S. Army) and the Natural Resources Unit of the Organization of American States. It has been very helpful to discuss these problems frequently with Peter Duisberg, Chief of the Natural Resources Division of the IAGS, and members of his staff, including Gilbert Caughran, Douglas Elliott, Roberto Gomez, Leon Laitman, and Louis Guzman. Wolfram Drewes, Arthur Heyman, Alan Randall, and Kirk Rodgers, of the OAS, have contributed much from their experience.

Peru and Chile each has a general resource information agency. These agencies and their relations with older specialized information agencies have had a special interest for me since they provide some actual experience with new forms of organization in the field of information. In the case of Peru, José Lizárraga R., head of the Oficina Nacional de Evaluación de Recursos Naturales, has responded to my questions with the greatest frankness and has permitted me to consult with members of his staff. I have had the same pleasant experience with Miguel Ruiz-Tagle P., head of the Instituto de Recursos Naturales in Chile, who, because he is located in the same city in which I have been working, probably has received an unduly large number of visits from me. In each country, the specialized resource information agencies have been most helpful in discussions of their problems.

I am indebted to Reynaldo Börgel O., of the University of Chile, for giving me the opportunity to participate as an observer in the deliberations of the Committee on Basic Natural Resources of the Pan American Institute of Geography and History, in August 1966, in Mexico City.

Adolfo Dorfman and the members of his natural resources group in ECLA have been a constant help not only because of their technical competence but also because of their knowledge of Latin America.

Within the Instituto, I can mention only a few of the many people who have aided me. Cristóbal Lara B., Norberto González, and Osvaldo Sunkel have given me the benefit of their incisive comments on several occasions. Francis Shomaly has seen to it that physical facilities and secretarial help were always more than adequate. I have worked most closely with three persons, however. The first is Estevam Strauss, who has been interested in the problems of this study from the start. My indebtedness to him is indicated at only two points in the text, but actually I have drawn on his experience and my discussions with him at many points in the study. Carlos Plaza V. has been an always available source of information on natural resource activities in Latin America and on Latin American problems in general. Unlike some bilingual persons, he has been willing to converse in his native language, a valuable opportunity for me. Cornelio Marchán has performed a wide range of tasks and is responsible for the assembly of a great deal of the information on which the study is based. More important, however, has been the opportunity to get to know well a young Latin American economist and to compare our views on a wide range of problems.

Exceedingly helpful comments on an early draft of the study were received from a varied group of experts, including W. Keith Buck, Gabriel Dengo, Wolfram U. Drewes, Peter Duisberg, Edgar S. Dunn, Jr., James Eckles, Irving K. Fox, Morris E. Garnsey, Arthur Heyman, Henry Jarrett, David L. Jones, Allen V. Kneese, Christian de Laet, Walter Langbein, Roland McKean, Vincent McKelvey, Donald MacPhail, R. S. Nakra, Michael Nelson, Harvey S. Perloff, Alan C. Randall, Anthony Scott, R. M. Strock, Robert L. Thomson, Gilbert White, and Nathaniel Wollman.

Finally, I am grateful to Joseph L. Fisher and Cristóbal Lara B., heads, respectively, of Resources for the Future and the Instituto Latinoamericano de Planificación Económica y Social, for making this study possible and facilitating the work in every possible way.

Only the author is responsible for what is said in this study. The fact that Resources for the Future and the Instituto have sponsored the work indicates neither agreement nor disagreement with the views expressed here.

July 1968   ORRIS C. HERFINDAHL

Contents

List of Tables

Introduction

The development and improved use of natural resources obviously can make an important contribution to the economic development of a country. Before more resources can be brought into use or their present productivity raised, however, additional data on their physical characteristics and related economic and social information must be assembled. The constant stream of decisions on the additions to be made to this stock of information poses a difficult and challenging problem in management. On the one hand, there are pressures toward the amassing of a great deal of information in order to facilitate later decisions and to reduce uncertainty, but clearly it is possible to go so far in this direction that much information will be developed prematurely. Some may never be used. On the other hand, the pressure for action opens the way to premature commitments to resource development projects without enough information at hand to evaluate them adequately.

To avoid both of these dangers, those concerned with the economic development of a country must be reasonably certain that additional gain will, in fact, accrue to economic development if they spend a certain proportion of their budget on producing more information about natural resources.

Some key questions are: How much should be spent on each type of resource? What parts of a country should be worked on first? There are various ways by which certain types of information can be gained; what should be the allocation among them? These questions cannot profitably be discussed without considering other elements of the situation in which the natural resource information will be used. Some attention must therefore be given to information which is different in kind from that dealing with the physical characteristics of natural resources but which must be coupled with it to use it effectively. Similarly, effective use of natural resource information requires some attention to organizational arrangements. No simple, direct answers to these questions are possible. However, it is the hope of the author, who is not a technical specialist but an economist, that in the following pages at least the groundwork will be laid for finding useful answers.

The first order of business will be a discussion of the role of natural resources in economic development, including an analysis of the process by which information comes to be generated and related finally to decisions on investment and production. With this common framework of ideas, we can proceed to examine some of the ways of gaining information about natural resources and become acquainted with the capabilities and limitations of that information and the cost of acquiring it.

Some guidelines for decisions on natural resource information programs are proposed, considering such matters as time and the productivity of capital, location, and other factors needed to make effective use of information about natural resources. Organizational problems are especially difficult in this area. They are discussed first in general terms and then with special attention to the problems of small countries and to the lessons to be had from the experiences of Chile and Peru, whose natural resource information programs have much to offer that is instructive.

The analysis of these problems turns out to be independent, to a considerable extent, of the more general views one holds on the process of economic development and the measures appropriate to its pursuit. Perhaps the main reason for this is the fact that, as elsewhere, the necessity to economize is present in the management of resource survey activity; thus, problems of economizing tend to get analyzed with the aid of the same body of principles regardless of political persuasion or one's theory of social development.

The appropriate division of functions between government and private enterprise does not bulk very large in this discussion of natural resource survey problems, for many of the functions served by such information can be performed only or better by government. It is clear, of course, that in the process of developing resource information it will sometimes be convenient for government to purchase services from the private sphere.

The reader will note that the ensuing discussion envisions a system in which decisions and actions are constantly revised on the basis of new information. We do not end up with a prescription for determining, once and for all, a program for natural resource information. Instead, the result is a series of suggestions concerning a way by which the information program gradually can be directed more closely to needs. It is impossible to know definitely whether this way of proceeding comes close to an optimum path through time, but very likely it does not. We can be more confident that incrementalism (that is, a series of adjustments based at each point in time on what is known with reasonable assurance) does enable us to avoid the possibly large losses that may be incurred when action is based on unreliable attempts to forecast far into the future. In line with this reflection, it is important to search out and develop information by which the effectiveness of policy can be evaluated, for only thus can mistakes be corrected. The small facet of development policy explored here is no exception. The keynote is successive change as demands change, resources change, and capabilities change.

All countries share the problem of how to manage the activities that produce information about natural resources, but this study is written with the problems of developing countries in mind and, in particular, those of Latin American countries. Latin American experience has been drawn on at a number of points, both to illustrate and to provide evidence for the assessment of certain organizational arrangements.

I: The Role of Natural Resources in Economic Development

In order to clarify the purpose of gathering information about natural resources, it is necessary to be clear about their economic significance. Failure to follow the dictates of common sense in thinking about the economic significance of natural resources may result in considerable mismanagement. The purpose here is not to put forward a theory of economic development or even to indicate adherence to one of the many current versions. Instead, the much more limited goal is to point out some aspects of the exploitation of natural resources that are important and with which any useful view of the process of economic growth ought to be consistent.

Natural Resources as a Capital Stock

To start with, no particular type of natural resource is essential to a high level of national income or to economic progress. We can assert with confidence that a country's endowment of natural resources need not exercise a determining influence on the course of its national income over time—if it is able to trade. "All" that is necessary for economic progress is the availability of a substantial quantity of services of capital and labor—with a considerable part of the capital embodied in persons—plus a social system with certain characteristics favorable to systematic improvement of production practices. And the more capital per person the better. The truth of this observation is evident from the economic success of countries with limited natural resources and the success of countries with greatly different natural endowments. To enjoy economic success, a country must have *access* to natural resources, but this can be had through trade with other nations with a different or better natural endowment. It is not necessary to economic progress that a nation have iron ore, good soil, forests, or any particular one of the natural resources.

At the same time, it is clear that possession of natural resources can have a favorable influence on the level of income and its growth. Generally speaking, more is to be preferred to less in things economic, and this is no less true of natural resources. Some writers, it seems, hold the view that lack of variety in natural resources leading to a "one-crop economy" is inimical to economic development. So far as economic history is concerned, the argument probably has some validity. It may well be that where methods and institutions were geared to the exploitation of one crop, it was difficult to make the changes necessary to bring about a type of economic progress capable of accommodating a population larger than that associated with the one-crop industry. Be that as it may, natural resources that are worth anything get used, and few countries have chosen deliberately not to use the services of a natural resource in order to avoid specialization. Furthermore, in this day and age when we know how to avoid some of the undesirable features of specialization, there seems little reason to postpone use of a natural resource in order to force diversification.

At the same time, when one compares diversification with greater specialization in a situation where the total value of natural resources is the same in both cases, diversification is probably advantageous. This is clearly the case if a government believes that trade involves undue penalties, perhaps because it requires rapid adjustment to changes originating outside the country or because it threatens to bring in foreign influences considered to be undesirable. In such a case a country will be fortunate indeed if it possesses a variety of natural resources, and the more the better. But few governments have chosen deliberately to avoid full utilization of the services of a natural resource in order to avoid entanglement with foreign trade.

From the economic point of view, natural resources are simply a part of the capital stock of a country; they are to be regarded as pieces of "equipment" which render productive services. Hence, the more a country has of them and the higher their quality, the better off it will be, other things being equal. Natural resources have their peculiarities, however, and it is from these that comes such unity as is possessed by the problem of assembling pertinent information.

Locational distribution plays a dominant role in the exploitation of natural resources. They are movable only to a limited extent as compared with other forms of capital, although their products can and do move long distances. The quantity of the resource at particular locations generally is limited, although from a practical point of view some materials or potential materials—sea water and granite, for example—are without limit relative to demand.

Since man had no part in the placement of natural resources, we can not go, say, to a registry of past natural resource production to find out how much was produced and where it was stored. Instead, information about their location and characteristics must be painstakingly accumulated as it is needed.

These two characteristics of natural resources—that you must accept them as they are since they were not made to the user's specifications and that information about them is incomplete—make it convenient to think of them as partly finished capital goods. That is, additional outlays are required before the natural resources can yield their productive services. Part of these outlays is made along with the release of the services of the natural resource. In agricultural operations, for example, expenditure on labor and tractor services is a necessary part of the immediate production process. But another part of the outlays is in the nature of a long-term investment, in the sense that the fruits of this expenditure are enjoyed not immediately but only over the periods that follow. This investment outlay is of two sorts. First, related pieces of capital may need to be constructed: land may need a drainage facility, or a mine a shaft. But second, investment outlays are necessary to find out where the resource is, how much of it is there, and what characteristics it has. From the point of view of the production process, these outlays are investment just as is the outlay on a mine shaft.

If, in view of these two types of investment outlays, it is proper to think of natural resources as unfinished capital goods, it is clear that investment in information on natural resources should be subject to the same general criteria that govern investment in any type of capital good. The question always should be whether the streams of services or products associated with the investment opportunity are worth more than the outlays so associated. To make this comparison, we must recognize in some way the fact that investment in any particular project involves foregoing the opportunity of making other investments which could have yielded a future surplus over the outlays. The generalized measure of the productivity of investment is expressed by the percentage rate of return on investment. The way we make sure that a particular investment is not using up funds that would yield more elsewhere is to require that an investment yield not only enough to cover the outlays, but enough to cover them with interest. The simplest and best way to determine this by calculation is to accumulate or discount all revenues and outlays to the same point in time, using the rate of return to investment in the economy at large as the discount rate.[1]

After doing this, a surplus of revenues over costs indicates that the particular investment opportunity is yielding at least as much as investment in general. Unfortunately, the existence of a surplus does not show that the investment opportunity is yielding as much as possible. Perhaps a better way of using the opportunity could be found, one that would yield a higher return. This problem, by the way, is a very serious one in the

---

[1] For an explanation of the process of discounting, see Appendix to this chapter.

administration of publicly owned resources because of the absence of a market for the resource. While the private owner of farm land knows that his operations plan must yield something over and above the interest on the market value of his land, no such quantity exists in the case of many public investment opportunities. Thus a plan that demonstrates that one particular way of using a dam site yields a positive net present value tells us only that this plan would be better than "doing nothing." It can not be concluded that the plan is in fact desirable until something like the full range of all the different ways of using the site have been explored and the calculations made. The plan with the highest net present value for the site should win the day.

Product and outlays should be understood to include *all* real products and costs (valued in money), even though there is no money payment and even though it may be difficult to value them. Investment in works of infrastructure are to be evaluated and do not constitute an exception. Nor are government employees costless outlays unless the real product sacrificed (i.e., not produced) because of their work for the government is zero.[2] For some types of projects, outlays on infrastructure and government employees will be an important part of the total. The proper social evaluation of the investment will require their inclusion. In short, society is interested in social product and cost, which in some cases (monopoly, for example) will differ from private product and cost.

The numerical evaluation of natural resource information outlays is difficult or impossible in many cases. Nevertheless, this model of investment decision should be our guide. It is the purpose of this study to point out some of the implications of the general investment criteria for the particular problem of investment in natural resources.

How Large Should the Natural Resource Industries Be?
Let us return to the question of the general role of natural resources in economic development. The facts that quantities of any resource at particular locations are limited and that quantities within a country may be

---

[2] Note that this is not quite the same as saying, ". . . unless the value of their alternative employment is zero." The question is not whether the particular employee in a particular case would or would not be employed in the absence of employment by the government, but whether the hiring of one more person by government means that nongovernmental product is lower than it otherwise would have been. It might be noted also that if, say, 5 per cent of the labor force will be unemployed with or without the increased employment by the government, there is a real alternative cost attached to hiring one more employee even though that particular employee was drawn from the pool of the unemployed. This would imply, incidentally, that the forces that determine the percentage of the labor force that is unemployed in a "normally" functioning economy are independent of the ratio of governmental to private employment.

small[3] in relation to the demand for products produced with the aid of the natural resources, have an important consequence for the development of the "natural resource industries."[4] This is that for many countries and many products the size of the domestic industry is dependent mainly or wholly on supply conditions that are confronted with a demand curve that is practically horizontal. That is, the price at which the country can sell the natural resource product is not affected, for all practical purposes, by the quantity it puts on the market. Consider, for example, a country that is exporting a natural resource product to a world market that it does not dominate. The quantity that it ought to produce in the years immediately ahead certainly should not depend on domestic demand for the product, but only on the predicted long-run world price (which does not change rapidly for commodities whose markets are not too much interfered with) and, most important of all, the scope and richness of the units of the natural resources that could be brought into production. What domestic demand should determine in this case is the allocation of sales between the domestic and foreign markets. The situation is the same, *mutatis mutandis*, if a country is an unimportant importer of a natural resource product. That is, its domestic production should depend only on the world price and the size and richness of the domestic natural resource involved.

A product may be on neither an import nor an export basis, and there may be quite a large range of prices over which this is so. In this case the problem of production planning within the range of prices over which there are neither imports nor exports (and it makes no difference whether the planners are private or public) is to match output to demand in such a way that price is just sufficient to induce supply for the quantity demanded. But even here there is likely to be a difference between the natural resource and other products in that the qualities and quantities of a particular domestic natural resource can easily be so limited that an increased demand will raise the price of the commodity in question to the import point; and this increase may be substantial if transfer costs are large. Sizable downward movements are less likely for natural resources that must be found, although surprises can occur which are not completely unrelated to increases in demand, and these surprises can result in declines in price.

To reiterate, the proper rate of activity for natural resource industries will depend heavily on the quantity and quality of the natural resources

[3] That is, small in relevant economic terms. The relevant terms are not a simple matter from the conceptual point of view.
[4] There are not very many "purely" natural resource industries. In this study the term simply means an industry that produces a product in whose production some natural resource plays an important role.

involved, in contrast to "ordinary" commodities whose supplies can be increased or decreased with little change in cost.

But isn't all of the preceding discussion obvious? Apparently not. For example, not a few government officials will give assent to the view that exploration and development effort should be the greatest for those mineral products whose trade balances are the worst; thus, if a country imports all of its lead and zinc, it should look diligently for deposits of these metals. But this is illogical, since the prospects for finding these metals may be very poor. Indeed, the fact that domestic deposits good enough for exploitation have not been found is an excellent indication that this is the case, granted that it is not conclusive. If one is looking for a simple criterion by which to allocate exploration effort, he could begin by making a trial allocation to those directions of exploration that have been experiencing recent success. A less satisfactory criterion, but one somewhat easier to apply, would be to allocate according to the value of deposits by industry (or perhaps net profits), on the ground that the known presence of valuable deposits indicates past success in finding them and that past success points, imperfectly, to future success. However, once thinking along this line has begun, a continued questioning of why money should be spent in one way rather than another should lead quickly to the right answer, which is that prospective return is the proper criterion.

More or less the same error is often committed in the name of "saving imports." The thought seems to be that if a country consumes a great deal of petroleum, for example, it should devote much effort to increasing its own output of petroleum or petroleum substitutes, because this will save imports. Very likely so, but we need to remind ourselves that the fundamental objectives of a country's economic activity embrace the size, growth, and distribution of its real income. "Saving imports" is a good thing only insofar as it contributes to these objectives. So far as size of income is concerned, it will pay to undertake an action that saves imports (say oil) only if the value of the additional oil produced is greater than the value of the products a country no longer can produce because it is devoting more of its productive power to oil.

In a system in which prices reflect costs (including competitive return on investment), such allocations of investment can be made on the basis of prospective profits. Once again, the question is whether a prospective investment will pay: that is, will the product be worth to society what has to be given up (the value of other products) in order to undertake the investment? Thus, changes in circumstances will make it advisable to "save imports" at certain times, but to "spend" or, rather, increase them at others.

One last example of how not to allocate investment, including investment in information, to the natural resource industries: By using techniques more or less sophisticated, depending on the equipment, data, and audacity available, it is possible to calculate the "requirements" for the products of the various natural resource industries for some years in the future, with the calculation necessarily incorporating flat assumptions about many things that are as yet beyond prediction. So far as our problem is concerned, the use of the word "requirements" provides a verbal trap for many otherwise sophisticated people in that it tends to suggest that domestic outputs ought to be adequate to meet "requirements." This would be a correct position for an isolated economy, provided it is understood that "requirements" really means demand, and that the quantity demanded ought to depend on the cost of producing the product acting through the medium of price. But in an economy that can trade, domestic production need not match domestic demand. What the production of any particular product should be depends on the whole range of productive opportunities, including those of the natural resource product in question, the terms on which goods can be imported or exported, and the economy's entire range of competing demands for productive services.

Principles Governing Investments in Information

While natural resources are to be regarded as capital for purposes of economic analysis, they often are not ready for use, for outlays must be made to find out more accurately their quantities and various qualities. The goal is not to find out everything about the natural resources of an area, but only as much as is necessary to make efficient use of them in production.

From a practical point of view there is no difference between a particular bit of natural resource about which more knowledge is needed—and which requires more outlay—and any piece of unfinished capital equipment. The fact that in many cases the information gained results in no visible change in the resource has no economic significance. Nor does any special problem arise when information acquired about a piece of a natural resource results in a decision not to use it because it isn't good enough. The expenditures in such a case are not wasted, but are simply a part of the cost of locating and getting into usable condition those natural resources that do turn out to be good enough to use. With the above points in mind, we can turn to a closer examination of the way expenditure on natural resource information fits into the production process. Two different types of information will be distinguished on the basis of their role in the production process.

Types of Information

The structure of knowledge on which productive activity is built rests, at bottom, on a network of principles, some of them "basic" in the sense that they are of wide applicability and possess a high degree of generality, and others less basic.

At the mundane level of production, basic and less basic principles have been utilized in determining "recipes" for production. These recipes, called production functions, form one of the conceptual tools of economics. A production function is nothing more than a statement of the relation between inputs into a production process and the output to be had therefrom. That is, if certain quantities of materials and specified services of labor and machines are combined *in a certain way*, a certain quantity of product will be obtained; that is, we can not get more than the quantity specified in the production function from the combination of inputs in question. There may be more than one product, of course. It is important to note that a production function reflects a certain *state* of information about production processes. Technological progress consists in a change in the stock of this type of information so that for a given set of inputs it becomes possible to get more output.[5]

But production decisions can not be made on the basis of a production function alone. Once the myriad physical *possibilities* for production are known, selection among them must be made on the basis of cost. In a market system or other type of economic system making effective use of prices, productive services acquire prices which reflect their usefulness or worth in making various types of products. Thus when considering the production of any particular product, since productive services have to be paid for, some ways of producing turn out to be cheaper than others. It is the job of the producer to find *the* method of production that is cheapest, given his circumstances.

Note that the method that is cheapest may change as a result of changes in the prices of the productive services. After all, if the price of one particular productive service rises a lot, it is only sensible to use less of it if some cheaper input can be used in its place. Also it is obvious that the cheapest method of production can be changed by a change in the production function—that is to say, by a change in our understanding of *how* to produce.

[5] There are physical limits beyond which we can not possibly go, of course. But in most processes we are far from being so efficient (in a physical rather than an economic sense) as all that. Some industrial processes are within striking distance of this limit in certain limited aspects, however.

Outlays to develop information on natural resources are on the same footing as outlays for any other input, so far as their economic significance is concerned. They are to be distinguished from outlays made for the purpose of changing the production function, since they are spent to produce information that will be "used" as the "finished" natural resource yields its services within an already existing understanding of how to produce the article in question.

Consider, for example, the job of "producing" a mineral deposit. The applicable production function involves outlays to produce information (e.g., geological studies, geophysical work of various types, drilling, etc.), but there is no economic difference between these outlays and the outlays more directly and obviously connected with developing the mineral deposit, such as stripping or sinking a shaft. However, in the case of outlays made to change the production function—i.e., outlays that are intended to add to our knowledge of *how* to produce—the results are usable not only by the production unit making the outlay but by all similar production units.

Although a natural resource scientist or technologist may call his information-generating activity research, its economic significance is quite different from research whose purpose it is to change production functions. The latter is directed toward changing the methods of producing natural resource information, including research on the instruments used, but it is to be distinguished from the survey or inventory type of work considered in this study.

The distinction between the two types of outlay, one of which changes the production function and the other which does not, involves a distinction between what are known in economics as "private" and "public" goods. These words are often given special technical meaning, thus: A private good is one whose benefit accrues only to the firm making the outlay required to get it or produce it. With the public good, on the other hand, production of a unit redounds to the benefit of all.[6] That is, the product (in this case the product is production knowledge) can be used by any number of producing units without reducing the quantity of this product available to the economic unit that produced it.

It should be noted that some types of natural resource or inventory type activities have limited external effects, effects which the pure public good has without limit. This is especially the case with geological studies and various types of geological information. Since the ground owned by each of the production units may be smaller than the area covered by the geological phenomena involved, information generated by one firm may

---

[6] In the case of private research on production methods, this may be prevented for a limited period of time by patents.

be valuable to other firms operating nearby. This is especially true of studies of regional geology and is one of the main reasons why many governments find it advisable to do such studies themselves, making the information available to anyone who wishes to use it.[7]

Long-run and Short-run Decisions

Production decisions often are divided into two classes: investment decisions versus current production decisions; in the terminology of economics these are known as long-run and short-run decisions. In the short-run or current production case, a situation is envisaged in which many elements are fixed for the time being and cannot be changed readily. These fixed elements are called the "plant," by analogy with a manufacturing plant, which ordinarily does not alter very much from day to day. The essential notion, however, is one of fixity. The idea is applicable to a far wider variety of situations than manufacturing operations.

In the long-run, or investment, situation, the full range of inputs is subject to the control of the decision maker and can be changed. Thus, the number of possibilities open to him is greater than in the short-run case.

When people speak of natural resource surveys, what they commonly seem to have in mind is the use of this information for investment decisions. When the goal is the initial development of a natural resource, it is clear that an investment decision is involved. In this case, the word investment simply means that the natural resource will yield its productive service in the future. So far as outlays on natural resource information are concerned, the pattern of return over the future can vary greatly, depending on the type of information involved. If you are locating fish with sonar, you had better reap the return right now, for it won't be there later on. On the other hand, to find out that your soil lacks a certain element may enable you to enjoy a perpetual return to this outlay on information by taking appropriate steps. Conversely, a mineral deposit will yield its productive services only for a limited period which will not extend beyond that point in time at which it no longer pays to work the mine, loosely called the time at which the mine is exhausted.

---

[7] The provision of free information for mineral exploration tends to shift the exploitation of mineral deposits forward in time and is a source of inefficiency in allocation over time. So far as the private participants in the process are concerned, free information is the same as any other cost reduction. At first glance, at any rate, it would appear possible to devise a tax on mineral production to cover government outlay on exploration information that might at least partly correct this misallocation. I do not advocate such a tax, but mention the problem for those economists with an interest in this aspect of efficiency.

To Sum Up

We have seen that, so far as general economic considerations are concerned, the management of natural resource industries is no different from that of other industries. The objective of this management must be firmly tied to the general economic objectives of the whole economy—the size, growth, and distribution of real income. Are natural resources "essential" to economic well-being and development? The answer to the question as it stands must be "no," but the smaller are a country's stock of capital and the skills of its labor force, the greater will be the importance of its natural resources, for they may provide a ready-made stock of capital which can permit the country to leap over the years that would be required to accumulate the same stock of capital out of income.

But natural resources do have certain characteristics that give their management some peculiarities not shared with other types of capital. They are localized by nature, particular resources may be quite limited in supply, and investment may be required to learn their location and other characteristics essential to their use.

The last few pages have emphasized the similarity between outlays on natural resources and outlays on other production inputs from the point of view of general economic significance. Emerging from the discussion are certain characteristics that are especially important for the study of natural resource information. Not all of these features are peculiar to natural resources, but they seem frequently to be lost sight of, as will be seen in detail later in this study.

1. The terms on which the services of natural resources can be had (i.e., what do the services cost?) are often not known but have to be found out. In the case of most inputs the cost of finding out the price is very low—a few letters or telephone calls, perhaps, if a piece of capital equipment is involved. But in the case of natural resources, where it is a matter of finding out the quantity and quality of a resource in a particular place, the problem of deciding how much to spend can be difficult.

2. In the case of flow resources which can not be appropriated, information about resource characteristics is a public good in the sense that its use by one does not diminish the quantity available for use by others. Climatological information is a prime example.

3. We have said that the production function is a statement of relationships between inputs and outputs. But what *is* the production function that is known or understood by the person who is making the production decisions? This points to an important problem in the use of natural resource information, especially in agriculture, for it indicates the need to find a means of acquainting farmers, say, with the production possibilities that exist.

4. Since some of the inputs into the production process in natural resource industries are variable in quantity and not subject to control—weather, for example—product is going to be variable, too. The problem of economic evaluation is considerably complicated by this.

The Theory of Discounting

To understand the nature of the process of discounting, we must first realize that at all times a society has the option of investing another $1,000, say, in a capital good of some sort which will return a sum greater than $1,000—but only at a later point or points in time. In a market economy, this return will tend to be the same for all lines of investment.

The return will be the same in a special sense, however. The longer the period between the investment and the return, the greater must be the return. And it must be greater in a very special way if the following two situations are to be equivalent:

	Now	*One year from now*	*Two years from now*
Situation A:	Invest $1		Receive $1 plus return for 2 years $= S_2$
Situation B:	Invest $1	Receive $1 plus return for 1 year $= S_1$	Receive S_1 plus return on S_1 for one year at the rate of $(S_1 - 1)$ per dollar invested $= S_1 + (S_1 - 1) S_1$
		Invest S_1	

The initial investment is the same in both situations. Hence competition in the market should insure that the sum of money available two years from now should be the same in both situations. That is, competition will insure that

$$S_2 = S_1 + (S_1 - 1)S_1$$
$$= S_1 + S_1^2 - S_1 = S_1^2.$$

Now let us substitute $(1 + r)$ for S_1. We now have:

$$S_2 = (1 + r)^2.$$

For equivalence among investments of different periods, this relationship must hold not only for two periods as compared with one, but for any pair of periods. That is, $S_n = (1 + r)^n$.[8]

---

[8] In order to facilitate explanation of basic ideas, it has been assumed that the one-year return to investment is the same in both years. This need not be the case. If change in the return to investment can be foreseen, this should receive recognition in the dis-

Because of the very existence of the opportunity to invest now and to secure a return on this investment later, a dollar spent or received now should not be regarded as having the same value *as of now* as a dollar spent or received at some other time. As we have just seen, a dollar spent now should be regarded as equivalent (in terms of present value as of now) to $(1 + r)$ spent one year from now and as equivalent to $(1 + r)^2$ spent two years from now, and as equivalent to $(1 + r)^n$ spent n years from now.

This process by which dollars spent or received at different times are made comparable by converting them to "present value" as of *a given date* is called discounting. For example, to convert $10 to be received in 1970 to dollars of present value of 1967, we divide $10 by $(1 + r)^3$.

$10 received in 1970 has a present value (P.V.) as of 1967 of:

$$\frac{\$10}{(1 + r)^{1970-67}} = \frac{\$10}{(1 + r)^3}$$

For example, if the rate of interest is 20 per cent per year, then,

$$\frac{\$10}{(1 + .20)^3} = \frac{\$10}{1.728} = \$5.58$$

to the nearest cent.

On the other hand, $10 received in 1967 has a P.V. *as of 1970* of $10 *multiplied* by $(1 + r)^3$

$$= \$10(1 + r)^3 = \$10(1.728) = \$17.28.$$

In calculating the profitability of an investment, all expenditures and receipts must be converted to a present value as of some given date. The timing of the receipts and expenditures is of very great importance, as the following example illustrates. Suppose that an investment opportunity involves the following products and outlays, all at the end of the year designated:

	1966	*1967*	*1968*	*1969*	*Total*
Product	$ 0	$90	$160	$54	$304
Outlay	100	70	60	42	272

Without discounting, the value of product exceeds the outlays. To compare product and outlay correctly, however, we must discount them to the same date. Any date will do, but let us pick the end of 1968. Then if the rate of

counting process. For example, the discount "factor," $(1 + {}_0 r_2)$, for a two-year period from $t = 0$ to $t = 2$ should be the geometric mean of the discount factors for the separate years, $(1 + {}_0 r_1)$ and $(1 + {}_1 r_2)$. That is, $(1 + {}_0 r_2)^2 = (1 + {}_0 r_1)(1 + {}_1 r_2)$.

discount is 20 per cent per year, the 1966 outlay of 100 has a 1968 value of $100(1.20)(1.20) = 100(1.20)^2 = 144$, because the 100 could have produced a capital good which would have yielded, say, 144 after two years.

The 1969 outlay has a 1968 value of $\dfrac{42}{1.20} = 35$.

The complete values discounted to 1968 are as follows:

	1966	1967	1968	1969	Total
Product	$ 0	$108	$160	$45	$313
Outlay	144	84	60	35	323

Thus when proper account is taken of interest, the investment does not pay.

II: The Capabilities and Limits of Information Programs

Up to this point, the discussion has dealt with information about natural resources in quite general terms; but to make any progress in analyzing problems in managing information programs, we must distinguish between different types of information in more detail and on a more practical level. These differences, both with respect to uses of information and to methods and costs of obtaining it, play an important part in shaping and using the programs.

In this discussion of the different types of natural resource information there is no pretense of providing a guide to methods for developing information on natural resources themselves. Each of the various fields— geology, soils, forestry, for example—has long been the domain of the specialist, and he must be consulted for any discussion that would give a reasonably complete view of his particular field.

The objective is more limited. Since this discussion is directed to people who have to make decisions on the size of information programs in relation to other programs, and who are concerned with relations between these programs and the use of their results, the intention is to specify what kinds of information various types of programs can generate. In the process, some of the things these programs can *not* do will also be clearly indicated.

Since the purpose of the discussion at this point is to describe simply the potential accomplishments and limitations of natural resource information programs, questions of economizing—how much should be spent on what—are dealt with in later chapters. Our concern here is with the types of governmental activities that generate physical information about natural resources. For the most part, these activities have developed into information programs or have attained a separate identity because of the supposed advantages of having organizations specializing in such activities. Our discussion is restricted to topographic and related mapping, geologic information, and soil-vegetation information, that is, information that generally is collected by the use of methods already known. With respect to a given type of information and resource, the collection will be repetitive in nature, using the same methods for different areas.

As a point of departure, let us start from the often heard position that with modern techniques we finally are in a position where we can generate information on natural resources so copious that we can speak of having an inventory which, it is claimed, will be invaluable to us in planning the exploitation of our natural resources. The questions of whether an inventory is possible, desirable, and useful are deferred to Chapter III. In the present context, however, one can not escape the fact that techniques occupy a dominant position in these matters. Techniques for gathering information have changed enormously, decade by decade, and indeed are on the verge of making another large leap. The facts that technique is so versatile, that surprising and spectacular things are frequently accomplished, and that the rate at which some tasks can be performed is much higher than formerly was possible, are a principal source of unguarded statements to the effect that "now we can develop all the information we need." It is an easy step from here to the erroneous view that physical information about natural resources is the key to their development and, in the minds of a few benighted souls, to economic development itself.

It is an observable fact that natural resources are spread out over the land with the consequence that efforts to find out about them must always involve some operations at their site. Before the days of the airplane, the sheer necessity of covering ground made this activity very expensive, especially in areas with poor or no transportation facilities. The great surveys of the western United States, for example, produced information substantially only for their lines of march and a few miles alongside, valuable though this small quantity of reliable information turned out to be. Geologists could map only a small area each year, and even the production of topographic maps could proceed only very slowly.

Changes were in evidence between the two world wars, but the real revolution in method came during and after World War II. Perhaps the principal change has been the use of the airplane as a platform from which to take photographs; but other advances—in photographic equipment, films, photogrammetric instruments, and instruments for measuring electromagnetic fields and radiation, among others—have been important. The necessity for expensive work in the field has *not* been eliminated, especially when a high degree of accuracy is demanded. Reduction in the amount of field work required has been so great, however, that it is now rather easily possible to develop tremendously large quantities of facts, both useful and useless. Still, not everything is possible, nor can all the different types of information be derived from equipment carried in one plane.

We should bear in mind the ultimate objectives in relation to economic development that are to be served by natural resource information. In line with the earlier discussion of the place of natural resource information in the economic process, these objectives boil down to three, with a fourth "non-economic" objective to be added:

1. To aid in the evaluation of investment prospects.

2. To provide factual information which can be used to improve the way in which a natural resource is being used, that is, to improve its current use.

3. To satisfy direct consumer demands.

4. To aid in the performance of certain governmental activities in which natural resources are involved but not used by the government.

The third category contains such things as direct consumer demands for maps used for recreation activities. The principal item in the fourth group is the use of land capability classifications (resting on data on soil, climate, water, and vegetation) for administration of land taxes.

Our interest in this study lies mainly in the first two objectives for the accumulation of resource data: the evaluation of investment prospects and the improvement of the current management of a resource. In each case, the resource under examination may be owned publicly or privately. Similarly, the information may be used by governmental agencies or by private owners or users of natural resources.

The same type of natural resource information may be useful both for the evaluation of investment prospects and for current management, as is clearly the case with geological and soils information, for example. Information may be collected with varying degrees of detail and accuracy, however. With some types of information, the lower the levels of detail and precision, the less useful is the information likely to be for management purposes. This is clearly the case with soils and geological information, for example. If one applies the term "coarse-grained" to information with a low level of detail and precision, it might be said that the whole process of investment evaluation will use both coarse-grained and fine-grained information, whereas current management will use fine-grained information.

The process of evaluating investment prospects, as viewed here, is quite comprehensive. Almost any natural resource information activity might be a part of this process. The attempt to develop some general ideas on the characteristics of an "unknown" area—types of vegetation, types of landforms, and so on—is a part of this process even though particular investment projects requiring detailed evaluation have not yet been identified. The attempt to form very rough ideas of the economic potential of a region is also a part of the process, because it is necessary to induce potential investors to give the region some attention and to make a search for particular investment opportunities.

Viewed in this way, evaluation of investment opportunity will include information activities that are a long way (figuratively speaking) from the evaluation of a particular project. Small-scale planimetric and topographic maps fall here, for example, as would also broad-brush studies of geomorphology and vegetation in order to give some clues to the nature of the soils in the area under study.

It is useful to view the process which results in the evaluation of particular projects[1] as one that proceeds from the general to the specific. The initial information will often be wrong for smaller areas and it may even be wrong—to a lesser degree, naturally—for larger areas. On the basis of initially imprecise information, tentative investment opportunities (which might consist, for example, only in the identification of certain areas as being more favorable than others) are identified, with later and more detailed information activity concentrated on these areas.

Note well that the above description is of the *process* by which detailed investment evaluations are reached. While natural resource information activities will show a similar tendency, I believe a serious error is involved in thinking of resource activity as proceeding from complete-coverage general information to more detailed and more precise information. The reason is that in deciding what natural resource information to gather, the answer will depend in part on the state of existing information. By this time in history, it is hard to imagine cases where nothing is known of an area. The limited information that exists will often permit a less than complete survey to be made—in many cases much less—although there certainly will be cases in which a complete areal coverage survey will be appropriate.

Some General Considerations

The possible combinations of the different elements involved in developing information about natural resources are enormous. It is important to understand this if only to realize the need for competent and *disinterested* advice at an early stage in the process of obtaining this information, whether its development is purchased from private firms or is undertaken by government agencies. It is important to realize that the phenomena involved are complex and that the particular situations are very different from each other. In spite of this complexity and diversity, a diligent search will show, in many cases, a disinterested consensus on the appropriate steps in proceeding from small-scale, general information to more definite and detailed information. What is said here is definitely not intended to bring the reader to the point of making such judgments, but to give him a few orienting ideas that may help him to develop the ability to discriminate between competent and poor or self-interested advice.

---

[1] Let us remind ourselves again that the most precise evaluative statement we can make, which should orient all investment activity and toward which we should strive, is of the following nature: "Project No. 123 has a present value of social benefits minus cost of $1.20 million." The goal should be to be able to make statements of this type for both "final" projects, such as a dam, and for "preliminary" projects whose purpose is to scan an array of possibilities and ultimately eliminate a part of them.

In the cases we are interested in, information about various natural characteristics is transmitted over some portion of the electromagnetic spectrum—the visible portion, infrared, the magnetic field of the earth, or the portions involved in the disintegration of atomic nuclei. In some cases we can capture this information with apparatus carried in a plane, thus permitting rapid coverage of large areas of the earth. Recording the strength of the magnetic field and similar variables will probably be done graphically and be coupled with some type of system to relate reading and location.

Some Fundamentals of Aerial Photography

The most common medium for obtaining the needed information is photographic film. The image on the film must be interpreted, of course. In some cases, its significance for the information of interest is clear and unambiguous. Where it is not, it often will be possible to connect puzzling features observable on a photo with reliable information that has been developed on the ground. For example, a certain texture and pattern on a photo may indicate a certain type of crop, as verified by sample ground checks. Or in a certain locality tree crown size may be found to be associated with trunk volume.

The reliability of a given type of information produced by the combined use of air photos and ground check ordinarily can be increased, up to a point, by enlarging the scale of the photo so that more detail is shown—or by increasing the density and possibly the accuracy of the checks that are made on the ground. The management problem, as has been emphasized earlier, is one of specifying the type of information needed and of choosing the appropriate level of precision in view of the costs and benefits involved. For some purposes, information of a low order of precision will be sufficient. Contour lines may not be needed at all, for example. But for other purposes, contour lines that are within a foot of accuracy may be very useful.

The accuracy of information presented in the form of a map should not be confused with the scale of a map. In particular, a large-scale map need not imply that the information presented is of a high order of accuracy. For example, a small-scale map prepared from "generalized" information that is correct only "on the average" can be enlarged to any scale desired, but enlargement does not increase the accuracy of the underlying information.

The film can register the visible spectrum (plus some of the non-visible at the upper end) with some possibility of controlling the relative emphasis on various parts of the spectrum by means of filter. Infrared can also be registered on a special film. Sensitivity (speed) and resolving power of the film can be chosen. Design and choice of lens open up another complex range of considerations, as does also the highly specialized camera itself. Also to be considered is the plane and crew available. Focal length of the lens and the height of the camera above the terrain being photographed determine the scale of the negative. (For example, if 400 meters on the ground register as a centimeter on the film, the scale is $\frac{.01}{400}$ or $\frac{1}{40,000}$. This is not an uncommon negative scale.)

Aerial photographs nowadays are mainly vertical, i.e., taken with the camera pointed at the center of the earth. Oblique photos, while useful for a variety of well-localized problems, pose some difficult problems for making topographic maps and for many types of interpretation. The scale of the photograph need not be the same as the scale of the negative, of course. Reduction poses no technical problems, but the degree of enlargement that is useful depends on the quality of the negative, the information sought, and the equipment available. Photo scales needed for different uses will be discussed in the next section.

If a vertical photo is taken of a square, flat surface from an airplane, a line one mile long directly beneath the plane will register as the same length on the negative as a line one mile long at the edge of the square. There is no distortion in this respect. However, if the surface being photographed is not flat, then objects at different heights will register at different scales (scale depends on focal length of the lens and the height of the lens above the object being photographed). What is more, objects not on the "reference plane"[2] and not directly below the camera will not be in correct relative positions on the film. By one definition, a map is a projection of points straight downward to the mapping plane (contracted to usable size), but light rays entering a camera lens in an airplane are vertical only when coming from objects directly beneath the camera. The important ratio here is the ratio of airplane height to the "relief" (distance between altitudes of highest and lowest points) of the subject. While these characteristics of photographs make impossible any simple, direct use for which great precision is required, they do not at all prevent the making of highly accurate maps. The derivation of a true map from photographs is the photogrammetrist's stock in trade. He has at his command a highly developed body of principles, equipment, and practice which permit an adequate solution of these problems with comparative ease.

It should be noted that photos taken from satellites, which we probably shall be using for mapping purposes before very long, will involve light

---

[2] We might think of the imaginary horizontal plane containing the lowest object in the photographs being considered.

rays so close to vertical that the problem of misplaced relative position
will become very small indeed.[3]

A considerable part of the value of photos, both for the making of
topographic maps and for the compilation of natural resource information,
arises from the fact that two photos of the same object or objects taken
from different vantage points (properly chosen, of course) can be used for
stereoscopic viewing. That is, the human visual system can blend the two
images so as to permit quite accurate judgments of the relative distances
of objects from the viewer, just as it blends two images in ordinary vision.

One may think of a giant, for example, the lenses of whose eyes (two
camera lenses) are, say, 5,000 meters above the ground. The retinas of his
eyes (analogous to the film in two cameras) are, say, 9 inches from the
lenses in his eyes (9 inches is the focal length of the camera lenses). His
eyes are as far apart as the two cameras (actually only one camera will be
used, but two pictures will be taken with the camera and plane in different
positions). Just as depth perception can be enhanced by using prisms on
binoculars to widen the distance between the objective lenses, so also is it
possible to enhance depth perception in stereo photos by increasing the
distance between camera positions for the two stereo photos. When the
two stereo photos are viewed in a stereo viewer, we are in effect putting
ourselves in the position of the giant with eyes 5,000 meters above the
earth and using our whole perception and interpretative apparatus (i.e., the
brain) to see what he could see.

When stereo photographs are being used as an aid in interpreting some
aspect of the environment, the interpreter commonly views the two photos,
called a "stereo pair," through a stereoscope, which is a device that permits
the simultaneous viewing of one photo with one eye and of the second
photo with the other eye. Interpretation generally can proceed quite
efficiently with this simple arrangement. In the use of stereo photos for
some purposes, especially for the making of topographic maps, the equipment used is far more complex.

The potential user of this photographic activity may use its product at
any one of several stages, some of which have already been indicated.
He may use the *negatives* themselves, but usually not directly. They are
used simply for making prints or transparencies (probably slides on glass)
for viewing and/or measuring equipment of one sort or another.

Prints may be contact prints of the same size as the negative (usually

---

[3] A "true map," in the sense of a vertical projection of points on the earth's surface to a
reference plane, may be approximated for areas small enough for the curvature of the
earth to be neglected. For larger areas, projection to a plane or even to a reference
sphere or other shape must necessarily misrepresent some aspect of the earth's features
if presented as a flat map.

9 × 9 inches) or enlargements. Stereo pairs for stereoscopic viewing generally will be contact prints.

Single prints viewed directly and not as stereo pairs are extremely useful for many purposes, even when used by persons with no special training. Either contact prints or enlargements may be combined to form *photo mosaics* covering an area larger than that covered by one photo. If the photos have been printed directly from the negatives, the mosaic is called an "uncontrolled" mosaic. In such a mosaic, scale may not be the same where the different photos are fitted together. A variety of reasons can be responsible, including tilt of the camera, change in altitude of camera, different registration of given *vertical* distances (not horizontal distances in a given horizontal plane) on film and print because of changes in view from different camera positions. One of the results will be that straight roads and other linear features may have jogs in them.

The defects of an uncontrolled mosaic can be eliminated to a considerable extent by making what is called a "controlled" mosaic. The procedure consists largely in modifying the prints so as to minimize scale differences arising from the various sources before piecing together the different photos. The photos are placed so that the center of each is in correct relative position. Thus errors of scale do not accumulate.

A controlled mosaic is not a map because the view is from straight above only at the center of each photo, but it has the great advantage, for some purposes, of being a photograph, with all the infinite gradations of tone and the information this can convey. The map, with its lines and smaller number of tonal differences, conveys fewer types of information, but with greater precision. Compare, for example, altitudes as shown by a photo with the contour lines of a good topographic map.

Various kinds of interpretative information, such as soil types, land use capability classes, and property lines, can be indicated directly on mosaics —a procedure that is often convenient for the user.

Maps are especially useful in presenting particular types of information. Almost any information with a locational aspect can be represented on them by means of lines, symbols, and shade differences on an underlying representation of true (more or less) relative locations of various objects located in the area. For example, soil classes or forest types might be represented on either a planimetric or a topographic map.

Planimetric and Topographic Maps

Today, planimetric maps, which do not show altitudes, and topographic maps, which commonly show altitudes by means of contour lines, are almost always based on air photos, and for a very simple reason: given the standard of precision, the photo is generally the cheapest method to use.

While there are sometimes circumstances that make the use of air photos infeasible—for example, the mapping of ground surface on a large scale under a dense canopy of trees[4]—these cases are exceptional.

A substantial amount of ground work is still required, however, for establishing horizontal and vertical controls and for checking cultural features and place names if these are to be indicated on the map. The extent of such work depends on many factors. In a settled area there may be an established network of locational controls, but in an unsettled area no such controls may exist. The cost of establishing them will vary greatly with the type of terrain. Also, the scale of the map and the purposes for which the map will be used will have a determining influence on the density and accuracy of the control network that is desirable. For some special purposes, large horizontal and vertical inaccuracies can be tolerated. For general purpose maps, however, the level of precision for ground controls is commonly set at levels that surely must impress a layman as being quite high.[5]

What purposes are served by planimetric and topographic maps? It is clear from the composition of the clientele of map agencies in economically advanced countries that the general public finds many uses for them, both as aids in making business decisions and in consumer activities. With respect to the development of natural resources, topographic maps are especially important among the variety of tools with which a person forms his mental images of an area or a country and on the basis of which he constructs many types of information relating to its economy. In countries or regions where there is a possibility of extensive economic development, a topographic map is essential to an evaluation of prospective undertakings. In such cases topographic information is especially useful, because in the past terrain so often has played an important role in preventing development.

Conventional maps also are important in providing a framework within which various specific types of natural resource information can be placed.

---

[4] But streams will show "through" trees on infrared film.

[5] The precision of the control network is to be distinguished from the precision of relative horizontal locations and representations of altitudes on the maps themselves. A reasonably careful visual comparison of maps with landscape in terrain with substantial relief will easily reveal that (1) contours on small-scale maps are "generalized"—a fact that is not surprising, for detail can not be represented on small-scale maps unless we are prepared to use microscopes in making and reading them; and (2) contours are often substantially in error even on fairly large-scale maps. The ground control may be up to standard, but this can not of itself insure accuracy of all the altitudes indicated on the map.

A check on the horizontal accuracy of a map is not accessible to direct visual inspection unaided by instruments unless errors are very large indeed.

While it is possible to reduce all types of natural resource information to a number that has no direct locational reference (for example, the number of acres in certain soil classes, or the volumes of water in reservoir sites), for all practical uses one must be able to return to the point for which the information is presented. Information without a locational tag is not worth very much. True, it is not necessary to record the locational reference of natural resource information in association with maps, but if the quantity of information is substantial it is economical to do so from the start. For general use, map scales as small as 1:250,000 (one centimeter to 2,500 meters, or about four miles to the inch) appear to be suitable. Both the United States and Canada have, or shortly will have, complete coverage at this scale.[6]

Although even smaller scales are used on some maps, most specific applications that go beyond general orientation require planimetric or topographic maps on a considerably larger scale. For example, regional surveys of several types can make good use of conventional maps with scales around 1:40,000 or 1:50,000. This scale may frequently be close to that of the negatives.[7]

Photos for agricultural surveys often need or commonly use a still larger scale, say 1:20,000. According to MacPhail, almost all the photography for the U.S. Department of Agriculture has been at this scale in recent years.[8]

For engineering uses such as roads, buildings, or dam construction,

---

[6] See H. Arnold Karo, "Maps as a Basic Requisite for Economic Development," in *Natural Resources*, Vol. II, U.S. Papers Prepared for the United Nations Conference on the Application of Science and Technology for the Benefit of the Less Developed Areas (Washington: U.S. Government Printing Office, 1963); and R. A. Stewart, "Aerotriangulation Procedures for National Mapping of Canada," *Photogrammetric Engineering*, Vol. 30, No. 1 (January 1964).

[7] See the discussions of W. Schermerhorn, "Planning of Aerial Surveys for the Over-All Development of the Natural Resources of a Country," *Proceedings of the United Nations Seminar on Aerial Survey Methods and Equipment*, Bangkok, 1960 (UN Mineral Resources Development Series No. 12), p. 68; and D. A. Stellingwerf, "Forestry Requirements in Integrated Surveys," paper given at the 1964 Toulouse Conference on Principles and Methods of Integrating Aerial Survey Studies of Natural Resources for Potential Development (UNESCO, Department of Natural Sciences).

Choice of negative scale depends on many things, however, and whatever combination of lens, focal length and airplane height is chosen, the photographic product must satisfy interpretative needs for single photo coverage and detail. With the availability of super wide angle lenses in recent years, the range of options has increased. For example, it is now possible to take both 1:70,000 and 1:21,000 pictures from 6,200 meters. See p. 6 of Stellingwerf's discussion.

[8] Letter of May 26, 1967, from Donald MacPhail, professor of geography, University of Colorado.

much larger-scale base maps are needed. One expert suggests that even for a reconnaissance survey of route alternatives in rugged country with little or no land use the map scale should be 1:6,000 to 1:12,000 with contour intervals of 15 to 30 meters. For preliminary survey and design of a highway in the same type of area, map scale could be twice as large and contour intervals half as small.

Whatever the application of the topographic or planimetric map, often no ready-made map will satisfy the particular need. This is especially apt to happen when investigations are aimed at mineral or forest resources as well as when engineering is involved. In these cases a base map will have to be specially produced, either by governmental cartographers or by a private company under contract to the government.

Geological Investigations

What kind of things can a program for geologic information tell us? So far as the relation of geologic information to natural resource development is concerned, five types of activity can be distinguished. The most general is the study of regional geology, which forms a basis for major fields closer to application: search for minerals, search for petroleum, ground-water investigation, and geological studies for engineering applications and mine design and operation.

Studies of regional geology have as their object a general understanding of the geology of a substantial area, that is, identification of the rocks of the area, their structure and layering, and an understanding of the history and processes that have preceded the situation observed. In short, how did the area under study come to be what it is? Was there volcanic activity? Was there opportunity for magmas to enter the area? What was the sedimentary and erosion history? What crustal movements and deformations have taken place? In working out the answers to these types of questions the study necessarily involves a large area, because the geological processes and events out of which has come the present situation have taken place on a very large scale. Consider, for example, the scale of sediment deposition, crustal raising or lowering, crustal deformation, erosion, volcanic activity, and the like.

An understanding of the regional geology of an area is important in the search for minerals and petroleum. In the first place, mineral and petroleum deposits are loosely associated with certain geologic processes and structures. If the places where these processes and structures took place can be identified, the area of search can be greatly narrowed, as Lacy and Swayne have emphasized:

In spite of the adage "ore is where you find it" the distribution of minerals is not random, but is in orderly patterns related to the geologic history of the earth's crust. Therefore, an intelligent minerals-exploration program must be based on understanding of the distribution of elements in the earth's crust and the processes by which they are concentrated into ore deposits. . . . An initial requirement for comprehensive minerals-exploration programs is determination of regional geological environment.[9]

And Fischer, of the U.S. Geological Survey, has pointed out, "A large percentage of known mineral deposits is associated with faults or fractures."[10]

Regional geologic study has been affected greatly by aerial methods, although not to the same extent as topographic mapping. Geology is still geology, and a good deal of work on the ground is still necessary. Although possession of good aerial stereophotos cannot replace geologic insight, the pace of work now can be much faster than formerly. And, what is perhaps more important, aerial photos are more than merely a substitute for field work, for they make it possible to examine the surface of the earth with a breadth of view that encompasses all or most of an area affected by a given geologic process. It is easy to understand the difficulty of the task of piecing together the nature and sequence of geological events from the worm's eye view of a man on the ground when some of the features he is trying to identify may involve a good many tens of miles. In fact, the view provided by air photos in some cases permit the identification of features and interpretation of events that would be missed with ground methods alone. Faults, for example, which are important as indicators of zones of mineralization and which have an obvious significance for construction projects of all kinds, can be identified by means of aerial photos, because they often are indicated by change in color or tone of a linear character, frequently expressed as alignments of natural features such as trees, streams, and so on. Fracture intersections are especially significant by reason of their association with mineral concentrations.

Aerial photos are also useful in detecting other characteristics that are associated with mineral deposits such as outcrops of favorable host rock and zones of alteration as indicated by change in tone or color. The view from above is useful in desert and other areas where the ground surface is well exposed. But perhaps it is of even greater use in areas with dense ground cover, for structural units that may be most difficult to perceive

[9] R. J. Lacy (American Smelting and Refining Co.) and W. H. Swayne (The Anaconda Co.), "Integrated Mineral Exploration," in *Natural Resources*, Vol. II, U.S. Papers Prepared for the United Nations Conference . . . for the Benefit of the Less Developed Areas, p. 134.

[10] William A. Fischer, "Interpretation of Geology from Aerial Photographs," in *Proceedings of the United Nations Seminar on Aerial Survey Methods and Equipment*, p. 102.

by ground investigation alone often leave their imprint on the outlines and tonal differences of vegetation and surface as it appears in an air photo.

The scale of the air photos must be small enough, as has been pointed out, to permit the stereoscopic viewing of large enough areas to see evidences of extensive geologic processes. Lacy and Swayne suggest, for example, that a scale of 1:62,500 (about a mile to the inch) is quite suitable for the study of regional geology and that it can serve other purposes as well.[11] A mosaic permits one to view a large area, but the view is not stereoscopic. Furthermore, recognition of the traces of certain processes is hampered by the abrupt, even if slight, changes in tone at the boundaries of the individual photos. Nor can the situation be remedied by "dodging" (i.e., altering exposure at boundaries so as to match tones on adjacent prints) when making the prints, for this will inexorably change tonal relations between the dodged and adjacent portions of the same print.

These considerations have led some experts to think that photos taken from satellites will have great importance for the recognition of certain geological features. A print will contain a large area on one negative or photo, all of it with the same sun angle, characteristics that facilitate recognition of features of great length or area. For some features it may be a positive advantage not to be distracted by the detail shown in larger-scale photos. A mechanically reduced low altitude photo will not show the same patterns as a high altitude photo.[12]

All this is not to suggest that studies of regional geology will be done from satellite photos in the future or even that photos taken from an airplane are now the exclusive route to geologic understanding of an area. Conventional observation on the ground, perhaps supplemented by observation from a helicopter, is still necessary. The problem is to adjust the proportions between the different types of observation to the particularities of each situation.[13]

In the search for minerals and petroleum, one of the important functions of the general examination of the geology of a large area is to separate those portions which, on the basis of past experience, are unlikely to yield

[11] Lacy and Swayne, p. 135.
[12] See Paul D. Lowman, Jr., *A Review of Photography of the Earth from Sounding Rockets and Satellites* (Greenbelt, Md.: NASA, Goddard Space Flight Center, August 1964).
[13] In addition to the references cited above, some of which contain papers by persons in addition to those cited here, the non-professional who wishes to learn something of the technical aspects not only of studies of regional geology but of most of the other technical matters discussed in this study will find the following two volumes to be very helpful: *Manual of Photographic Interpretation*, 1960, and *Manual of Photogrammetry*, 1952; both published by American Society of Photogrammetry, Washington, D.C. Each of these volumes contains authoritative discussions directed, not to the specialist in a specific technical field, but to the person with more general interests.

eventual successes sufficient to justify further expenditure from those which do have such potentialities. Some of the indicators useful in making this separation have already been mentioned.

The economic object of this procedure, as well as of other "siftings" that follow, is to reject as many of the initial possibilities as possible by the use of cheaper methods of investigation, and reserve the more expensive methods (but always more definitive methods if we consider only those methods in the sequences of methods actually used) for prospects which, as a class, are estimated to have a positive present value, as discussed earlier.

It should be clear that there must be a sifting stage before that of regional geologic studies, for if the area of a country is at all great, such studies cannot be made all at once. Hence, there will have to be a choice of areas in which these studies are to be pursued first. Furthermore, geological phenomena are complex, and geological investigation is costly. The emphases that are given to regional studies should depend on potential uses for the information, estimated on the basis of whatever information is at hand. The degree of detail and level of precision also depend on the likely uses for the information. But let us suppose that some regional studies have been completed for some areas and that within these areas some have been selected as warranting further investigation. How are they to be investigated? Some very local locations may be selected because of highly specific information from outcrops, some of which may have been the sites of earlier mining activity.[14] Apart from these sites, one of the possible steps nowadays is to survey a part or all of the area by geochemical methods, studying the locational variations, often along streams, in concentrations of elements of commercial interest or of their associates. These data will be joined with other information of many varieties, such as standard geologic maps, locations of known mines, and so on.

Regional geologic work may be followed or pursued simultaneously by the airborne measurement of some characteristic whose magnitude varies either with the presence or absence of a mineral deposit or of some substance that is commonly associated with a mineral or petroleum deposit. In the case of petroleum, where the immediate goal is the delineation of underground structure, the variable chosen for measurement probably will be the force of the gravitational field, perhaps supplemented by measurement of the earth's magnetic field.[15]

---

[14] Such information may have been important in selecting the priority areas for regional studies.

[15] See the excellent summary discussion by D. Trumpy and C. Sallé, "Petroleum Prospecting Techniques," in *Techniques of Petroleum Development* (New York: United Nations, 1964). Most of the aspects of the operations of the petroleum industry are discussed in this volume in a series of papers by different experts.

In the case of mineral deposits the choice will probably be the earth's magnetic field. The idea here is that certain types of mineral concentrations produce changes in the reading of a magnetometer as it passes over. Some types of iron and nickeliferous minerals are cases in point, as is also bauxite via the magnetic expression of the parent syenite. Unfortunately, such anomalies are also caused by variations in rock composition that are not associated with concentrations of minerals with potential commercial value. What is more, there is no unique structure of bodies associated with a particular set of magnetic or other airborne readings, although collateral information—regional geology, for example—may serve to reduce the field of possibilities to *useful* proportions.[16] Thus mineral deposits can not be located in any final sense by a magnetometer survey. The results must be interpreted in the light of all other available information, after which it may be possible to pick some locations that warrant even more intensive work.

While a magnetometer survey can be taken from any height to which a plane can carry the apparatus, the usefulness of high altitude survey is limited. Dempsey suggests that a regional survey at very high altitude (say 25,000–30,000 feet) may be of some use in interpreting structure.[17] But he, as well as other experts, look on magnetic surveys primarily as a means for locating and measuring the strength of localized magnetic anomalies which may be caused by certain types of mineral deposits. Surveys with this objective are flown at a very low height, perhaps 500 feet for a detailed survey ranging up to as much as 3,000 feet for a reconnaissance survey. These heights, also required for other geophysical airborne measurements, are incompatible with the heights needed for most photo interpretation purposes, including topographic map making. It does not appear feasible to do both things at the same time. This is apart from the cost of taking geophysical measurements over large areas with no special indication of having possible mineral deposits. The low height required for magnetic survey to delineate local anomalies makes them impracticable in terrain with great relief.

Only certain types of mineral concentrations will produce a magnetic anomaly. But some of the others will produce anomalies that can be detected by other instruments which can be carried in a plane. The two methods are the electromagnetic survey and the measurement of the rate of radioactive activity.

[16] William J. Dempsey, "Airborne Geophysical Surveys," in *Proceedings of the United Nations Seminar on Aerial Survey Methods and Equipment*, p. 128; and Trumpy and Sallé, p. 68.

[17] Dempsey, p. 127. Another good discussion of methods for finding minerals is Raoul Giret and Leon Bouvier, *L'Inventaire des Ressources Minerales; Methodes Permettant de le Realiser* (Paris: Compagnie Général de Géophysique, apparently 1960).

In an electromagnetic survey a current is induced in the ground from the aircraft. This current has an associated electromagnetic field which can be measured by instruments in the plane. The response will vary with the nature of the material in which the current is induced. In particular, sulphides will often produce a detectable response with this method, whereas there is no magnetic effect. Electromagnetic methods are more expensive than magnetic methods and are used in present practice only in quite detailed search in areas already determined to be especially favorable for mineral concentrations.[18] There is, however, a large body of experience with electromagnetic methods. L. W. Morley, Chief of the Geophysics Division, Geological Survey of Canada, has estimated that as long ago as 1960 two million line miles had been flown in Canada alone and that at least ten major orebodies with no surface indications had been found with the use of this method plus, it surely must be added, information generated in other ways.[19] Morley states that many informed geologists believe the problem of estimating the metal values of a massive sulphide deposit before drilling to be more difficult than the problem of finding the deposit.

All the airborne geophysical measurements can also be made on the ground, usually with more precision. Where power is required it can be furnished in large quantities, and instruments can in some cases be more accurate. But ground activity is expensive, and especially so in remote areas.

The array of geophysical measures used in the search for petroleum is somewhat different from that used in the search for minerals. There will be more interest in gravity survey than in magnetic or electromagnetic surveys. In addition, for highly localized work, the search for petroleum will make frequent use of artificial seismic disturbances to aid in the location and delineation of structures associated with petroleum. And geophysical measurements will be continued in a variety of ways once it becomes possible to lower instruments in a hole and thereby get more direct access to material far below the surface.

To sum up, geologic knowledge serves a variety of purposes, some of which, such as the exploitation of ground water and the planning of engineering projects, including irrigation projects, have barely been mentioned here. Aerial methods have come to occupy an important place

[18] See W. B. Agocs, "Aerial Natural Resources Evaluation Procedures and Costs," in *Proceedings of the United Nations Seminar on Aerial Survey Methods and Equipment*, p. 141.

[19] L. W. Morley, "Prospecting for Massive Sulphide Deposits with Airborne Electromagnetic Devices," in *ibid.*, p. 164.

both in the study of regional geology and in the search for mineral and petroleum deposits. But the "new" methods do not permit the location of the economically viable deposits of a region simply by flying some instruments over it, which seems to be the mistaken impression of many wishful thinkers. What has happened in recent decades is that the searchers for both mineral and petroleum deposits are able to accumulate relevant knowledge more cheaply than before, and in a number of cases far more cheaply. Understanding of the environments in which deposits have developed has advanced. Thus, the process of locating deposits in an area of given potentiality is, without doubt, much cheaper now. In particular, it is now possible to reject more effectively than formerly areas thought to be unsuitable, reserving the most expensive and most effective means of verification, drilling, for quite good prospects. The cost of drilling is high even in settled areas. For areas with difficult access, these costs multiply rapidly, hence the importance of methods that will effectively reject unsuitable acreage as compared with the costs of the methods.[20]

Soil Surveys and Related Studies

Soil, vegetation, land use, and land capability surveys, all of which are closely related, cover a large range of precision and have a correspondingly large range of objectives. But the common purpose of assembling information of the types contained in these surveys is to aid in predicting what will happen when land is used by man in specified ways, especially in agricultural activity. Is the soil in this area suitable for use as irrigated land? How much lime should be added to this field? What type of agriculture can be conducted in a particular area or semi-tropical forest?

To understand the role of the surveys in helping to answer questions like these, it is important to realize that the factors determining the outcome of a particular type of land use are complex to an extreme degree. First of all, the soil itself at a given moment of time is the end result of processes that have been going on for a very long time. Ponder, for example, some of the explicit or implicit suggestions of the definition of soil given in the authoritative soil manual of the U.S. Department of Agriculture.

Soil is the collection of natural bodies occupying portions of the earth's surface that support plants and that have properties due to the integrated effect of climate and living matter, acting on parent material, as conditioned by relief, over periods of time.[21]

---

[20] For further discussion of the general search process see the appendix to this chapter.
[21] U.S. Department of Agriculture, Soil Survey Staff, *Soil Survey Manual*, Agricultural Handbook No. 18 (Washington: U.S. Government Printing Office, 1962), p. 8. The text is the same as in the edition of August 1951.

The range of factors determining the particular characteristic observed is truly impressive, including, for example, the nature of the parent material, the geologic history of the particular materials, especially the stage of the locality with respect to geological erosion (relief), chemical composition, pattern of precipitation (e.g., seasonal pattern, distribution of intensity), vegetation (not only present, but past), organisms in the soil, and so on. It is the function of soil science and other disciplines to explain the processes which bring a certain type of soil into being and to explain how a certain group of forces (these might be natural or man-made) acting through time will change the characteristics of a particular soil.

In addition to the soil itself, there is another group of disciplines—a whole hierarchy, in fact—devoted to the study of the many aspects of agriculture which have as their end result predictions of what will happen if certain plants are planted in a given soil environment and handled in a certain way. The principles and relations uncovered by these sciences are applied and used by farm managers or anyone else who wishes to predict outcomes of certain combinations of action in these fields.

Soil surveys are involved in the whole process in the following way. Suppose there are some research results that say that the largest wheat yield on land with a certain specified type of soil is obtained when variety X is used. Now if we knew the location of all soil of the same type, we would know that this same conclusion applies to all of these locations without having to go through the varietal research for each plot.

A soil survey attempts to do exactly this: it attempts to identify and classify the characteristics of the different soils of an area into types and subtypes that are useful when this information is joined with other information to predict what will happen under certain circumstances. What is wanted is not a separate description of the soil under each separate square inch of surface. Nor is this needed, for soil characteristics are uniform (with respect to agricultural purpose) over much larger areas than this. What the soil survey aims at is locating the boundaries between the significantly different soil types.

How many different types are there? This will depend on the purpose of the classification. The *Soil Survey Manual* suggests that in one county of the United States where, to take an example, counties average about 570 square miles in the state of Iowa, there might be some 150 types that would be significantly different for farm management purposes.[22] This would be a detailed survey. The different soil types may be spatially related in simple ways or in a manner so complex that all occurrences can be represented only on a map of large scale.

---

[22] *Ibid.*, p. 34.

Soil surveys are to be distinguished from land use surveys and from land capability surveys. A soil survey is a classification of soils according to groups of physical characteristics. But the spatial distribution of land use, say agricultural use, will reflect not only soil, certainly one of the principal determinants of land use, but also climate plus a host of economic and cultural factors. Land use will be affected, for example, by distance from markets, prices of inputs and outputs, and the level of competence of the farm managers.

A land capability survey must necessarily specify the circumstances in which the capability of the land is being assessed. Is water for irrigation to be available or not? What type of farming practice is envisioned? How much capital will the operator have at his disposal? What prices for outputs are envisioned and what prices for inputs? While it may seem that some classification schemes are independent of any assumptions about prices, costs, and other economic aspects of farm operation, it is difficult to see how they can be avoided, for without their specification there are no limits on the quantities of inputs except for physical limits in some cases, and these may be so far beyond the economically practicable as to have no significance. If land is classified as to capability by reference to "prevailing practice" in an area or according to a specification of "good practice," it is clear that some very definite assumptions about economic factors are being made, implicit though they are.

A consequence of all this is that the pattern of land capability and land use may and probably will change over time as a result of changes in technical knowledge available or prices of outputs and inputs. A soil map will not change over time because of these factors, though a soil might be assigned to a different class after a period of time because of changes in the soil produced either by man's activity or natural processes. Erosion caused by denudation would be a case in point.

With these basic notions in mind, we are in a position to look a little more closely at the various types of surveys, the methods by which they are conducted, and to examine, if only very briefly, some of their limitations.

The cost and method of making soil, vegetation, land use, and land capability surveys, all of which are closely related, have been much affected by the use of aerial photos and methods just as have been the geologic and mineral surveys discussed earlier. There are differences of objective, however, that have important consequences.

In the case of the regional geology and related studies, the information desired is quite coarse grained, in that the particular facts portrayed relate to fairly large areas. What is more important, many of the final uses of these studies involve only a very limited portion of the area initially studied. This is most clearly the case with mineral deposits, where the object of the program is finally to select a few sites that will be subjected to the most intensive type of study, either by a government agency or a private enterprise, depending on the way the mineral industry is organized in the country concerned. With soil and related studies in an area with existing agricultural activity, on the other hand, the object commonly is not to find a few acres which finally will be studied intensively but to develop information of sufficient detail and accuracy to be useful in solving the management problems of each of the individual farming units. Information that is correct "on the average" for units of a square mile or of ten or a hundred square miles simply will not do for this purpose, although it may be useful for other purposes.

Some of these surveys, however, may have objectives more analogous to those of the search for minerals—for example, surveys directed to the examination of a large unexploited area for settlement and exploitation possibilities. Here there will be a similar process of elimination of unsuitable areas on the basis of preliminary information, but, unlike the minerals case, eventual success in the search will result in intensive study not of just a few small points but of a considerably larger area. Even in the case of areas already under exploitation, if there is a possibility of a substantial change in the manner of exploitation that would involve substantial public investment—for example, the institution of irrigation—less precise soils and related information may be useful as a part of the process of making a preliminary evaluation of the project.

Soil and related surveys can be made with widely varying degrees of accuracy. So far as reconnaissance surveys are concerned, expert opinion seems to hesitate to call them soil surveys. To begin with, the object of investigation, the soil, is commonly hidden from the view even of a person standing on the ground. Hence to obtain reliable information on soil characteristics necessarily involves a certain amount of digging and examination of particular sites.

Nevertheless, information can be gathered at a reconnaissance level of precision on factors that are related to soil characteristics and the production possibilities of the soil which can be useful for determining that some areas do not warrant more detailed investigation, at least as of the moment. For example, Buringh suggests that where soil conditions are not well known it would be best to make a physiographic map in which the different units are described in terms of terrain characteristics.[23]

James L. Haynes has made a study, "First-Approximation Location of

[23] See P. Buringh, "The Applications of Aerial Photographs in Soil Surveys," in *Manual of Photographic Interpretation*, p. 663.

Potential Settlement Areas in Brazil," which provides an interesting example of what can be done with very general information in the absence of detailed soil data.[24]

Having in mind settlement possibilities beginning with low-capital traditional agriculture but with later transition to a more highly capitalized modern agriculture, Haynes first uses information on vegetation types and geology to estimate locations of soils with renewable fertility. As screening rules, the presence of fully developed forests along the seaboard or south of 13° S. Lat. was taken to indicate renewable fertility, but not for forests north of the 13th parallel.

Areas without fully developed forest and with over 1,200 millimeters of rainfall were classified as lacking renewable soil fertility.

Next, outside the semi-arid zones, soils over sedimentary geologic formations were rejected since soils with renewable fertility generally do not occur over such formations in Brazil.

Length of growing season served as the next elimination criterion. Health considerations were noted as relevant but were not used to eliminate potential areas.

Haynes started with some 950 million hectares of potential settlement land. The vegetation criteria eliminated 400 million hectares. The geological criteria reduced the remaining 450 million hectares to 170 million. Growing season considerations eliminated another 10 million, leaving about 160 million hectares. Of this total, 60 million hectares are already populated, leaving around 100 million hectares. Perhaps some 25 to 30 per cent of this land would turn out to possess the desirable settlement characteristics. He estimates that some 1.6 million new families might eventually be supported, including those engaged in supporting service activities.

Haynes presents his estimates with much caution and is acutely aware of their approximate nature. An important question is, of course, whether the areas eliminated do in fact contain substantial areas of soils with renewable fertility. The bases for Haynes's sifting criteria seem adequate to make this unlikely. But whatever the actual situation turns out to be, this study illustrates very well the type of use that can be made of the most general sorts of information. At a minimum, what Haynes has done is to raise, in an effective manner, the possibility that settlement opportunities

[24] This brief study, which is based on earlier studies by Haynes, is Supplement I to *Aspects of Frontier Settlement in Northern Brazil*, Report of Interagency Reconnaissance Team (Washington: U.S. Agency for International Development, June 1964, mimeo). The team leader was Peter Duisberg, Chief of the Natural Resources Division of the Inter American Geodetic Survey.

in Brazil are far less abundant than they are often thought to be, even by experts in "development." The reorientation of thinking that should follow could not but be salutary.

For more precise information, however, a survey is needed which can properly be called a soil survey, that is, a survey with a certain density of field observations, with the significance of these extended and enhanced by the judicious use of aerial photos. To an economist, the difference between "detailed" and "semi-detailed" surveys seems to be the difference between the densities of the field observations. The lower the density, the greater must be the reliance on interpretation of aerial photos to interpolate between the field observations.

The general procedure is to start out with aerial photos and photomosaics of the survey area.[25] These can be used to gain a general familiarity with the area, the landforms present, and an idea of the soil formation processes that have been at work. Tentative locations for detailed field observations can be located and the scheduling and routing of field work worked out.

As soon as soils at some field observation points have been assigned to their detailed classes, the aerial photos can be used to delineate boundaries between the different soils. The soils man interpreting the photos has a wide assortment of characteristics associated with soil differences that will show up in the photographs. In general, these will be differences in tone and texture, but, more specifically, soil differences will frequently be associated with vegetational differences, soil deposition or forming processes acting over considerable areas, terrain characteristics of different types, and so on.

If the density of field observations is very great, the aerial photos will be used largely to determine boundary lines between soil types, relying on the association between soil type and characteristics of the types described above. However, with lower densities of field observations, the use of the photos will have to be more daring, with a more frequent use of the reasoning that the soil at point B is the same as that observed on the ground some distance away at point A because of the similarity of relevant characteristics observable on the photos (e.g., tone, texture, mode of deposition, origin, similar topography, and so on). The fewer the field observations, the more frequent and more serious will be errors, given the level of detail with which the soils are being described. The maximum gain from a given number of field observations is not to be had by uniform spacing of the

[25] A. P. A. Vink suggests that it is often cheaper to order new photo coverage than to use old photos which will yield incorrect or incomplete results. See his "Aerial Photographs and the Soil Sciences," paper presented at the 1964 Toulouse Conference (UNESCO/NS/90, Paris, February 28, 1964), p. 21.

observations, of course. A large area that appears to have uniform characteristics on the photos needs fewer field observations than a complex area of highly varied soils.

In assessing the limitations of the use of photos in the making of soil and related surveys, it is important to keep in mind the purpose for which the survey is to be used. Generally speaking, the more closely these purposes are related to the management problems of particular small units of land, the more precise and more detailed must be the information if it is to be useful.

In the case of crop survey, it is difficult, for example, to distinguish small grains from each other.[26] With respect to soils, Buringh states that regional soil differences are not detectable from photos. Nor can the proper soil group be deduced from a photo alone. Even the simultaneous use of vegetation and climatic information will not permit this except in special cases. Nor can soil texture be predicted from photos.[27]

Of course, these and many other difficulties in interpretation can be overcome if one is willing to spend enough money on films, equipment, highly skilled personnel, etc. In the case of small grains, for example, color film, spectrographic analysis, much larger-scale photos, and a few other aids might resolve the problem. But the fact that something is technically possible does not make it economically desirable. Still, granted the limitations of air photos in soil work, their use is essential and results in sizable cost saving even in rather detailed surveys, as we shall see later when costs are discussed. In surveys of a highly reconnaissance nature, aerial photos permit one to do now what would be impossible without them, that is, to gather information that is admittedly inaccurate in the small but which can help to develop ideas on the characteristics of areas larger than management units.

Some Other Uses of "Land Surveys"

In areas already under exploitation, surveys far less ambitious than the detailed soil survey information needed for improvement of management of particular plots can yield useful information for the planning of erosion

---

[26] *Manual of Photographic Interpretation*, p. 577. A recent discussion of the problem is Marjorie Smith Goodman's article, "Criteria for the Identification of Types of Farming on Aerial Photographs," *Photogrammetric Engineering*, Vol. XXX, No. 6 (November, 1964), p. 984.

[27] See Buringh's discussion in *Manual of Photographic Interpretation*, p. 640. R. N. Colwell, professor of forestry at the University of California, Berkeley, is of the same view. See his "Aerial Photo Interpretation for the Evaluation of Vegetation and Soil Resources," in *Natural Resources*, Vol. II, U.S. Papers prepared for United Nations Conference . . . for Less Developed Countries.

control programs and for two purposes less directly related to production—
land taxation and land registration.

A survey on a less than "detailed" scale can not yield the type of information required for determining a suitable operating program for a unit
with respect to soil conservation and profit objectives.[28] But it can show,
with a level of detail dependent on the elaborateness of the survey, the
severity of the erosion problem by location, information clearly necessary
to the design of a program to combat erosion. It should be noted also that
repeated surveys, perhaps of sample areas, can serve to measure erosion
progress and the effectiveness or lack thereof of erosion control programs.
Once again, however, air photos can not reveal all and must be coupled
with ground observations. In particular, Vink reminds us that some very
active forms of sheet erosion are not clearly evident in air photos.[29]

That aerial "land" surveys might have a contribution to make to land
taxation and land registration may not be immediately evident, but the
experience of Chile, which will be discussed in more detail in Chapter VII,
at least indicates the possibility. In the case of land taxation, for instance,
suppose that a country has a land tax system in which land is supposed
to be taxed according to its market value. If assessment procedures function poorly, there is a possibility that a land classification survey, done by
a combination of air photo interpretation and ground checks, can result
in assessed valuations which are both closer to the criterion of market
value and which are more acceptable to landowners than former assessments. That is, by the use of personnel hired for survey purposes, who
may tend to have a more professional outlook than the traditional assessment personnel, two things might be accomplished: First, a more accurate
delineation of property boundaries for tax purposes can be obtained; by
using a controlled photomosaic, one can be rather sure that every acre of
ground will be assigned to at least one, but not more than one, owner.
Second, the assignment of land to classes according to its "capability" for
various types of agricultural activity, while certainly a Procrustean bed as
compared with a refined determination of market values, may represent a
great improvement over traditional assessments.

[28] It would be better to refer simply to "profit objective," which by itself will encompass
soil conservation objectives if information and understanding are adequate and there
is a well-functioning land market. That it is very difficult to develop these conditions is
obvious.

[29] Vink, p. 90. For an application of aerial survey photos to the erosion problem, see
Evaluación de la Erosión (Santiago: Instituto de Investigación de Recursos Naturales,
August 1965); and *Inventario de Dunas en Chile, zona 29°48'–41°50' Latitud Sur*
(Santiago: Proyecto Aerofotogramétrico—Chile, 1964). The Instituto is the successor
organization to the Proyecto.

In a country with a good rural land market, land survey information, especially soil survey and related information, is of obvious utility to the assessor who has the task of "interpolating" to determine the value of a farm that has not changed owners recently but which is near some that have. Soil survey information can help to determine how and to what extent the farm in question differs from its neighbors.

In a country with a good cadastral survey, aerial "land" surveys have little to contribute to land registration. But good cadastral surveys are lacking in many parts of the world, and here the possibility exists that air photos can serve as the basis for the land registration system, constituting a convenient and possibly a sufficiently accurate method of description. After a preliminary examination of this possibility for Peru, for example, Fahr concluded, "From the legal standpoint I do not believe existing law forbids the use of aerial photos in making inscriptions, and I believe sufficient accuracy can be had by skillful use of existing photos to satisfy all requirements."[30]

Now let me try to summarize this effort to give some impression of the uses of "land" surveys. First, the detailed soil survey, with a large part of the effort devoted to field work, is potentially useful for the improvement of management practices on individual farms.[31]

Soil surveys on a somewhat lower level of detail have proved to be adequate for the assessment of the viability of irrigation and other agricultural projects in the view of Buringh. He applies the term "semi-detailed soil survey" to the case in which photos of about 1:20,000 scale are used and in which the reporting scale is between 1:40,000 and 1:63,360 (1 inch to the mile). Soil mapping units may be soil series, but are mainly complexes and phases. Soils are grouped in mapping units as in reconnaissance surveys, but the grouping is more detailed. Field observations are made throughout the whole area, but not on uniform spacing.[32]

In contrast, the lesser degree of precision in the Chile aerophotogrammetric project provided soil and land capability data useful for comparison of sizable areas and for taxation purposes, but not of sufficient accuracy

---

[30] Samuel Fahr, "The use of Aerial Photographs in Land Title Registration in Peru," Misión Iowa (Iowa State University), August 6, 1965, hectograph, p. 12.

[31] The data are only potentially useful, however. It is also necessary that the farm operators have the capacity to use the information. The importance of this point was strongly emphasized in conversation by Roberto Gomez (Natural Resources Division, Inter American Geodetic Survey), with reference to his experience in the southwest United States after World War II, where certain classes of operators were unwilling to make the effort necessary to learn how to apply this information. The problem would be far more widespread and difficult for an underdeveloped area.

[32] Buringh, pp. 655–57.

for irrigation project evaluation and, of course, not for highly local management problems.

At the very general level of Haynes's study of Brazil, there is no question of using the results as the basis for a commitment of funds to a substantial investment, but the results can serve to orient thinking, especially with respect to certain quantitative aspects of the problem, and to orient later and more detailed investigation of soils.

Forest Surveys

Surveys of forests, like those of soils, can be directed toward objectives of varying degrees of specificity. There is what might be called the "inventory" objective, for which species composition, volume, and condition of forest lands are estimated. Obviously, estimates of this kind can be made at various levels of detail and with various degrees of precision. At one extreme are those, derived from exploratory surveys, of the spatial distribution and densities of broad classes of trees and other vegetation. At the other extreme are estimates of volume by species, with sufficient information on spatial distribution, density, and terrain to estimate costs of exploitation and determine broad areal sequences of exploitation. Such estimates merge into the still more detailed and precise information required to prepare management plans involving determination of methods and equipment to be used, location of roads, location of auxiliary facilities, disease prevention programs, and perhaps reforestation.

As in the case of soils and geologic work, forest surveys often can be made much more efficiently with a judicious use of air photos combined with sampling on the ground than by ground work alone. The amount of information that can be developed by a survey using aerial photos depends on the type of forest surveyed. Tropical rain forests offer the greatest problem: here, identification of individual tree species from photos is usually impossible because of the very heterogeneous species composition and the absence of clear differentiating characteristics on the photos.[33] The difficulty lies not in a heterogeneity "on the average" over large areas with separate plots of uniform composition, but in an intimate intermingling of species with no sharp areal boundaries. There are special cases in which species identification from photos is possible—for example, where one species stands out by reason of height, form or color, secondary growth after fire, and, in unusual local climatic zones or local areas, soil peculiarities.[34] But these are special cases, and not sufficiently numerous

---

[33] D. A. Boon, "Aerial Photography and Forestry," in *Proceedings of the United Nations Seminar on Aerial Survey Methods and Equipment*, p. 118.

[34] I am indebted to Alan Randall, of the Organization of American States, for pointing this out and for other comments on the problems of forest surveys.

to upset the generalization that species identification from photos is difficult for tropical rain forests.

It is possible, however, to delineate different *forest types* from characteristics observable on photos. Consequently, aerial survey is a useful producer of information for tropical rain forests at what might be called the reconnaissance level.[35] If the purpose is to obtain estimates of volume sufficiently reliable to evaluate economic possibilities, however, a much heavier reliance on ground measurement and a greater density of sampling points will be necessary than in the case of other types of forest.

Photo interpretation problems are easier for forests in monsoon areas, and are still easier for forests of types found in much of the United States and Europe. Coniferous forests lend themselves especially well to the use of aerial survey methods. Hernández X. has summed up the situation as follows:

The techniques for the inventory of coniferous forests are well studied, presenting only minor problems of application. In contrast, it has only been in the last two years that the problem of inventorying forest resources in the hot-humid tropical regions has begun to be studied.[36]

While there is no doubt that good estimates of volume in temperate climate forests can be made with the use of photos, estimates with a high level of accuracy still will require a substantial amount of field work either in the area under study or in one known to be similar. To know when two forests are similar in the many different characteristics affecting volume per acre is not easy.

To see the problem, consider first a survey of volume made without systematic ground sampling of the whole area studied.[37] In a survey of an area without dense stands, and for which the photo scale is large enough to measure height and crown diameter of individual trees, the first step will be to classify the area into timber types, basing the classes on average height or some related quantity, perhaps crown diameter, and any pertinent variables available for the whole area under study which can be

[35] Boon, in *op. cit.*, cites Thailand experience where it was possible to distinguish four types of forest from existing 1:48,000 photos: mixed deciduous, semi-evergreen, dry dipterocarp, and permanent non-forested area. These distinctions were useful because teak occurs only in the first type.

[36] Efraim Hernández Xolocotzi, "Recursos Florísticos, Forestales y Forrajeros de Mexico y Centroamérica," UNESCO/CASTALA 2.1.2. VII. 3, (1965), p. 3. Although Hernández' paper is concerned with Mexico and Central America, the above remarks have a wider application. They no doubt refer to a rather detailed inventory.

[37] This brief discussion of volume surveys is based on the article, "Photo Interpretation in Forestry," in *Manual of Photographic Interpretation*, pp. 457–520, and attempts to summarize and use its points that are relevant to our interests.

observed on the photos or are available from other sources. These might include species or vegetation class, type of topography, and so on.

The next step is to obtain aerial tree volume tables. Existing tables thought to be relevant may be used or new tables may be constructed from limited field observations which are not, however, made systematically over the whole area studied. This table expresses tree volume, as measured in the field, as a function of tree height and crown diameter, with these measured from photos since the table is to be applied to measurements made on photos. These tables can then be applied to measures made of sample plots on the photos and an estimate of total volume derived.

In areas with stands so dense that individual tree measurements cannot be made from photos, a similar procedure based on stand density will have to be used. Measuring stand density by the percentage of crown closure, say, stand volume tables must be obtained or prepared. These will be used in the same way as described for tree volume tables, to prepare estimates of the volume of timber in the area under study.

Volume estimates made without systematic field sampling to derive the volume tables may be satisfactory for situations in which considerable error can be tolerated. However, there can be and is a great deal of variation from place to place in the relation between volume and the characteristics measurable on photographs. A need for precision will require systematic sampling, not necessarily uniformly spaced, to be sure that a more nearly correct volume table or relationship is being used. Clearly, the more detailed are the management or investment decisions the information is to serve, the greater will have to be the volume of field work. In addition, only large-scale photos will yield all the potential benefits of aerial photography for detailed decisions. Furthermore, other variables of interest, such as stem quality or defects, require field examination. Any precise appraisal or management objective will require an extensive field sampling program.

Potentialities of Satellites

A great deal of work has gone into investigations of the possibilities of using orbiting sensors to gather data that would be of value in a variety of fields; but, in the view of the author, apart from a few applications that already seem feasible, it is much too early to make definite judgments about the economic significance of remote sensors for natural resource information. Some applications for information of a "current management type" may be useful. Where sea surface characteristics can be viewed from a satellite—the tracing of ocean currents and the location of upwellings, for example—the information gained may turn out to be valuable to the fishing industry. Measurement of wave characteristics might be of some value in routing shipping to save time, fuel, and damage; but, so far as I know, the feasibility of such measurement from a satellite has not been demonstrated yet. The utility of satellite photos for weather prediction is said to be quite clear by now, most notably where little weather data are collected. Since, generally speaking, weather data tend to be poorer for ocean and sparsely settled areas, it might be expected that the use of satellite photos would improve the forecasts of weather approaching settled areas from oceans. So far, however, no systematic studies seem to have been made to measure the extent of the improvement, if any, in forecast accuracy. Another use for the satellite which promises to pay off if it turns out to be technically feasible, is in forest fire detection.

Concerning "survey" type information that is not used for current management purposes, two areas of application have already been mentioned in this chapter. One is in connection with geological studies, where satellite photos and data from the non-visible parts of the electromagnetic spectrum may permit perceptions not easily obtained from data collected from a plane or on the ground. (See page 30.) The other has to do with planimetric mapping, where the utility of satellite photos is clear. (See pages 26–29.) One could hardly ask for a better controlled photo "mosaic" than a single photo taken from an altitude a hundred times, say, the side of the square of ground covered by the image,[38] especially considering that the local relief would be at most on the order of a half per cent of the altitude of the camera.

The utility of satellite sensors for generating other types of natural resource information is more doubtful. We have only to recall the brief discussions, in earlier pages, of the limitations of aerial survey methods in soil and related surveys and in timber resource surveys to want firmer evidence before concluding that satellite sensors will be able to take crop censuses, identify diseased crop areas, or provide data for a timber resource survey. Problems of species identification may yield to a procedure that relies on more than just the visible or infrared portion of the spectrum, but it must not be forgotten that such sensors can be carried in a plane as well as in a satellite.

What is more, in industrially developed countries, especially, the satellite must compete not only with airplanes but with existing programs for gathering information. In many cases this information, especially that relevant to current operations, is collected more or less automatically as a part of other activities. That is, the savings to be made by *not* collecting

[38] See, for example, *Peaceful Uses of Earth-Observation Spacecraft*, Vol. III: *Sensor Requirements and Experiments* (Ann Arbor: University of Michigan, Willow Run Laboratories, Infrared and Optical Sensor Laboratory, 1966).

the data in the conventional way may be quite small. The marginal cost of collection is low.

On the other hand, in developing countries the economic management of natural resources requires not only information but a whole administrative system in which the information can be used. Even if a great deal of information were generated more or less relevant to "needs," the all-important question would be: How can it be put to work? This theme will be emphasized at length in Chapter VI.

It does not seem likely, then, that satellite sensors will make the task of managing natural resources radically easier, nor even that they will revolutionize the gathering of natural resource data over a very wide front. Satellites can do some things fantastically well, however. In general terms, additional opportunities for their use are most likely to be those requiring a synoptic view of large areas (as for weather prediction), rapid coverage of large areas, frequent coverage of particular or large areas, and coverage of areas which, because of distance or cloud cover, are inaccessible and therefore are comparatively costly to investigate by airplane or ground activities. But it is too soon to have acquired useful indications of the types of information activity that will be able to exploit effectively any of these advantages.[39]

[39] For a comparatively optimistic view of the resource applications of satellites, see National Academy of Sciences, *Space Applications, Summer Study 1967, Interim Report*, Vol. I (Washington: U.S. Government Printing Office, 1968).

APPENDIX TO CHAPTER II

The Question of Exploration Strategy

The strategy of using drilling only in the final stages of the sequence of minerals exploration activities, a strategy which seems to me to characterize all commercial operations that enjoy exploration success over a considerable period of time, has been called into question by Griffiths, a geologist, in a way that makes his advice peculiarly applicable to the developing country, for he ends up by strongly suggesting a vast program of drilling on equal spacing[40] to gain geological information and locate mineral deposits. The last paragraph of the article in question is so important that it deserves quotation:

Perhaps the most important question that this approach gives rise to is—what is the expected value of a unit volume of the earth's crust? A suitable precise estimate of this parameter *should*[41] form the basis for national and international planning for industrial development and may be used as a base for evaluating the natural wealth of areas of the earth's crust. Stable geopolitical units could thus be established on a sound fiscal basis.[42]

[40] Five-mile spacing is suggested at one point.
[41] Italics are mine.
[42] See John C. Griffiths, "Exploration for Natural Resources," *Operations Research*, Vol. 14, No. 2 (March–April 1966), pp. 189–209. An earlier article which made the same general type of argument is M. Allais, "Method of Appraising Economic Prospects of Mining Exploration Over Large Territories," *Management Science*, Vol. 3, No. 4 (July 1957), p. 285. This is a translation of an article appearing in *Revue d'Industrie Minerale*, Special issue 1R, January 1956. So far as I can see, my critical remarks about Griffiths' article apply also to Allais' article, although it is important to be aware of a fundamental difference between the two in that Allais does *not* recommend systematic grid drilling. He does recommend a more limited type of effort applied to a large area, such as the Algerian Sahara. Still, the factors I discuss with reference to Griffiths' article are relevant to Allais' article too.
  A paper given by Griffiths and L. J. Drew at Pennsylvania State University in April 1966, "Grid Spacing and Success Ratios in Exploration for Natural Resources," extends the fitting of binomial and negative binomial distributions to other petroleum basins, and also attempts to determine how the expected success ratio would change as systematic well spacing was changed. Although this paper appears to have been written after the one first cited, the *Operations Research* article is more closely directed to the problems in which we are interested.

The purpose of this appendix is to consider Griffiths' suggestion in the light of the considerations emphasized so far in this study.

An optimal exploration strategy ought to consist in a sequence of different actions such that with the expenditure of a given sum of money the present value of the deposits found is a maximum. Each of these actions, or activities, produces information about the likelihood of mineral deposits. Although individual firms may specialize in one type of information-producing activity or in one phase of the whole process, we can look at the whole process and ask whether, out of a given sum available for the whole process, the sequence of the actions is correct and whether the allocation of funds to each of the activities is correct. In the case of minerals, including petroleum, one might classify the possible actions into two groups: drilling and all other exploration activities. Then we can ask where drilling activity should come in the sequence of other activities. Should it be all at the beginning, the end, or intermingled? And how should the expenditure be divided between drilling and the other actions? It is easy to see that this problem, which can be posed in a few sentences, is very complex even on a theoretical level. And the application of a theoretical solution would be very hard because of the difficulty of developing quantitative descriptions of both the application of these activities and their results.

Nevertheless, the mineral industries and consultants in the exploration field have worked out an answer to this problem, an answer that by and large schedules drilling in the last stage of the actions taken to verify the presence of a deposit, granted that at times a limited amount of drilling is used to gain geological information at the earlier stages. The strong point of drilling is seen to be highly local verification of presence or absence. In conformity with this view, it is commonly said that drilling is "too expensive" to be used in the earlier stages of exploration activity. What is meant here is not that drilling a hole is more expensive than flying a magnetometer a mile—a comparison that is meaningless—but that, for example, drilling with the spacing of the holes just dense enough to provide the same quantity of information over a large area as would a study of regional geology conducted in the conventional manner, will cost much more.

While Griffiths' study makes some valuable points, important economic problems involved in selecting an exploration strategy are either neglected or are handled incorrectly. Since drilling is expensive, especially in countries with underdeveloped highway systems and overdeveloped topographic relief and/or jungle, the potentialities for misallocation of resources to which the suggestions of this article conceivably might lead are enormous.

Among the valuable contributions or points made in the article are the following—and I do not pretend to an exhaustive coverage:

1. The proper objective for exploratory activity is economic gain, not the finding of a particular type of deposit. As Griffiths points out, this is now the motivation of much private activity.

This objective is the proper one for a country, too, as has been emphasized in Chapter I of this book, where it is stated that outlays to gain information are investment outlays and should be directed toward the same objectives as other investment—maximization of economic gain.

2. The negative binomial fits the locational pattern of known oil wells in Kansas much better than does the Poisson distribution. The important point here is that the Poisson distribution presumes constant probability in all parts of the continuum in which the phenomenon of interest occurs whereas the negative binomial can be used to represent a contagion effect.

Griffiths suggests, no doubt correctly, that oil and mineral deposits are "contagious," i.e., that successes tend to cluster because of the existence of a genetic control. From the point of view of logic, however, even if oil deposits were in fact Poisson distributed it would seem possible for an observed "contagious" distribution to be generated in a situation in which (a) part of the drilling is random and (b) the remainder of the drilling is undertaken on the basis of the mistaken view that deposits are contagiously distributed.[43] I do not suggest that this is in fact the case but merely point it out as an interpretation that may also be consistent with an observed contagious distribution.

The major conclusion of the article—that one should drill on five-mile centers to provide the basis for a natural resource inventory—is based on oil well data for Kansas and Pennsylvania-Ohio. In the case of Kansas, Griffiths estimates that a systematic drilling program with five-mile centers would have had practically certain success since thirteen of the fields were so large or elongate that they could not have been missed. The systematic drilling program would have cost $200.5 million and would have yielded (basing the estimate on production up to only 1959) oil worth $4.2 billion valued at $3 per barrel, "leaving an ample margin for development costs."[44] In the case of Ohio and Pennsylvania a similar result is reached in that wells with six-mile spacing costing a total of $388.5 million would have been more than paid for by the Bradford field alone, worth $2.5 billion

---

[43] This possibility is recognized on p. 2 of the later of the two Griffiths' articles.
[44] The derivation of these numbers is not given. Cost of drilling appears to be low, although it would depend strongly on depth and size of hole. The $4.2 billion appears to be too low by 50 per cent.

with its production valued at $4 per barrel. This is the largest field in the area.

He also notes that in the simulations for Ohio and Pennsylvania the success ratios would have been better than the U.S. average over the period 1944–62 for wells drilled *with* technical advice (page 196) and almost as good as this for Kansas (page 198).

He concludes that if we take into account *all* the possible prizes—oil, metallics, non-metallics, water resources—"an exploration program by systematic grid drilling is likely to lead to a *commercial* success with probability approaching unity."[45] Furthermore, we should have a much better understanding of the geology of the first two miles of the earth's crust in the drilled area.

What's wrong with all of this? If there isn't something important that has been missed, then we must conclude that:

1. Exploration programs conducted by private enterprise are missing a good bet and are at present misguided, for private corporations certainly are not doing grid drilling regardless of other information already at hand or that could be developed. Also, that:

2. Government programs designed to develop mineral and water resources are proceeding in the wrong way, for they have persisted up to now in concentrating their efforts on such comparatively cheap methods as studies of regional geology done with the aid of air photos and helicopters instead of a drill.

One of the major faults in this argument is that time, which should have its economic manifestation here as a rate of discount, does not receive explicit attention. Thus the $4.2 billion of Kansas oil, which can't be produced all at once, would look a little different if discounted to the time when the exploratory wells are drilled on five-mile centers. The time when outlays are made and revenues are received is important and can be the decisive difference between the desirability of different economic projects.

What is more, the estimate of $4.2 billion for Kansas oil (at wellhead) is based on existing exploration practice and the resulting price. What would happen to the price of copper if, after putting holes all over the world, we found ourselves with twenty times as many copper deposits as we know of now? The procedure for evaluating Griffiths' drilling program ought to deal with this question explicitly. There seems to me to be no basis on which it can be assumed to be of negligible importance.

Clearly, all the wells can't be drilled at once. But if not all at once, what is to determine the rate and locations at which they are to be drilled? What are the relevant considerations? This major problem receives no

---

[45] Griffiths, p. 208.

attention. The impression one gets is that the drilling should take place quickly, for otherwise one would not speak of using the result of the drilling as the basis for "national and international planning for industrial development." But, once again, investment funds have an alternative cost. They could be used to produce capital goods that would yield a real return soon, whereas many of the deposits found under the extensive drilling program would yield their product only in the very distant future.

Let us suppose that the estimates of the results of a systematic drilling program for the three states studied are correct. What is their significance? First, Griffiths is applying his hypothetical program of systematic drilling to areas that are already known to be productive. The results are applicable to other areas only on some strong assumption about their productivity as compared with Kansas, Ohio, and Pennsylvania. This may or may not be true. Griffiths does not give us his position explicitly, but his conclusions seem to imply that other areas do compare favorably with these three states. Certainly the prevailing view is the opposite for most areas.

The all-important question is, how is a Kansas to be found? Part of the historical answer is that it was necessary to drill unsuccessful wildcats which served to lower the success ratio with which Griffiths compares the results of the hypothetical program applied to a known Kansas.

Hovering over the discussion are some important questions about the objective of an exploration strategy. Since they are not considered explicitly, these remarks may not be directed at Griffiths' true position but only at what his position might be. The objective of an exploration program should not be simply to find a program such that costs are covered, as some of his remarks seem to suggest. For private enterprise the goal is to *maximize* profit. Similarly, for a society the goal in the production of natural resource products is to maximize the present value of the year-by-year excesses of consumers' plus producers' surplus over outlays involved in their production. Thus, a program of exploration that just attained *commercial success*, if this means any outcome that covers costs, may be a very inferior program.

The most important result of the systematic drilling program is suggested as being the contribution to determination of the value of a unit volume of the earth's crust, this knowledge to be used for planning industrial development nationally and internationally.

Neither the course of industrial development nor its planning by public and/or private bodies appears to be hampered by inadequacies in estimates of the value of a unit volume of crust. It is not clear why such strong emphasis is placed on the estimate of this quantity, which seems to me to have little significance for private or public investment plans. No one bases his investment decisions on this quantity now, and it probably would not alter decisions even if it were reported that someone's estimate of the present average value had been doubled. The average value of a unit volume of the earth's crust is not, of course, a quantity that will stay the same if there were large changes in exploration strategy such as that proposed by Griffiths. How then are we to know when a correct estimate of average value has been reached?

This question has no answer. But there is an estimate of average value that would be *associated* with the best exploration strategy. The best exploration strategy almost certainly is not the one that will provide the most complete information for an estimate of average value of unit volume of crust or for the planning of industrial development. Our objective is not to maximize information or to minimize the dispersion of outcomes to industrial investments. Insofar as the size of real output sums up our social objectives, the subsidiary objective for exploitation of natural resources is, to repeat, the maximization of their contribution to real product. That is, systematic drilling can not be justified by showing that the information at our command would be much greater, or that certain planning tasks would be easier, or even that some mistaken investment decisions could be avoided. To justify such a program involves demonstrating that we will be better off in a socially relevant sense. This requires, in turn, consideration of the whole exploration process and explicit attention to the times when outlays are made and products are produced and the values attached thereto.

It is conceivable that a numerical evaluation of Griffiths' program that took account of the factors discussed in this appendix would show it to be the optimum program. In the case of Allais' program, which does not involve grid drilling at the first stage but less expensive methods, a numerical evaluation conceivably might show it to be optimum. In either case, a basic problem would be the adjustment of the program to prospective demand. The basic economic consideration, systematically dealt with by neither writer, is to avoid making outlays earlier than necessary to produce a given stream of product.

So far as evaluation of the different types of exploration programs is concerned, the correct criterion is the net present value of the deposits found by a given outlay on exploration. This net present value is the result of discounting to a common date all sales of metal produced from the deposits found, all costs of processing ore, and comparing the resulting figure with the discounted outlays on the exploration program. For the purpose of comparing different exploration strategies, one could assume a given discounted outlay on each strategy and compare the resulting product from the two strategies, or one could specify a flow of product and compare the minimum exploration *and* processing outlays required to produce it.

III: The Costs of Natural Resource Information

There is no single unit in which natural resource information can be measured, but only a number of different units in which various aspects of the physical environment are described. This raises difficulties for applying any neat and tidy costing formula to the various sorts of information-gathering means discussed in the preceding chapter. Yet, since the work involved in providing natural resource information usually is repeated over successive areas, it is useful and conventional to express these costs as so many dollars per unit area for a specified type of information.

The cost estimates to be discussed in this chapter are drawn from many sources and are often somewhat impressionistic. While no doubt intended by their originators to exemplify typical situations, in most cases there is no precise definition of what "typical" means. It is certain that the variation of costs for particular cases is substantial, but without the basic data precise estimates of this variation cannot be made. It is possible, though, to indicate the principal reasons for variation.

Having an obvious bearing on cost is the distance of the area under study from established sources of service supply. Clearly, it costs more to move men and equipment over long distances than short ones, but in addition the costs of providing each of the required services will vary as the "cost of living" varies from place to place. Climate, transportation difficulties, health problems, and level of wages for a given type of work are some of the factors involved.

The imposition of a deadline for completion of the work may be an important source of cost increase, whether the work is done under contract or by a governmental agency. The important question here is whether the completion date restricts the contractor or executing agency in planning the execution of the work. For example, if there is unused capacity, a contractor can easily handle the additional work and will be willing to undertake it at a price that will insure only some contribution to overhead over and above the extra outlays occasioned by the project. Other things being equal, a close deadline for completion is likely to give a contractor or an agency less opportunity to fit the required work into slack periods and will cost more. However, a requirement that work be performed within a certain week or month, a requirement that may be necessary where the object under study varies seasonally or where checks at fixed intervals are wanted, may not be very costly provided enough advance notice is given to permit economic scheduling of the whole workload. In short, it is better to buy when demand is low in relation to supply.

The cost of aerial photography will clearly be affected by the weather. The number of hours in the day that are suitable for photography are limited in any case because of sun angle, haze, and other factors affecting the quality of the images. Conventional black and white or color photography is useless through clouds, although clouds do not prevent some wave lengths of the spectrum, such as radar or infrared, from getting through. Certain areas—for example, parts of the eastern slope of the Andes—are so plagued by clouds that conventional photography is usually out of the question. Even where clouds are less of a problem, costs of the photographic operation that vary with the simple passage of time rather than flying time will vary inversely with the percentage of potential photographic time that is free of clouds. Cloud-free time varies greatly from place to place and is ordinarily not a high percentage anywhere. For example, in July the average number of days with 10 per cent cloud cover or less is under 10 for forty-one of the contiguous forty-eight states of the U.S.A., and even in Nevada is only 19. Vermont has only 1.6 days.[1] Many areas of Central and South America have very few cloud-free days.

The nature of the terrain will affect the cost of a particular type of investigation. In general, the more "complex" the terrain is with respect to the information under study, the higher will be the cost of investigation, assuming a given level of detail and precision. Contour mapping is more expensive for irregular mountainous areas than for plains. Areas with many soils in small patches will take longer to map than those with more uniform soils. Similarly, it is obvious that the cost of geological maps that give an accurate picture of the vertical dimension as well as of superficial features will vary greatly, depending on the complexity of the structures involved. Flat beds of sedimentary rocks, extending for tens or hundreds of miles, present easier mapping problems than the convolutions of an intricate mountain range showing the results of different processes and perhaps widely different geological periods within a short distance.

It should be remembered that specification of scale in any kind of map is only a part, though an important part, of the specifications that affect cost. The amount of detail and the accuracy of data presented can vary enormously among maps—of any given type—that are nominally of the same scale. What is more, some information terms are used *without* refer-

---

[1] Gene Avery and Merle P. Meyer, *Contracting for Forest Aerial Photography in the United States*, Station Paper No. 96 (St. Paul, Minn.: Lake States Forest Experiment Station, March 1962), p. 8.

ence even to scale. For example, what is a "mineral survey"? The range of variation in quantity and accuracy of information is obviously enormous.

Most of the above influences on cost are not given specific attention in the following series of tables, although there are a few cases where the estimators have taken rough account of one or other of them.

Photographic Coverage (Table 1)

Stereoscopic photographic coverage is one of the cheapest components of natural resource information, as measured by cost per unit area. Table 1 indicates that for sizable areas without special characteristics that would raise cost, the cost per square mile is $5 or less for a scale of 1:20,000.[2]

If we compare the estimates for those cases in which scale is specified, bearing in mind that the amount of flying for taking pictures (as opposed to flying for transport) will vary directly with scale,[3] it appears that the low estimates are those of R. N. Colwell and the *Manual of Photographic Interpretation.*[4] The estimates of the Food and Agriculture Organization of the United Nations (FAO), on the other hand, are distinctly higher.

Topographic Mapping (Table 2)

Topographic maps are far more expensive than the underlying photography, which W. T. Pryor, in Table 2, estimates to constitute only 5 to 10 per cent of the map cost. The effect on cost of the level of detail specified is evident from the table, the larger-scale maps and small contour intervals being very expensive. The one estimate for a map on a "reconnaissance" scale of 1:250,000 (about 4 miles to the inch) is $18–$26 per square mile. The costs for larger-scale maps of about 1:24,000 are much higher, although the estimates cover a considerable range, say, from $26 in easily mapped, accessible areas, to some $300, the upper limit of an estimate ascribed to the U.S. Geological Survey. Note that FAO puts the cost of planimetric maps, useful for many purposes, at only some 10 to 15 per cent of the cost of topographic maps.

[2] Miguel Ruiz-Tagle P., head of the Instituto de Recursos Naturales, Santiago, Chile, cautions that estimates based on the experience of a country with a well-developed aerial photography industry, such as the United States or Canada, must be increased substantially—perhaps 50 per cent or more—to be applicable to distant developing countries. The costs of many articles and services are higher and there is a variety of risks and delays that tend to raise cost.

[3] But some costs will vary with the time required for the whole contract. This will vary directly with photographic flying time, although probably not proportionately. Some costs will be rather independent of length of project or photographic flying time.

[4] I take it that the lower end of Colwell's range refers to "non-special" conditions, and that the upper end refers to cases involving special cost-raising factors.

Table 1. Estimates of Cost per Square Mile[1] of Stereoscopic Photographic Coverage

Source of cost estimate and date of publication	Area to be photographed (mi²)	Scale and cost per mi²			Locale
U.S. Forest Service[2] (1962)		*1:20,000*	*1:12,000*	*1:7,920*	United States
	25	$35.00	$42.00	$50.00	
	100	12.50	20.00	35.00	
	400	7.50	15.00	23.00	
	1,500	5.10	10.00	17.00	
	5,000	4.20	8.00	15.00	
	Excessive number of cloudy days may raise costs as much as two or three times. Infrared adds 5 to 25 per cent. Cost of ground control *not* included.				
Colwell[3] (1963)	Not specified	*1:20,000* $3.00–$20.00			United States
	Cost depends on size and shape of area, distance from airport, frequency of days suitable for photography.				
Leicester[4] (1964)	Not specified; probably large	$8.40–$16.80			Not specified; probably distant from home bases
	Scale not specified; estimate may include ground control and mosaics				
Manual of Photographic Interpretation[5] (1960)	"County" (e.g., average Iowa county is roughly 500 mi²)	*1:20,000* $2.50–$4.00			Probably United States
Buck[6] (1966)	60,000	*1:32,000* Can.$3.50–$6.00			Northwest Territories, Canada

Source	Area	Scale / Cost				Location
Morley[7] (1962)	5,000	*1:50,000* Can.$4.00–$6.00				Based on Canadian experience
FAO[8] (1963)	Not specified	*1:40,000* $3.20–$3.40	*1:20,000* $5.20–$6.50			Not specified
Peters[9] (1959)	50,000 25	*1:63,000(?)* $2.00–$8.00	*1:12,000* $20.00			United States
Visser[10] (1960)	Special projects (not whole country)	*1:40,000* $1.50	*1:20,000* $4.30	*1:10,000* $11.00	*1:5,000* $44.00	Iran

[1] To obtain cost per square kilometer, multiply cost per square mile by 0.39.

[2] Gene Avery and Merle P. Meyer, *Contracting for Aerial Photography in the United States*, Station Paper No. 96 (St. Paul, Minn.: Lake States Forest Experiment Station, March 1962), p. 11. These estimates by the U.S. Forest Service refer to stereoscopic coverage (commonly about 60 per cent overlap in line of flight and 30 per cent sidelap, yielding an effective 22 square inches per print of 81 square inches, see p. 4) and use of panchromatic film. Cost estimates commonly include delivery of two sets of contact prints on double weight paper and one or two photo indexes. The buyer owns the negatives, although he commonly will leave them in the physical custody of the photographic firm.

[3] R. N. Colwell, "Aerial Photo Interpretation for the Evaluation of Vegetation and Soil Resources," in *Natural Resources*, Vol. II, U.S. Papers Prepared for the United Nations Conference on the Application of Science and Technology for the Benefit of the Less Developed Areas (Washington: U.S. Government Printing Office, 1963), p. 320.

[4] P. Leicester, "Organization of Exploration," in *Techniques of Petroleum Development* (New York: United Nations, 1964), p. 131.

[5] *Manual of Photographic Interpretation* (Washington: The American Society of Photogrammetry, 1960), p. 27.

[6] Letter of June 7, 1966 to author. W. Keith Buck is Chief, Mineral Resources Division, Department of Mines and Technical Surveys, Ottawa, Canada.

[7] L. W. Morley, "Aerogeophysics and Its Role in Mineral Exploration," E/CONF. 39/A/100, October 10, 1962, p. 4. Paper given at United Nations Conference on the Application of Science and Technology for the Benefit of the Less Developed Areas. Controlled mosaics made as a part of the photographic operation are estimated to add 40¢–60¢ (Can.) per mi².

[8] Cited in "Los Recursos Naturales en América Latina, Su Conocimiento Actual e Investigaciones Necesarias en Este Campo," Economic Commission for Latin America (Mar del Plata, Argentina), General E/CN.12/670, April 20, 1963, p. 15.

[9] William C. Peters, "Cost of Exploration for Mineral Raw Materials," *Cost Engineering*, July 1959, p. 7.

[10] J. Visser, "Cost of Aerial Surveys," in *Proceedings of the United Nations Seminar on Aerial Survey Methods and Equipment*, Bangkok, 1960 (Mineral Resources Development Series No. 12), p. 93.

Table 2.   Estimates of Cost per Square Mile of Topographic Mapping

Source of cost est. and date of publication	Contour interval	Scale and cost per mi²	Comments
Pryor[1] (1964)	20 meters	1:20,000; $26–$104	Includes cost of ground control for highway, strip 22,000–60,000 m. wide
	10 meters	1:10,000; $65–$233	Strip 3,000–10,000 m. wide
	3 meters	1:5,000; $207–$1,160	Strip 1,600–3,000 m. wide

Aerial photography 5%–10% of above figures. Ground survey control 30%–60%, with the higher percentage accompanying the upper end of the ranges above.

Source of cost est. and date of publication	Contour interval	Scale and cost per mi²	Comments
U.S. Geological Survey[2] (1966)	Not specified	1:24,000; $10,000–$20,000 per map; assuming 67 mi² per map, cost per mi² is $175–$350[3]	Precise content of cost not known
Peters[4] (1959)	5 feet	1:12,000; $100–$150	25 mi²
FAO[5] (1963)	20 meters	1:250,000; $18–$26[6]	Includes cost of ground control; seems not to include cost of photography
		1:100,000; $26–$52[6]	"
		1:25,000; $115–$142	"
Wright[7] (1960)	10 feet 5 feet	1:4,800; $225 1:2,400; $750	Highway strip 2 mi. wide
Hemphill and Kidwai[8] (1963)		1:20,000; ¾ man-month per mi² if plane table method; 3/40 man-month per mi² with aerial photos, i.e., only a tenth as much	West Pakistan, 80 mi² area; 2,000 feet of relief in a mile is common

[1] William T. Pryor, "Evaluation of Aerial Photography and Mapping in Highway Development," *Photogrammetric Engineering*, Vol. XXX, No. 1 (January 1964), p. 121.

[2] Cited in *Peaceful Uses of Earth-Observation Spacecraft*, Vol. II: *Survey of Applications and Benefits* (Ann Arbor: University of Michigan, 1966), p. 18.

[3] At 42° latitude a quarter quadrangle (7′30″ × 7′30″) contains about 57 mi².

[4] William C. Peters, "Cost of Exploration for Mineral Raw Materials," *Cost Engineering*, July 1959, p. 7.

[5] Cited in "Los Recursos Naturales en América Latina," p. 15 (see Table 1, fn. 8).

[6] Planimetric—1:250,000, $1.95–$2.60; 1:100,000, $3.90–$7.80. Cost of photography not included. L. W. Morley (see Table 1, fn. 7) estimates the cost of 1:50,000 planimetric maps (5,000 mi²) at Can.$2–$3 per mi², not including the cost of photographs.

[7] Marshall S. Wright, Jr., "What Does Photogrammetric Mapping Really Cost?" *Photogrammetric Engineering*, Vol. XXVI, No. 3 (June 1960), p. 452.

[8] William R. H. Hemphill and Abdul H. Kidwai, "The Application of Photogeology and Photogrammetry to Geological Surveys of Natural Resources in Pakistan," in *Natural Resources*, Vol. II, U.S. Papers Prepared for the United Nations Conference on the Application of Science and Technology for the Benefit of Less Developed Areas (Washington: U.S. Government Printing Office, 1963), p. 198.

Studies of Regional Geology (Table 3)

Over the last decade and a half the Geological Survey of Canada has made a number of studies of regional geology in northern Canada, making extensive use of helicopters and planes. A comparison of the costs with those of the U.S. Geological Survey, when conducting similar studies in the United States, is shown in Table 3. Most of the Canadian Government work was at a scale of 1:500,000, although some was at 1:250,000, and one study in a different area (Cape Breton plateau) was at 1:63,000. Field costs, not including wages, equipment, or overhead, have run around Can.$2–$3 per square mile for the two smaller scales, although one study in a mountainous area cost Can.$6.73 per square mile. The more detailed study on Cape Breton, which covered a much smaller area than the others, was far more expensive, costing Can.$37 per square mile.

Non-field costs on these projects are estimated to range from about 25 to 80 per cent of the field costs.

L. W. Morley, Chief of the Geophysics Division, Geological Survey of Canada, probably drawing on the same experience, puts the typical cost of 1:250,000 geological mapping at Can.$5–$7. This figure would include both field and non-field costs. Note the much higher costs of the 1:50,000 geological map as estimated by Morley.

The apparent contrast between the Canadian experience and that of the U.S. Geological Survey is striking. Even if non-field costs were equal to field costs, the sum would be far less than the presumably comparable U.S.G.S. figures. How can the differences be accounted for?

First of all, seven of the ten Canadian Geological Survey cases listed here are completely or partly at a scale of 1:500,000 with only two at 1:250,000. The usual expectation would be that maps at half the larger scale would portray a narrower range of phenomena, and these with a lower degree of accuracy.[5]

---

[5] The comment is fairly frequent in Latin America that the U.S.G.S. standards, presumably referring to the range of phenomena covered and the degree of accuracy required for a given scale, are too strict to be appropriate for an underdeveloped country. This obviously is not a plea for slackness, per se, but reflects a belief that the economy will be better served if the survey teams available map more ground per unit time even if maps are of lower quality. Canada is not an underdeveloped country so far as level or rate of growth of income is concerned. However, because its mineral potential is very great, the same issue arises. It appears to me that there is some feeling that U.S.G.S. standards are in some respects stricter or more elaborate than those of the Geological Survey of Canada. Note that if this is in fact the case, it does not indicate that southern geologists are more able than those to the north. Nor would it indicate that either had made the wrong decision so far as standards are concerned. Indeed, in view of the literally more extensive opportunities in Canada, coverage acquires a greater importance, and this has been achieved by the Canadians at the reconnaissance level. At the same time, U.S.G.S. standards may or may not be appropriate to the circumstances of the United States.

Table 3. Estimates of Cost per Square Mile of Regional Geology Studies

Estimator	Location and type of terrain	Area (mi²)	Scale	Cost per mi²[1]
U.S. Geological Survey	N. Central Alaska[2]	28,000	1:250,000	US$ 16.10
	Esmeralda City, Nev. (1966)	3,570	1:250,000	48.50
	Nye County, Nev. (1966)	17,900	1:250,000	17.10
	Eureka County, Nev. (1966)	4,182	1:250,000	27.70
	N.E. Alaska[2]	18,000	1:250,000	29.20
	Southern Rocky Mtns.[2,3]	56,000	1:250,000	11.20
	Wrangell Mtns., Alas.[2]	1,200	1:63,360	346.00
	Montana-Idaho (1964)	400	1:62,500	250.00
	Idaho[4] (1965)	215	1:62,500	135.00
	N. Carolina (1966)	975	1:62,500	269.00
	Maine (1966)	200	1:62,500	560.00
Peters[5]	United States	Not specified	Generalized geologic interpretation from government photos.	US$1.00–$4.50
			Detailed interpretation from government photos	4.00–8.00
Government of Canada[6]	Keewatin, barrens (1952)[7]	207,000	1:500,000	Can.$ 3.63
	Baker, barrens (1954)[7]	67,000	1:500,000	2.15
	Thelon, barrens (1955)[7]	61,000	1:500,000	2.21
	Franklin, barren islands (1955)	100,000	1:500,000	3.17
	Fort George, bush and barrens (1957–58)	70,000	1:500,000	2.03
	Mackenzie, plains and mountains, 1957	100,000	1:500,000 and 1:250,000	1.68

Stikine, plateaus and mountains, 1956	25,500	1:250,000	8.65
Porcupine, mountains and plains, 1962	80,000	1:500,000 and	
		1:250,000	2.62
Ogilvie, mountains, 1958, 1961	15,000	1:250,000	6.73
Cape Breton, wooded plateau, 1954	850	1:63,000	36.94
Morley[8] Canada	5,000	Broad geological reconnaissance	Can.$2.00–$4.00
		Reconnaissance geological mapping 1:250,000	5.00–7.00
	600	Geological map 1:50,000	30.00–117.00

[1] U.S. cost figures include direct project costs, e.g., salaries, field expenses, map compilation and report writing, office rental, library, analytical, and paleontological support, and administrative and publication costs. The data were provided by David L. Jones of the U.S.G.S. (letters of June 27, 1967, and April 3, 1968).

Canadian cost figures do *not* include staff wages, cost of equipment, or overhead; neither do they include pre-field office planning or post-field preparation of maps and reports. All aircraft service was contracted.

[2] Report not completed as of April 1968.

[3] Extensive use of aerial photos in areas of exceptionally good exposure has probably greatly reduced the cost.

[4] Mapping project only. Did not include written report or extensive analytical or paleontological support.

[5] William C. Peters, "Cost of Exploration for Mineral Raw Materials," *Cost Engineering*, July 1959, p. 7.

[6] Geological Survey of Canada, Department of Mines and Technical Survey, *Helicopter Operations of the Geological Survey of Canada*, Bulletin 54 (Ottawa: Queen's Printer, 1959), p. 2 and *passim*.

[7] In each of the first three of the Canadian government projects non-field costs were estimated to be about the same. They ranged from 27 to 36 per cent of the field costs. On some projects they may be as much as 80 per cent. Information on non-field costs furnished by Keith Buck, Chief, Mineral Resources Division, Department of Mines and Technical Surveys, Ottawa, Canada (letter of June 27, 1966).

[8] L. W. Morley (see Table 1, fn. 7).

Second, there is a substantial difference between some Canadian and U.S. costs. This is definitely the case with respect to professional salaries and the wages of other help.

Third, the geology of the areas included in the U.S.G.S. cases may be more complex, but I raise this merely as a possibility, having no indication of significant differences in either direction.

From 1952 to 1960 the Canadian dollar was at a premium of 2.7 per cent; thus, correcting for this factor would increase the observed differences. In 1961 and 1962, however, the Canadian dollar sold at an average discount of 5.8 per cent. A possible remaining factor might be differences in the efficiency of the two services—an interesting and appropriate object of study, but one that is beyond the facilities available to this study.

William C. Peters' estimates for generalized and detailed geologic interpretation from government photos are considerably lower, but do not include a number of the functions included in the other estimates, notably back-up laboratory work and the preparation of a published report. Some type of report is necessarily involved, however.

Soil Surveys (Tables 4, 5, and 6)

As with other types of surveys, the cost of soil surveys depends on the degree of detail and precision of the survey. The common designations of detailed and semi-detailed have been used by P. Buringh[6] to characterize cost estimates based on extensive experience in Iraq. In the case of a detailed survey covering about 3,600 acres, with results reported on a scale of 1:25,000, he estimates that one party made up of one soil surveyor, one assistant, and two laborers can survey about 75 acres per day. It appears that a detailed survey is one that contains sufficient detail and is accurate enough to be useful in making detailed operating decisions for small parcels of land. It ordinarily would not pay to conduct more detailed investigations. A party making a detailed survey would have made use of aerial photographs for general orientation and for scheduling and organizing field work, but a great deal of the field work would be of the same nature as that required if air photos were not available.

This is more clearly seen in Buringh's figures (Table 4) for what he calls semi-detailed soil surveys for three Iraq projects totalling 530,000 acres. Even though Buringh characterizes these as semi-detailed surveys, field work accounts for 35 cents out of the 40 cents per acre attributed to soil mapping proper (or 35 cents out of 38 cents if the cost of aerial photography is excluded).

---

[6] In *Manual of Photographic Interpretation* (Washington: The American Society of Photogrammetry, 1960).

Table 4. Cost per Acre of "Semi-Detailed" Soil Survey on Three Iraq Projects (Buringh)

Activity	Cost per acre
Aerial survey[1]	$0.02
Preliminary field investigations	0.02
Aerial photointerpretation[2]	0.01
Field work	0.35
Total soil mapping	0.40
Soil capability classifications	0.04
Soil variability	0.22
Total soil survey, excluding overhead	0.66
Overhead	0.25
Total soil survey	0.91
Other planning investigations (irrigation, drainage, levelling)	1.93
Total project planning costs	$2.84

[1] Apparently 1:20,000 or so. The cost per mi[2] is about $11, which is quite high as compared with other estimates. However, this appears to include: a "few copies" of the photo index; one set glossy prints single weight; two sets matte prints on double weight paper; one glossy photo mosaic at contact scale; some matte mosaics on double weight, contact scale; some mosaics, matte, double weight, at 1:50,000. (See *Manual of Photo Interpretation* [Washington: American Society of Photogrammetry, 1960], p. 638.)
[2] Includes cost of training assistants.

Note also that soil mapping proper accounts for only 14 per cent of the total project planning costs—in this case irrigation projects.

The estimates by Buringh are in line with data for the soil surveys of the U.S. Soil Conservation Service, as indicated by Table 5. These are average figures, however, and reflect changes in the types of land surveyed. The Soil Conservation Service has prepared estimates of survey costs for

Table 5. Soil Survey Costs per Acre of U.S. Soil Conservation Service, Fiscal Years 1959, 1965, and 1968[1]

Year	Field mapping and related activities	Map compilation, editing, and printing
1959	$0.22	$0.11
1965	0.33	0.10
1968 (est.)	0.34	0.11

[1] Data provided by Louis Derr of the Soil Conservation Service, U.S. Department of Agriculture, Washington.

Table 6.   Estimated Costs (1965 Prices) of Detailed Soil Surveys of Different Intensities[1]

Degree of intensity	Soil work	Cartography	Editing	Printing	Total
High					
Total	$244,000	$35,000	$7,000	$12,000	$298,000
Per acre	55.0¢	7.8¢	1.6¢	2.7¢	67.0¢
Per cent	82%	12%	2%	4%	100%
Medium					
Total	$170,800	$23,000	$6,500	$ 9,000	$209,300
Per acre	38.0¢	5.1¢	1.5¢	2.0¢	47.0¢
Per cent	82%	11%	3%	4%	100%
Low					
Total	$122,000	$17,000	$6,000	$ 7,000	$152,000
Per acre	27.0¢	3.8¢	1.3¢	1.6¢	34.0¢
Per cent	80%	11%	4%	5%	100%

[1] Estimated for counties with 700 square miles of survey area. Data provided by Louis Derr of the Soil Conservation Service, U.S. Department of Agriculture, Washington.

Note: Mr. Derr has kindly made available revised estimates of "investment savings" *attributable to* the existence of the soil survey. The details of these estimates are not conveniently available for inspection, but it appears that the intention has been to sum up, without discounting, the annual changes in receipts and costs *attributable to* the existence of a soil survey. Only a detailed study of the estimates could permit an evaluation of these estimates. It is especially difficult to know what savings are genuinely attributable to the survey.

If we take the estimates at their face value and assume that the savings are accumulated continuously at a uniform rate over the life of the survey (twenty-five years), the estimated productivity of expenditure on typical soil surveys is enormous:

Survey intensity	"Investment saved" ($ million)	Survey cost ($ million)	Present value of investment saved minus survey cost at 10% rate of discount[a] ($ million)	Internal rate of return[b] (%/yr.)
Low	6.5	0.152	2.23	176
Medium	13.0	0.209	4.57	249
High	37.0	0.298	13.3	497

[a] With continuous compounding.

[b] Rate of discount required to equate present value of investment saved with survey cost.

If these estimates of productivity are anywhere near correct, it is clear that the intensity of each soil survey should be carefully examined to be sure that it is being carried to the point where the marginal net gain is zero. The analogy here is with the size of a construction project. Similarly, the size of the soil survey program needs careful examination to be sure that sizable opportunities for saving (in terms of present value of soil surveys) are not being forgone by having a soil survey program that is too small.

In any case, these estimates of benefits apply to the U.S. situation. That is, they presume the existence of institutions which permit the effective use of the information developed in a soil survey. For this and other reasons, these estimates would have no direct applicability to other countries.

In principle, what is needed to evaluate a soil survey (or any other outlay) is the following:
1) Estimate the "rent" for each year from $t = 0$ on as it would be *without* the survey

different levels of "survey intensity." For example, for a typical low-intensity county, 75 per cent of the land is assumed to be used for ranching, 15 per cent for dryland farming, 5 per cent for irrigated farming, and 3 per cent for urban purposes. Population growth is only 2 per cent over twenty-five years. In a medium-intensity county, 48 per cent might be cropland, 42 per cent range or forest, and 4 per cent urban, with 4 per cent population growth over twenty-five years. In a high-intensity county, 35 per cent of the land is assumed to be in commercial farming, 15 per cent forest, range, or recreation, 23 per cent urban, and 27 per cent other uses, with 27 per cent population growth over twenty-five years. Estimated costs of surveys for these three types of counties are given in Table 6.

Surveys of the kind shown in Table 6 are characterized by the Soil Conservation Service as follows:

The soil survey is a detailed physical inventory of the soil. It shows depth, texture, structure, drainage, stoniness, slope, erosion, and other land features that are helpful in classifying its use and capability. The soil survey of a county may show 75 to 200 kinds of soil, each of which are named and defined in the national system.[7]

Kirk Rodgers and his co-workers have made some careful estimates of costs for various types of soil surveys suggested for development of the Guayas River basin in Ecuador.[8] If estimated costs are classified as "direct" (those that are associated with a particular type of survey activity) and "overhead" (including some topographic map work, mosaics, drilling,

---

[7] *Department of Agriculture Appropriations for 1967*, Hearings before House Subcommittee on Appropriations (89th Cong., 2nd sess.), Part 2, p. 676. It is not clear whether the definitions of "detailed survey" as used by Buringh and the Soil Conservation Service carry the same meanings for level of detail and precision.

[8] Pan American Union, Department of Economic Affairs, *Survey for the Development of the Guayas River Basin of Ecuador, An Integrated Natural Resources Evaluation* (Washington, 1964).

Table 6 Note (continued)

available. The annual "rent" in this case is simply receipts minus outlays. With this procedure it is not necessary to distinguish between current and investment outlays.

2) Estimate for each year the *change in the rent calculated in Step 1 that would result from having the survey available*. Outlays will be changed in some years; e.g., there may be investments made as a result of the survey. Receipts may be changed in these and/or other years.

3) Find the present value of the changes calculated under Step 2. This is the value of the survey and is to be compared with the cost of the survey. One could also calculate the "internal rate of return" to the soil survey, i.e., find that rate of discount which will make the present value of the changes calculated under Step 2 equal to the cost of the survey.

If the changes in annual rents are estimated only for a limited period, such as twenty-five years, the present value of these changes must be increased by the present value of the value of the land with survey minus value of the land without survey (both taken at $t = 25$). This quantity often would not amount to much because of the long period over which it has to be discounted.

as well as the usual type of overhead), the latter amount to about 50 per cent of the former.

After some recalculation, the direct costs for each type of survey activity are found to be as follows.

Land use.....................................	$0.011 per acre	
Reconnaissance soils capability................	0.015 " "	
Semi-detailed soils capability.................	0.113 " "	
Detailed soils capability......................	0.358 " "	
Studies to select potential irrigation sites.......	0.083 " "	
Identification and evaluation of drainage and irrigation projects............................	0.032 " "	

The 36 cents per acre for the detailed soils capability study is substantially lower than the estimated cost of the Soil Conservation Service cited in Table 6. While the SCS estimate for a "low intensity" soils survey was 34 cents per acre, the Ecuadorian terrain for which the estimate was made is considerably more complex than the U.S. terrain surveyed and perhaps would be closer to the "high intensity" area so far as cost is concerned. Moreover, in the SCS lexicon, a soils survey includes only a description of physical, chemical, and other aspects of the soil which are relevant to the assessment of various capabilities. It does not include evaluations of land capability.

Buringh's estimate of the cost of semi-detailed soil mapping, given in Table 4 (40 cents per acre), is comparable with Rodgers' cost for a detailed survey. There may be a difference of definition involved here.

At the reconnaissance level, Buringh suggests that such surveys can be made for under 5 cents per acre, and perhaps as low as 3 cents per acre ($19 per square mile).[9] Rodgers' estimate for a reconnaissance study of soils capability again is lower—1.5 cents per acre. Differences in the level of precision envisioned may be involved.

Surveys need not present soils information directly; according to Buringh, they might show merely broad physiographic terrain units, suggesting that surveys of this type would be less expensive than reconnaissance soils surveys. The difference probably would be substantial.

Geophysical Surveys (Table 7)

Costs of geophysical surveys per unit area are much higher than they are for studies of regional geology done without geophysical information because the information sought is more specialized and involves measurement of a high order of precision.

The cost of geophysical surveys will depend on the phenomena being measured, the main ones being the natural magnetic field, induced magnetic

[9] In *Manual of Photographic Interpretation*, p. 663.

field, and radioactivity. Other important elements in cost are the level of detail (expressed in the height of the aircraft and the flight line interval), the type of aircraft used, and the purpose of the survey, that is, the place the geophysical survey occupies in the search strategy or sequence. Since measuring instruments must be fairly close to the earth for reasonably detailed measurement (i.e., measurement that will correlate closely with small surface areas), difficult terrain may require the use of helicopters, which are more expensive to use than fixed wing craft. Ground measurement, which can be very precise, is far more expensive than measurement from aircraft and will be used only for small areas in the later stages of the exploration process.

There are opportunities for reducing costs by combining surveys in those cases where more than one variable is to be measured, but combined surveys may not be desirable in many or even most cases. In the first place, the objectives served by the different types of measurement are themselves different. In some situations there will be little or nothing to be gained by a particular type of survey. In other situations the best flight heights and flight intervals for the different measurements may not be close enough together to permit one flight. And in any case, analyses of the data must proceed separately to a considerable extent. It should be noted that the value of geophysical information ordinarily will be greater if it can be combined with other types of geologic information for the area in question. One type of information can serve to fill in gaps in interpretations based on another.

Geochemical Surveys

Geochemical surveys, like geophysical surveys, can be made at various levels of intensity to give rather general indications of mineralized areas or to provide more specific indication of potential mineral deposits. Their cost, as with all types of survey, will vary with the degree of detail and precision that is sought and with the types of analyses wanted.

Estimates coming out of a recent United Nations seminar on geochemical prospecting indicate that the range is quite large. $14 to $42 per square mile (presumably including all costs) is suggested for reconnaissance surveys, but detailed surveys may vary from $280 to as much as $2,800 per square mile.[10]

C. Gleeson has provided data on the cost of a recent geochemical survey in Keno, Yukon Territory in northern Canada.[11] The field cost of this survey was $43 per square mile, including salaries of personnel in the

---

[10] *Proceedings of the Seminar on Geochemical Prospecting Methods and Techniques*, Mineral Resources Development Series, No. 21 (New York: United Nations, 1963), p. 5.

[11] Data are in letter of June 7, 1966, from Keith Buck, Chief of Mineral Resources Division, Department of Mines and Technical Surveys, Ottawa.

Table 7. Estimated Costs of Geophysical Surveys

Type of survey	Estimator	Type of craft	Area	Line interval	Elevation	Costs per line mile
MAGNETIC	Morley[1]	Plane	5,000 mi²	* (reconnaissance)[2]	*	40¢–60¢
		Plane	*	½ mi.	1,000 ft.	$10–$15
	Agocs[3]	Plane	9,300 linear mi.	*	*	$13–$19
	Peters[4]	Plane	*	⅙–¼ mi.	*	$6–$13
		Ground	*	100–200 ft.	*	$50–$130
	Engineering and Mining Journal[5]	Plane	*	*	*	$6–$10
	Davidson[6]	Ground	*	*	*	$110–$150
		Plane	*	*	*	$6–$9 petroleum[7]
						$8–$12 mineral[7]
ELECTROMAGNETIC	Davidson[6]	Plane	*	*	*	$10–$17
		Helicopter	*	*	*	$12–$25
	Pemberton[8]	Ground	*	*	*	$70–$100
						(+ $50–$75 if wood cutting necessary)
	Engineering and Mining Journal[5]	Plane	5,000 linear mi.	⅛–¼ mi.	*	$14–$18
		Helicopter	*	*	*	$20–$30
	Peters[4]	Plane	*	*	*	$10–$20
		Ground	*	*	*	$2,000 per mi²
		Plane	*	*	*	$10–$20
		Helicopter	*	*	*	$30–$40
		Ground	*	*	*	$100–$300
	Agocs[3]	Plane	9,300 linear mi.	*	*	$32–$45

RADIOACTIVITY	Agocs[3]	Plane	9,300 linear mi.	*	*	$8–$13
	Peters[4]	Plane	*	*	*	$4–$10
	Engineering and Mining Journal[5]	Ground	*	*	*	$35–$55
		Plane	*	*	*	$6–$10
MAGNETIC AND ELECTROMAGNETIC	Lacy and Swayne[9]	Helicopter	115 mi²	⅛ mi.	120 ft.	$40
	Pemberton[8]	Ground	*	*	*	$200
		Plane or helicopter	*	⅛–¼ mi.	*	$15–$50
	Morley[1]	Plane or helicopter	150 mi²	⅛ mi.	300 ft.	$266–$400
MAGNETIC, ELECTROMAGNETIC, AND RADIOACTIVITY	Davidson[6]	Plane	*	*	*	$14–$25
	Peters[4]	Plane	*	*	*	$15–$25

* Not specified.

1 L. W. Morley (see Table 1, fn. 7).

2 Reconnaissance survey to determine extent of area covered by igneous and metamorphic rocks and to delineate sedimentary basins and broad formations of volcanic and ultrabasic rocks.

3 W. B. Agocs, "Aerial Natural Resources Evaluation Procedures and Costs," in *Proceedings of the United Nations Seminar on Aerial Survey Methods and Equipment*, Bangkok, 1960 (UN Mineral Resources Development Series No. 12), p. 142.

4 William C. Peters, "Cost of Exploration for Mineral Raw Materials," *Cost Engineering*, July 1959, p. 7.

5 *Engineering and Mining Journal*, Vol. 157, No. 6a (Mid-June 1956).

6 D. M. Davidson, "Economics of Geologic Exploration" (New York: American Institute of Mining and Metallurgical Engineers, preprint No. 5819A3).

7 Flight lines commonly are longer on petroleum surveys.

8 Roger H. Pemberton, "Airborne Electomagnetics in Review," *Geophysics*, Vol. XXVII, No. 5 (October 1962), p. 698.

9 R. J. Lacy and W. H. Swayne, "Integrated Mineral Exploration," *Natural Resources*, Vol. II, U.S. Papers Prepared for the United Nations Conference on the Application of Science and Technology for the Benefit of the Underdeveloped Areas (Washington: U.S. Government Printing Office, 1963), p. 136.

field but not the costs of laboratory analyses. Half of the field cost was for helicopter charter.

This survey covered 1,900 square miles and involved the following number of samples:

6,000 stream sediment...........	3.2	samples per mi²
550 heavy mineral............	0.29	samples per mi²
1,000 water...................	0.53	samples per mi²
500 rock....................	0.26	samples per mi²

Timber Survey

The study for a survey of the Guayas River basin, in Ecuador, cited earlier in this chapter in connection with the section on soil surveys,[12] contains an estimate of the cost of taking a pre-exploitation forest inventory—7 cents per acre.

Integrated Surveys

Because economies are possible by combining surveys, the cost of an "integrated" survey requires some attention. Unfortunately, there is no standard content for an integrated survey; hence, each cost figure reflects the product composition of the survey in question as well as the particular circumstances under which the survey was taken.

In the case of the Guayas Basin study, the total cost of the study would be $1.4 million[13] applied to an initial study area of 8,800 square miles. The average cost would be about $150 per square mile or 23 cents per acre. But the area that would finally undergo some development would be far smaller than the original 8,800 square miles. Thus, the cost per square mile to be "borne" by the resulting projects would be much higher than 23 cents per acre.

The information required of the Guayas Basin survey program was to provide sufficient data to permit the planning and evaluation of irrigation and colonization projects and for the development of plans for sustained yield logging. In addition, data on land use, tenure, and capability were to be provided for the entire proposed area of study.

A Chilean aerophotogrammetric project, which included work on soils, land capability, and property identification, among other things (see Chapter VII for a fuller discussion), had a cost of about $5.5 million by its termination date in 1964—an average of $106 per square mile as compared with the $150 estimate for the Guayas proposal. The product of the two projects is not comparable, however, because the Guayas project

---

[12] Pan American Union, Department of Economic Affairs.

[13] *Ibid.* Includes $100,000 for two preliminary studies conducted in July 1962 and July 1963.

involves a substantial block of work on a more detailed level which would provide data rather directly usable in project design and evaluation.

Christian and Stewart have provided some information that bears on the cost of the type of reconnaissance survey the Australian government has been doing recently.[14] Information is commonly presented on scales of 1:500,000 or 1:1,000,000, with smaller areas occasionally portrayed at 1:250,000. The central core of the information is the joint description of the "land system." This description will embrace genetic factors (geology, geomorphology, climate), overall resources (e.g., water), and possibly man-made factors. Smaller-scale maps showing geomorphic regions, distribution of broad soil groups, land use, water resources, and vegetation communities also may be prepared. Where appropriate, investigations are made of forest, pasture, and underground water resources. Mineral resource assessment is restricted to collation of existing material.

Christian and Stewart state that a survey of one field-season in the humid lowland tropics (New Guinea) will cover about 2,000 square miles and will require from fifteen to eighteen team-months:

Pre-field work
    (collection of existing information, preliminary air
    photo interpretation, selection of sampling sites, and
    planning of field itinerary)........................ 3 months
Field work... 3 months
Final air photo interpretation......................... 3 months
Evaluation of field data and co-ordination of land system
    descriptions..................................... 3–4 months
Preparation of report............................... 3–5 months

       Total time................................ 15–18 team-months

The average production rate for this type of survey and area is, then, around 120 square miles per team-month. The number of professionals working on the project no doubt varies from stage to stage, but there are said to be three key members of all field teams: a geomorphologist, a soil scientist, and a plant ecologist. Other specialists may be involved at other stages and perhaps at the field stage. More detailed information would be necessary to calculate output per professional man-month.

Survey output is much higher in arid areas for a variety of reasons. The land is less variegated in many respects and access and transport are far

[14] C. S. Christian and G. A. Stewart, "Methodology of Integrated Surveys," paper given at the 1964 Toulouse Conference on Principles and Methods of Integrating Aerial Survey Studies of Natural Resources for Potential Development (UNESCO/NS/NR/94, Paris), pp. 95 ff. Christian is member of Executive Commonwealth Scientific and Industrial Research Organization, and Stewart is Chief, Division of Land Research and Regional Survey in the same organization.

simpler. An Australian arid zone project of about 140,000 square miles required two field-seasons of work. If the other types of work also doubled this would mean about 4,300 square miles per team-month.[15]

Obviously, the cost of an "integrated" survey is going to vary with the types and degree of detail of the data gathered. For this reason there is not much point in discussing its cost. It should be noted, however, that the cost of a minimal integrated survey is far from negligible. This can be illustrated by adding up the costs for separate surveys. Naturally, the total will be too large, for some economies will result from joint conduct of different surveys, but it is unlikely to be so out of line as to negate the contention that the cost of a "comprehensive survey," even on a fairly small scale, is not negligible.[16] For example:

Photography........................	US$ 4 per mi^2
Topographic maps 1:250,000 (20-meter contour interval)..........	22 per mi^2
Regional geological studies with mapping at 1:250,000..............	6 per mi^2
Soil survey—reconnaissance level, 1:250,000........................	25 per mi^2
	$57 per mi^2

In relation to the value of land that is being used, $57 per square mile is not exorbitant, but if unused lands are to be surveyed the picture is quite different for two reasons. The future investment to which this type of information can contribute will involve only a small part of the area surveyed. What is more, the information is on a rather small scale, and hence is useful only for general orientation, rough screening of areas, and perhaps as a background against which imagination can play in conceiving a range of development possibilities. The point is not that small-scale reconnaissance surveys should never be undertaken, but that they should not be undertaken where enough is already known to conclude that there is small probability of their disclosing specific investment opportunities that will recover the costs not only of the later investment but of the survey as well.

[15] See Christian and Stewart.

[16] One of my most helpful geologist critics believes that the "typical" cost estimates for geologic mapping are too low. He feels that soils mapping is a much simpler task at a given scale than geologic mapping, because the latter is concerned not only with the composition of the materials exposed at the surface, but with composition, structure, age relationships, etc. of surface and subsurface materials—and, it might be added, sometimes of materials that disappeared long ago from the area under study.

One matter at issue here is the definition of soils maps and geologic maps with respect to the level of detail and the degree of accuracy wanted.

IV: The State of Natural Resource Information
in Latin America

Relative to complete coverage, the natural resource information for Latin American is quite limited, especially in its detail. But, as has been emphasized in Chapter I, complete coverage is irrelevant to any decision to develop or not to develop a resource. To what extent and to what depth natural resource information should be gathered is a question that cannot be answered by a simple-minded comparison of a certain percentage coverage with 100. Other matters are involved, including the probable presence of desirable physical characteristics in the resources and the institutional capability of using information about them. This should be borne in mind while examining the bare facts of natural resource information in Latin America.

Coverage by Photography and Maps[1]

When we examine that part of natural resource information consisting of aerial photographs, topographic maps, geological maps, and soil maps of varying scales, it is found that a larger percentage of total area in Latin America is covered by small-scale photographs and maps of all these types than by medium- or large-scale ones. The breakdown by country and by type and scale of coverage is shown in Table 8, but it

---

[1] The main summary sources on map coverage in Latin America are the *Annotated Index of Aerial Photographic Coverage and Mapping of Topography and Natural Resources*, published for the various countries during or after 1964 by the Organization of American States; and reports of the Inter-American Committee for Agricultural Development, *Inventory of Information Basic to the Planning of Agricultural Development in Latin America* (Washington: Pan American Union). There is a volume for each country and also a summary volume.

The *Annotated Indexes* have been published within the last four years. The *Inventory* volumes refer to 1962 in the main, although some later data have been included if available at the time of publication. Used here especially are the summary volume for América Latina (1963), América Central (1965), Paraguay (1963), Brasil (1964), Argentina (1963), Mexico (1964), Ecuador (1963), and Peru (1963).

Other sources on the state of information for Latin America include the following: "Los Recursos Naturales de América Latina: parte I, Los Recursos Minerales y parte V, Los Suelos" (Santiago: Economic Commission for Latin America, 1963, mimeo.); "The Soil Resources of Latin America," UNESCO and ECLA, Conference on the Application of Science and Technology to the Development of Latin America (Paris: UNESCO, 1965, mimeo.); "La Cartografía en el Perú" (Lima: Oficina Nacional de Evaluación de Recursos Naturales, February 1966).

Table 8. Per Cent of Surface Covered by Aerial Photographs and Topographic, Geological, and Soil Maps in Latin America

Country	Aerial photographs (vertical) Scale:[1]			Topographic maps Scale:[1]			Geological maps Scale:[1]			Soil maps Scale:[1]		
	small	medium	large	small	medium	large	small	medium	large	small	medium	large
Argentina	65-70%	8-10%	1-2%	100%	50%	15-20%	65-70%	15-20%	1-2%	75%	4-6%	1-2%
Bolivia	70-75	*	*	100	2-4	1	3-4	45-50[2]	4-5	—	1-2	*
Brazil	60-65	20-30	1	100	5-8	1	40-45	25-35	1	—	1	*
Colombia	75-80	15-20	2-4	2-3	45-60	28-32	45-50	15-20	3-4	15	2-3	*
Chile	75-80	20-25	4-5	100	40-50	15-20	100[3]	4-6	1-2	8-10	1-5	*
Ecuador	40	10		100	10-12	6-8	100[3]	4-5	*	10-12	1	—*
Paraguay	45-55		1	100	8-10	*	100[3]	4-5		—		—
Peru	70	5	1	45-55	14-16	1	100[3]	8-12	*	4.4	1.6	*
Uruguay[4]	7-10	3-4	1-2	—	1-2	4-5	100	70-75	*	100	*	*
Venezuela	65-70	—	—	100	35-40	1	100	10-12	5	50	6-8	7-8
Costa Rica	90	7	1	100	30	25	100	5	4-5	10-12	4-6	*
El Salvador	100	60	—	100	100	5	100	15-20	4-5	100	25-30	1
Guatemala	100	—	—	100	40	10	100	40-50	*	100	—	*
Haiti	100	4-6	4-6	100	100	70	100	100	2-3	100	5-8	—
Honduras	90	15-20	1	100[3]	20-25	*	100	*	*	60	6-7	*
Mexico	60	18	*	100	45-50	2-4	35-40	3-4	5-6	8	5	*
Nicaragua	90	20-25	4	100[3]	30	1	100	3-5	*	35-40	*	*
Panama	80	20-25	—	100	15-18	40-45	100	2-3	—	100	15-18	—
Dominican Republic	100	15-20	3-4	100	50-55	15-20	100	20-22	40-45	0	*	1-3
Latin America[5]	36	10	1	60	18	20	95	2	0.1	6	3.5	0.5

Sources: See page 75, fn. 1.

* Less than 0.5 per cent.

1 Definitions of scale are as follows:

| | Aerial photographs | Maps | | |
		Topographic	Geologic	Soils
Small scale	<1:30,000	1:500,000 to 1:100,000	<1:250,000	1:500,000 to 1:100,000
Medium scale	1:30,000 to 1:10,000	1:100,000 to 1:50,000	1:250,000 to 1:50,000	1:100,000 to 1:25,000
Large scale	>1:10,000	>1:50,000	>1:50,000	>1:25,000

2 This coverage is mainly a map with scale 1:250,000 issued by Bolivia's Ministry of Mines and Petroleum in 1955.

3 Scale: 1:1,000,000.

4 Coverage of planimetric maps is complete in small and medium scales.

5 The percentages for Latin America as a whole are not comparable with those for individual countries. The former are from *Inventory of Information Basic to . . .* (see p. 75, fn. 1.) and include only maps of high quality available for use. Percentages for individual countries are, in general, from the OAS series, *Annotated Index . . .*, and include old and low-quality maps as well as those of high quality. In many cases the area covered had to be estimated from other sources. The resulting estimates in this table are only approximate because of imprecision in the verbal description of the map's coverage.

should be pointed out that the percentage figures shown in this table can only be regarded as approximate, due to the varying ways in which the source materials have been gathered and presented. The coverage of medium-scale topographic maps varies a great deal among the countries of Latin America, reaching 50 per cent or more in several cases. But for geological maps the coverage at medium scale is much smaller, and for soil maps it is smaller still.

Large-scale topographic maps show a very small coverage except in a few countries where some unusual circumstance has induced their use. And so far as geological maps are concerned, those that are large scale cover only a small portion of Latin America. This is also characteristic of large-scale soil maps.

If one hazards a comparison between a large geographic region and individual countries, map coverage in Latin America is low compared with that of the United States, although by no means complete for the latter. In the United States in 1958, topographic maps at a scale of one inch to the mile or greater (about 1:63,000 or greater, corresponding to the medium- and large-scale maps referred to in Table 8) had a coverage of 51 per cent; in 1966 it was 73 per cent; it is expected that by 1970 coverage will reach 86 per cent and by 1976 will be complete. So far as the 1:250,000 topographic series is concerned (classified as small scale in Table 8), U.S. coverage is complete.[2]

A partial list, prepared by the U.S. Geological Survey in 1967, indicates how the coverage by the 1:63,000 scale of topographic map varies among countries and regions.[3]

U.S.S.R.	100%	Cuba	100%
United Kingdom	100	India	90
France	100	Spain	95
Japan	100	Pakistan	75
Italy	100	United States	74
Greece	100	Finland	60
Switzerland	100	Sweden	50
Norway	100	Central America	50
Thailand	100	Canada	20
Denmark	100	Africa	20
West Germany	100	Mexico	10
Benelux	100	South America	10
Portugal	100	Australia	10
Nationalist China	100		

[2] See Hearings before Senate Appropriations Subcommittee, 89th Cong., 2nd sess. (1966), Department of the Interior and Related Agencies Appropriations for Fiscal Year 1967, Part I, pp. 577 and 578; and Hearings before Senate Appropriations Subcommittee, 90th Cong., 1st sess. (1967), Department of the Interior and Related Agencies Appropriations Fiscal Year 1968, p. 412.
[3] Hearings before Subcommittee of the Committee on Appropriations (House), Department of the Interior and Related Agencies Appropriations for 1968 (1967), p. 190.

Turning to geological and soil maps, the various percentages of area covered, shown for Latin America in Table 8, may be compared with information available for the United States. According to the U.S. Geological Survey, in 1966, 20 per cent of the connected forty-eight states had been mapped at a scale of one mile to the inch or larger[4]—a far lower coverage than that for topographic maps. And in mid-1965, 38 per cent of the U.S. land for which detailed soil surveys are regarded as being needed had a detailed soil map, this rather large coverage reflecting an intense program of long standing. All the same, if the planned rate of mapping for 1967 were maintained, fifty-seven years would be required to map the whole area involved.[5]

Coverage by Precipitation Gauges and Stream Gauges

Some idea of the extent to which information of a hydrologic nature is available in Latin America can be gained from the data on the degree of coverage by precipitation gauges and stream gauges in twenty countries, shown in Tables 9 and 10.

The variation in the number of station-years per 1,000 square kilometers that have been recorded is quite large; this can be seen under "coefficient of coverage" in the last column of Table 9. The record in this regard is substantially higher for Central American and Caribbean countries than for the countries on the continent, reflecting in part the difficult access to large areas in the Andes and the Amazon basin.

For stream gauges, coefficients are far lower than they are for precipitation gauges, as is evident in Table 10. Some idea of the coverage can be gained by comparing the index for Mexico which, with 9.7 years of stream gauge data per 1,000 square kilometers, is the highest in Latin America, with the index for the United States—32.5 in the fall of 1966.[6]

[4] Hearings before Senate Appropriations Subcommittee, 89th Cong., 2nd sess. (1966), p. 621.

[5] See Hearings on Department of Agriculture Appropriations, House Appropriations Subcommittee, 89th Cong., 2nd sess. (1966), Part 2, p. 677.

[6] Coverage for the United States is calculated from data supplied by the U.S. Geological Survey collected for purposes of hydrologic study. Alaska and Hawaii were included in both the number of station years and the number of stations, but the numbers are so small a part of the total that the effect on the ratio calculated is negligible. Land area of the conterminous states was used to calculate the coefficient of coverage.

The U.S. data suggest that measures involving the number of gauging stations may have little definite significance. In the United States there were about 8,500 river discharge stations active in the U.S. Geological Survey network in 1966, but there was an equal number of discontinued stations that had made their contributions in the past to the 1966 total of 250,000 station-years. Stations are discontinued for a variety of reasons, such as flooding by a reservoir, change of site, accumulation of sufficient data for a particular decision, and so on.

It should be noted that there are numerous sources of streamflow data in the United

Table 9. Coverage of Latin American Countries by Precipitation Gauges as of the Early 1960's

Country	Number of stations	Average number of years of data	Density[1] per 1,000 km²	Coefficient of coverage[2] (*station years per 1,000 km²*)
Argentina	3,613	24.1	1.3	31.33
Bolivia	200	19.8	0.19	3.76
Brazil	2,577	26.6	0.30	7.98
Colombia	510	9.8	0.60	5.88
Chile	479	19.0	0.65	12.35
Ecuador	86	7.6	0.33	2.51
Paraguay	—	—	—	—
Peru	993	4.0	0.8	3.2
Uruguay	547	—	2.92	—
Venezuela	1,016	11.0	0.11	12.21
Costa Rica	128	10.1	2.65	26.77
Cuba	188	24.0	1.64	39.36
El Salvador	95	16.1	4.75	76.48
Guatemala	149	19.0	1.37	26.03
Haiti	100	—	3.60	—
Honduras	62	8.6	0.55	4.73
Mexico	2,035	26.0	1.15	29.90
Nicaragua	60	26.0	0.41	10.66
Panama	112	19.7	1.48	29.16
Dominican Republic	208	20.8	4.27	88.82

Sources: "Los Recursos Hidroeléctricos en América Latina: Su Medición y Aprovechamiento," *Boletín Económico de América Latina* (Santiago), February 1962; and "Los Recursos Hidraúlicos del Perú" (Santiago: Economic Commission for Latin America, December 1965).

[1] 1,000 km² equals 386 mi² (equivalent to a square with sides 19.6 miles long).

[2] This coefficient is the product of average number of years of data multiplied by density per 1,000 km². This equals average station years per 1,000 km² if definitions used were as follows:

$$\begin{pmatrix} \text{Average number of} \\ \text{station years} \\ \text{of data} \end{pmatrix} \times \frac{\text{stations}}{\text{per 1,000 km}^2} = \frac{\Sigma \text{ station years}}{N} \cdot \frac{N}{\substack{\text{Total area} \\ \text{in 1,000 km}^2}} = \frac{\text{Station years}}{\text{per 1,000 km}^2}$$

States other than those reporting to the U.S. Geological Survey. Among these are irrigation districts, urban water supply agencies, and various arms of state governments. The situation is no doubt similar, to varying degrees, in other countries.

Some isolated cost data for U.S. gauging stations may be of interest to some readers. In the Columbia River basin (in the Pacific Northwest), the average cost of construction per gauging station was $8,500. This presumably is historical cost. Annual operating cost runs between $1,400 to $2,000 per station. In the Delaware River basin (Eastern Seaboard), average construction cost was $3,100. Annual operating cost runs from $1,600 to $2,000 per year.

Conclusions to be Drawn

What is the significance of this recital of coverages and comparisons for the natural information programs in the various countries? Does the fact that Latin American coverage by stream gauging stations is in every country far below that of the United States mean that an enormous effort should be made to expand this coverage? Does the extremely low coverage by detailed soils maps in almost all of Latin America indicate the desirability of a ten- or twenty-fold expansion in the rate of soil mapping?

Table 10. Coverage of Latin American Countries by Stream Gauges as of the Early 1960's

Country	Number of stations	Average number of years of data	Density[1] per 1,000 km²	Coefficient of coverage[2] (*station years per 1,000 km²*)
Argentina	537	26.0	0.2	5.2
Bolivia	85	8.7	0.08	0.7
Brazil	1,287	17.9	0.15	2.7
Colombia	227	7.0	0.20	1.4
Chile	260	13.0	0.30	3.9
Ecuador	18	4.0	0.10	0.4
Paraguay	—	—	—	—
Peru	216	12.3	0.17	2.1
Uruguay	—	—	—	—
Venezuela	248	8.0	0.3	2.4
Costa Rica	15	3.8	0.3	1.14
Cuba	26	—	0.22	—
El Salvador	41	2.6	2.05	5.33
Guatemala	8	9.0	0.07	0.63
Haiti	29	—	1.05	—
Honduras	40	2.7	0.36	0.97
Mexico	965	10.4	0.93	9.67
Nicaragua	16	13.0	0.11	1.43
Panama	47	7.2	0.62	4.46
Dominican Republic	10	—	0.21	—

Sources: Data for Bolivia, Colombia, Argentina, Chile, Ecuador, and Venezuela are from *Los Recursos Hidraúlicos de América Latina: III, Bolivia y Colombia* (New York: United Nations, 1964). Data for Peru are from "Los Recursos Hidraúlicos del Perú" (Santiago: ECLA, December 1965). For other countries, "Los Recursos Hidroeléctricos en América Latina: Su medición y aprovechamiento," *Boletín Económico de América Latina* (Santiago), February 1962.

[1] See Table 9, fn. 1.
[2] See Table 9, fn. 2.

Whether the answers to these questions are yes or no (and they almost surely are no, in my judgment), coefficients of coverage by themselves comprise only a small part of the information needed when one must decide whether to expand soils survey activity, increase the number of stream gauging stations, and so on. All that such coefficients can do is to give some idea of the present state of natural resource information, and they can do this only very imperfectly. As will be discussed further in Chapter VI, decisions on expansion or contraction of information-producing activities require detailed information on the present status of soil surveys and the like. This much is obvious. What may not be so obvious is that the decision to expand or contract requires more than these data. There is no escape from evaluating—even if only in the most approximate way—the return to be expected from additional expenditure to develop information. This will depend not only on the physical opportunities that will be uncovered by better and more complete information but also on the capacity of the country to use and apply the information. Thus, a low level of coverage of natural resource information in a country with large areas that are not currently utilized and that probably will not be utilized for many years may not indicate a need for an expanded information program. Similarly, where there are inadequate personnel and organization for putting natural resource information to use, a country may not be harmed by a low coverage of survey information. It will need to advance on both fronts—information and administration—simultaneously, for these two types of investment are complementary at this stage in a country's development.

Some people take the view that since expenditure on natural resource information is a form of investment, the desirable rate of expenditure should be more closely related to a country's national income or rate of gross investment than to its area or to some standard level of information "density." Even so, such a relationship, if it could be derived, must involve great variation among countries, for there is little reason to expect that investment or income will reflect very closely the opportunities for investment in more natural resource information. This would be the case for expenditure on all types of natural resource information taken together and more so for separate types of information. Consequently, any simple rule to guide investment outlay on information, such as a standard percentage of national income, is too rough to be useful. What can be done is to develop guidelines for information expenditures and for organization and procedures that will make possible considerably better decisions on investment outlays, even though estimates of returns are imprecise. Chapters V and VI deal with these two areas that are basic to the development of any natural resource information program.

Present Natural Resource Information
Activities in Latin America

The foregoing has dealt with the present *state* of natural resource information in Latin America. The availability of information bearing on this topic is attributable mainly to the efforts of the staffs of the Economic Commission for Latin America and the Organization of American States. It is a far more difficult task to assemble a picture of the activities that are under way in the various information fields. At best the materials for such a picture are fragmentary and dispersed among many agencies or institutions. The task of centralizing and co-ordinating the separate pieces of information and classifying activities by a system of uniform definitions has not yet been accomplished, but a beginning has been made. Since late 1966 the Committee on Basic Natural Resources of the Pan American Institute of Geography and History[7] has been making efforts to assemble systematic and detailed information on natural resource information activities. Data on the types, rates, locations, financing, and organization of information-producing activity are being gathered by questionnaire from governmental organizations of each of the Latin American countries and also from international organizations operating in Latin America. The results of this comprehensive survey should give us a much better picture of public natural resource information activities in Latin America than has been possible up to this time. Private activity that increases the stock of knowledge about natural resources is not covered in this survey.

In the meantime, information is readily available on at least the summary aspects of natural resource information projects that have been financed in part by the Special Fund of the United Nations and in part by the government of each country involved. Since its establishment in 1959, the Special Fund has contributed to a large number of such projects, some of them of a survey type and others designed to aid in the evaluation of projects. A United Nations unit, perhaps the Division of Natural Resources and Transport of the Department of Economic and Social Affairs,[8] or a unit from the Food and Agriculture Organization, usually is designated as executing agent, and the project ordinarily is administered jointly by international and national personnel.

These Special Fund projects are grouped by type in Table 11, which also

[7] This effort of the Committee, a part of the Commission on Geography, was begun under the chairmanship of Professor Reynaldo Börgel O. of the University of Chile.
[8] For a description of the activities of this unit, see its paper, "La Experiencia Recogida en Las Actividades de Las Naciones Unidas en América Latina en Cuanto a Recursos Naturales por la División de Recursos Naturales y Transportes del Departamento de Asuntos Económicos y Sociales de las Naciones Unidas" (UNESCO/CASTALA/2.1.8. Paris, August 13, 1965).

gives the source of funds, average size of project, and average length of time the projects have been in operation.

Soil surveys have accounted for only 3 per cent of the total expended, whereas forests and minerals account for 40 per cent. A careful examination of the efficiency of this allocation would be valuable. An important factor in such an evaluation would be an examination of opportunities for development investment outside these projects but related to them. It should be remembered that other information activities, not financed by the United Nations, are going on all the time. Hence an apparent imbalance in UN-financed activities may not be evident in the larger view.

To give a more detailed idea of the kind of work undertaken, the projects summarized in Table 11 are listed separately in Table 12, together with a brief description of each, its source and amount of finance, UN man-years involved, authorized beginning date, and planned duration. In some cases it is possible to calculate a cost per unit area. These numbers are not very useful to the general reader, for they do not apply to a standardized commodity and can not be combined to derive a meaningful average cost figure. Moreover, some of the projects for which such a figure has been calculated contain elements that are not related to area, thus clouding the significance of a number for cost per square kilometer. But persons who have some familiarity with the results of particular projects may find the figures for cost per square kilometer to be useful.

Table 11. United Nations Special Fund Projects in Natural Resources in Latin America, Classified by Type

Type	Funds provided by		Average project expenditure (*million dollars*)	Average duration (*years*)
	United Nations (*million dollars*)	host government (*million dollars*)		
Forests	11.0	14.6	2.13	4.4
Minerals	13.1	10.9	1.50	2.7
Fisheries	5.5	9.2	3.68	4.8
Soil	1.7	2.4	1.70	2.2
Meteorology and hydrology	8.1	7.7	2.63	4.5
Irrigation	5.8	9.4	2.16	3.7
Water resources	8.0	6.4	1.20	2.5
Other	5.9	4.7	1.51	2.2
All	59.1	65.3	1.86	3.3

Table 12.   United Nations Special Fund Projects in Latin America

Country	Purpose	Funds provided by — United Nations (thousand dollars)	Funds provided by — host government (thousand dollars)	Cost per km² (dollars)	United Nations man-years	Authorization to commence execution (date) and project duration (years)
	FOREST SURVEYS					
Chile	To establish an institute for research and training in forestry industries	1,268	900	—	44	August 1961 / 4
Paraguay	To carry out a forest inventory over an area of 30,000 km², prepare forest development plans	1,037	422	48.6	22	na / 5
Honduras	To carry out a forest inventory over an area of 7,000 km²	422	580	143.0	9	January 1962 / 3¾
Mexico	To assist in the survey of the forest resources of Mexico and to study inventory methods for tropical forests	418	1,044	—	na	May 1961 / 4
Mexico	To strengthen the National Institute of Forest Research to enable it to assist in formulating and developing a forestry plan	1,685	6,000	—	36	na / 6
Panama	To carry out a detailed inventory over an area of 2,000 km² (including aerial photographs, topographic and vegetation maps)	883	525	704.0	na	na / 4
Venezuela	To carry out a survey of forest resources over an area of 25,000 km² in order to prepare a forest industries development plan	599	1,123	68.9	14	December 1963 / 4
Nicaragua	To carry out a survey of agricultural and forestry resources over a pilot area of 2,000 km² and prepare a development plan of the Pto. Cabezas-Río Coco zone	852	439	645.5	25	January 1963 / 4

Table 12 (cont.)

Country	Purpose	Funds provided by		Cost per km² (*dollars*)	United Nations man-years	Authorization to commence execution (*date*) and project duration (*years*)
		United Nations (*thousand dollars*)	host government			
	FORREST SURVEYS (cont.)					
Colombia	To carry out a survey of selected forests in the Magdalena Valley, to prepare a forest development plan, and to establish a research and demonstration center	937	1,140	—	25	June 1964 4
Ecuador	To carry out a forest survey over selected areas in order to prepare a forest industries development plan; the project will study 10,000 km²	826	895	172.1	19	November 1963 5
Guatemala	To carry out a forest survey over an area of 13,000 km² to prepare a forest industries development plan	767	893	127.8	18	August 1963 5
Guyana	To assist the government in determining the extent and composition of accessible forests, and to develop suitable methods of extraction, processing, and marketing of forest products	1,308	685	—	34	na 4
		11,002	14,646			
	MINERAL SURVEYS					
Guatemala	To assess the mineral potential of two selected areas of 20,000 km²	801	469	63.5	17	March 1966 3
Chile	To carry out intensive ground investigations to assess the mineral potential of promising areas	1,161	610	na	13	na 2½
Nicaragua	To carry out intensive investigations of a promising area of about 18,000 km² to assess its mineral potential	739	355	60.8	11	August 1963 2½

Country	Description					Date	
Panama	To assess the mineral potential of the Azuero Peninsula and its northern extension; project area: 21,000 km²	823	546	65.2	14	October 1965	3
Mexico	To obtain geological and economic data on promising iron ore zones of 59,000 km²; to accelerate the technical training of Mexican staff in techniques of mineral exploration	897	1,850	46.6	na	July 1962	3
Ecuador	To assess deposits of metallic and non-metallic minerals of 20,000 km² and to build up the National Department of Geology	820	572	69.6	18	December 1964	3½
Bolivia	To carry out pilot demonstrations in petroleum exploration and production, undertake corollary research, and train technical personnel	795	645	na	18	na	3
Bolivia	To assist in the development of gold production in the Tipanui area by improving techniques of extraction and by assessing new reserves	787	418	na	16	na	4
Chile	To assess the technical and economic feasibility of exploiting minerals over an area of 30,000 km² of Coquimbo province	507	298	26.8	16	April 1964	2
El Salvador	To access the mineral resources of selected areas (6,500 km²) and to train professionals for the National Geological Service in the use of modern techniques	591	342	143.5	13	na	3
Argentina	To carry out aerial and ground surveys over a cordilleran area to assess its mineral potential; project area, for detailed investigation: 50,000 km²	1,167	1,244	48.2	28	October 1963	3½
Argentina	To obtain, through detailed geophysical investigations and drilling, information on the mining potential of porphyry copper type mineralization in the provinces of Mendoza and Neuquén; project area: 14,000 km²	1,158	956	151.0	9	na	1½
Guyana	Intensified ground investigation of prospects revealed by earlier airborne surveys and execution of supplementary airborne geophysical surveys	1,036	1,077	na	18	na	3

Table 12 (cont.)

Country	Purpose	Funds provided by		Cost per km² (dollars)	United Nations man-years	Authorization to commence execution (date) and project duration (years)
		United Nations (thousand dollars)	host government (thousand dollars)			
	MINERAL SURVEYS (cont.)					
Colombia	To study the possibilities of developing coal deposits in the Cauca Valley	217	120	na	na	February 1963 ¾
Bolivia	An intensive survey of 40,000 km² located south of Cochabamba	922	685	40.2	19	November 1961 4
Guyana	Through aerial geophysical surveying of promising areas, to delineate smaller areas whose mineral potential will be assessed through ground investigations; project area: 6,000 km²	641	700	223.5	na	June 1962 3
		13,062	10,887			
	FISHERY SURVEYS					
Peru	To assist in the further development of the fishing industry through a study of anchovy stocks and surveys of new resources	855	2,110	—	24	na 4
Central America	To assist in the strengthening of fishery administrations, development and proper management of various fisheries, in improving processing and marketing, and in carrying out an off-shore resource survey	1,829	2,170	—	49	September 1965 6
Venezuela	To assist in the development of fisheries through surveys, research and experimental fishing	1,340	4,145	—	40	na 5

Caribbean	To contribute to the development of the Caribbean fisheries through exploratory fishing, demonstrations and training of professionals	1,448	773	—	39	August 1965	4
		5,472	9,198				

SOIL SURVEYS

Chile	The project will consist of four parts: (a) detailed soil surveys over an area of about 10,000 km², (b) soil fertility studies, (c) investigations related to soils and their productive capacity, (d) training of personnel	815	1,688	250.3	22		
Colombia	To survey the soil of the northern part (168,884 km²) of the Llanos Orientales to determine soils capability and land use possibilities of the area	371	318	4.1	na	October 1960	3¾
Guyana	To assist in carrying out a soil survey of certain coastal and other areas of Guyana; project area: 4,000 km²	491	388	219.8	21	December 1960	3
		1,677	2,394				

METEOROLOGICAL AND HYDROLOGICAL SURVEYS

Central America and Panama	To establish a comprehensive regional network of 870 hydrometeorological and 270 hydrometric stations	2,915	3,257	—	20	na	5
Ecuador	To expand the existing meteorological and hydrological services of the country	406	797	—	na	July 1960	4
Brazil	To develop procedures for modern weather and flood forecasting and to train technicians to carry on expanded meteorological services in the northeast	1,087	727	—	11	na	4½
Caribbean	To improve the Caribbean meteorological network and to establish a regional institute for training and research purposes	1,622	818	—	20	na	4

Table 12 (cont.)

Country	Purpose	Funds provided by		Cost per km² (*dollars*)	United Nations man-years	Authorization to commence execution (*date*) and project duration (*years*)
		United Nations (*thousand dollars*)	host government (*thousand dollars*)			
	METEOROLOGICAL AND HYDROLOGICAL SURVEYS (cont.)					
Chile	To improve and expand the existing network of hydrometric and hydrometeorological stations	613	1,200	—	na	July 1960 4½
Brazil	To obtain regular hydrological information for the Upper Paraguay River basin and to investigate the behavior of the Pantanal hydraulic system and its influence on the Paraguay River regime	1,506	880	—	28	na 5
		8,149	7,679			
	IRRIGATION SURVEYS					
Peru	To carry out technical and economic surveys for irrigation in the Pampa de Olmos; area: 75,000 km²	786	967	23.4	22	December 1962 3
Peru	To conduct technical and economic surveys for agriculture and irrigation in Huaura River basin	808	920	na	23	na 3
Argentina	To survey land and water resources for irrigation development; the surveys will cover the entire area of the Viedma Valley (80,000 km²)	762	624	17.3	19	July 1963 4
Panama	To conduct feasibility studies for an irrigation project in the La Villa River basin; project area: more than 10,000 ha	970	782	—	23	na 5

Country	Description						
Haiti	To survey ground-water and surface-water resources for irrigation and to conduct trials and demonstrations in irrigated agriculture in the Gonaives Plain	666	470	na	16	November 1963	3
Brazil	To determine the physical and economic feasibility of introducing large scale irrigation in the lower-middle reaches of the San Francisco River basin; project area: 60,000 km² (Phase I)	974	990	32.8	na	na	5
Brazil	Survey of the San Francisco River basin (Phase II): to assist in the establishment of two pilot irrigation schemes on the basis of preliminary studies (Phase I) now nearing completion	865	4,640	na	16	na	3
		5,831	9,393				

WATER RESOURCES SURVEYS

Country	Description						
El Salvador	To assess the amount of groundwater available in the metropolitan area of San Salvador and to create a ground-water development service; project area: 600 km²	686	743	—	17	October 1965	3½
El Salvador	To assess the ground-water potential in the Valley of the Lower Río Grande de San Miguel	348	563	—	—	April 1961	2¾
Argentina	To investigate and assess ground-water resources in the arid and semi-arid zone of Argentina, and to train Argentine staff in modern techniques; project area: 20,000 km²	674	650	66.3	17	February 1965	4
Panama	To carry out a pre-investment survey of water resources for generation of hydroelectric power and use for irrigation in the Chiriqui and Chico river basins	419	91	—	2	November 1963	2
Dominican Republic	To carry out feasibility studies for hydropower and irrigation development in the Yaque del Norte and Yaque del Sur river basins	1,292	1,589	—	na	October 1965	2

Table 12 (cont.)

WATER RESOURCES SURVEYS (cont.)

Country	Purpose	Funds provided by		Cost per km² (dollars)	United Nations man-years	Authorization to commence execution (date) and project duration (years)
		United Nations (thousand dollars)	host government (thousand dollars)			
Guatemala	To assist in the survey of the country's hydraulic resources for purposes of electrification and irrigation	634	250	—	na	August 1961 / 2
Jamaica	To assess possibilities for ground-water development in selected areas and to estimate ground- and surface-water resources for development of irrigation	810	344	—	10	April 1965 / 3
Ecuador	To undertake hydrological surveys of the principal rivers of Manabi Province and to study their possible use for agricultural purposes, and to investigate the ground-water supplies of the valleys through Central Manabi	488	253	—	9	October 1962 / 2
Venezuela	To assist in carrying out agricultural surveys of two river basins through the provision of experts, fellows, equipment and contractual services	799	1,000	—	25	August 1962 / 3½
Guyana	To make a comparative study of alternative methods of augmenting the supply of electric power to meet increasing demand	876	292	—	3	May 1966 / 2
Argentina	To define the probable trends of power demand on the various systems in Argentina during the next 10-year period and to assess different supply configurations	250	50	—	na	September 1959 / ½
Brazil	To assist in the study of a hydrological project and to assess availability of the hydroelectric power resources in the state of Minas Gerais	753	560	—	na	October 1962 / 3
		8,009	6,385			

Other Types of Surveys

Mexico	To undertake feasibility studies for the development of the state of Oaxaca	693	750	—	24	na	2
Argentina	To undertake a survey of the physical and socioeconomic conditions affecting the development of the Comahue region	570	700	—	15	na	2
Paraguay	To carry out a road plan to open up those areas in southern Paraguay which have the best prospects for agricultural development	392	140	—	na	May 1964	2
Peru	To determine areas appropriate for colonization or resettlement, the agricultural patterns suitable to each, and to train local personnel to conduct such surveys	183	—	—	na	March 1961	2
Chile	To investigate the geothermal resources of northern Chile; project area: 108,000 km²	1,648	1,012	24.6	9	na	3½
El Salvador	To investigate and evaluate the potentiality of geothermal energy for electric power generation over an area of 250 km²	996	479	5,900.0	5	January 1966	2½
Peru	To undertake a general survey of the Central Huallaga, Chiriyacu and Nievas river basins to prepare overall development plan	1,377	1,600	—	40	September 1965	4
		5,859	4,681				

na = not available.

Sources: The figures corresponding to the columns "Funds provided by" and "man-years" were taken directly from "Recomendaciones del Director General" in the individual project writings prepared by the United Nations. The dates were taken from "Status of Projects in the Special Fund Sector" as of June 1966, United Nations Development Program.

V: Scheduling Expenditures
for Natural Resource Information

Information, like other inputs, costs money. With more information, returns to investment in natural resource projects can be increased. This increase in return comes about in various ways—perhaps by avoiding agricultural investment where climate is inappropriate or by designing dams, bridges, and irrigation works more in accord with the true characteristics of the site.

The return that information produces does not rise indefinitely, however, but diminishes as more and more information on an investment opportunity is assembled. Thus, the return to more information behaves in the same way as the return to any other input: after a point it begins to rise at a less rapid rate. The problem is to decide how far to go beyond this point. It is possible to accumulate so much information that more will not increase the total return at all.

Because expenditure on information is subject to diminishing returns, it is possible to spend too much on it. Obviously, the goal should be to increase expenditure on information to the point where additional return generated is balanced by the cost of the information—but no further. It is the purpose of this chapter to discuss some of the considerations involved in this problem. Simple examples of increasing complexity will be used, but because readers who are not economists may find the modes of expression in these examples different from those to which they are accustomed, the leading ideas will first be presented in a non-technical way.

Information on natural resources is of two kinds. If there are no records from the past, the first type can be gathered only by waiting for more data to unfold with the passage of time. Streamflow and climatological data are of this type. Gathering the second type of information is much closer to being independent of time, being exemplified by soil and other surveys in which pieces of ground are examined successively for certain characteristics. For the time being, attention will be confined to the first type of information. If it is not available when needed, we shall have to wait. If we want to have it when needed, we shall have to anticipate this need, usually by a good many years.

Consider what would happen in a large number of cases in which irrigation dams are to be built on similar sites but with no data on the amount of water available at the time of each decision to build. The only way to find out how much water is available is to wait for nature to perform. But how long should we wait? On the one hand, the flow is variable from one year to the next. If we don't wait very long, our estimate of what the flow will be over a long period of time may be greatly in error simply because the next few years may be unusually wet or dry. There is no way to tell whether a particular sample of, say, three years is unusual or not, but we can be sure that the estimates of the long-run flow made on the basis of a large number of five-year samples will cluster much more closely around the true value than would the estimates of a large number of three-year samples.

Now consider what happens to the stream of annual receipts[1] minus outlays when the estimate on the basis of which the dam is designed is in error. If the estimate of flow is too low, the project will be too small and receipts will be lower than with a project designed to take full advantage of the water available. There may also be damage from occasional high flows. On the other hand, an erroneously high estimate of water available will result in the construction of works that will not be used to their full capacity.

The advantage of having a more accurate estimate of water available can be had only by waiting for a larger sample of data to develop. But waiting brings with it two kinds of costs. First, although nature will perform without our buying an admission ticket, a quantitative record of this performance costs money. Equipment and people are required to record stream behavior. Second, the damsite is only the most evident part of a site that must be thought of as a piece of (natural) capital which can yield a return to society when combined with man-made capital goods. If we sit around waiting for more data to develop, the stream of potential net revenues from this site, or piece of natural capital, is also delayed.

We conclude that waiting another year for more data to develop is justified only if the increase in the value of the stream of net revenues, because of better design, is more than enough to offset the cost of collecting another year of data *and* of the postponement of the stream of net revenues.

To make this comparison, we need a way to express the value of the stream of net revenues as a single number associated with a given date. That is, we need a method for comparing sums of money received or paid at different dates, for the annual receipts and outlays of a project are spread out over the whole life of a project, with a large part of the outlays being made at the time of construction, of course.

---

[1] In some cases, receipts must be thought of as benefits (in money terms) for which no payment actually is made.

The appropriate method for making this comparison is called discounting (discussed in some detail in the Appendix to Chapter I). The basic fact involved here is that funds invested to produce real capital can earn a real return over and above the sum initially invested. This return is expressed as a rate of interest, or discount. Thus if $100 invested in a certain economic activity will be worth $120 a year from now, the rate of interest is $\frac{120}{100} - 1 = 0.20$, or 20 per cent per year. If the $120 were left in this activity for another year, it would be worth $144 = 120 + 0.20(120) = [100(1 + 0.20)] (1 + 0.20) = 100(1 + 0.20)^2$.

To compare $144 received at the end of, say, 1970, with a sum received two years earlier, we can *discount* the $144 to the earlier date by reversing the "accumulating" procedure of the preceding paragraph. Thus the $144 of 1970 is worth $\frac{144}{(1 + 0.20)^2} = 100$ as of 1968.

Now let us return to our problem. Suppose that if a large number of similar projects is constructed with design in each case based on a sample of five years of data, the average value of the projects with the streams of net receipts discounted to the time of construction (say, January 1, 1969) is 100. If in these cases we wait for one more year of data, the opportunity to start the stream of receipts on January 1, 1969 is foregone. What is the value of this foregone opportunity as of January 1, 1970? Simply $100(1 + 0.20) = 120 if the appropriate rate of discount is 20 per cent.

What else is foregone by waiting? The products that could have been produced and consumed or invested with the money used to collect the additional year's data, say $3.

Now we can decide whether to wait or not. The value of the project with the additional year of data is, say, $127 as of January 1, 1970. We must ask if this is greater than the value of the foregone opportunities: $127 > 120 + 3$.

The answer is yes, and we should wait one more year. If we express the above inequality in general terms, we ask if

$$V_{70} > (1 + r)V_{69} + k$$

or $$(V_{70} - V_{69}) > rV_{69} + k.$$

That is, a wait of a year for more data is justified only if the increase in the value of the project as of the date of construction is greater than interest on the value for the earlier date plus the cost of collecting another year's data.

In contrast with the preceding case, suppose that the time of construction of the project can be foreseen. How much earlier should we start collecting data? Here there is no question of postponing the start of the stream of net receipts by beginning to collect data one year earlier, but the increase in the value of the stream of net receipts must be at least as great as the cost of starting to collect data one year earlier, say, k, *cumulated at the rate of discount to the date of construction.* That is, the increase in the average value of projects with, say, six years of data must be greater than that with five by at least $k(1 + r)^6$. In general terms, if starting data collection one year earlier means going to the nth year before the date of construction, the increase in project value must be at least as great as $k(1 + r)^n$.

In both of the preceding cases, the data collection program should be undertaken only if the program of optimum length yields a surplus after taking into account all data collection costs cumulated at the rate of discount to the date of construction. It might be, for example, that extension of a program from four to five years would increase the value of the project by just enough to cover the cost of the fifth year of data, but with the cost of all five years of data greater than the value of the project.

Although the development of a number of types of natural resource data is not rigidly connected with the passage of time, the basic factors involved in deciding on the quantity of information to generate and when to generate it are the same, with one addition, namely, that the cost of generating information depends in part on the rate at which it is generated. It still takes time to generate information, however. Hence, we still want to balance the gain in project value from more information against the cumulated cost of getting it plus any interest cost arising from delaying the start of the project's stream of net revenues.

Information whose generation is not rigidly connected with time is of two different types. The first is information connected with a localized project site, such as information on the characteristics of a potential damsite. The problem of determining the quantity of different types of information is not very difficult for many of these cases. With less than the "standard" quantity, risk of serious loss is incurred, for example, risk of structural failure, whereas beyond a rather well-defined point more information will be of no help in improving design or operation. The problems here are to avoid premature generation of information and to manage the rate at which the work is done to minimize its discounted cost.

The second type of information not rigidly connected with time is that used as part of a sifting process, perhaps best exemplified by information aimed at finding minerals. In the early stages of search in an area not previously investigated, the function of the information is to aid in rejecting certain areas (provisionally, of course) and in selecting others for more intensive investigation. Once the decision to make a survey of this type is made, there is great freedom in planning operations to minimize discounted cost, but the decision to undertake the survey or not presents serious difficulties. The emphasis given earlier to the importance of the time when expenditures are made, which receives expression through the process of discounting, is very appropriate to extensive surveys, too. If undertaken prematurely, costs are increased greatly because of interest on the outlays. If the rate of interest is 10 per cent per year, $100 spent now is equivalent to $259 ten years later. The availability of good investment opportunities carries the immediate implication that it is very costly—*in terms of real product sacrificed*—to squander money on investment in capital goods, including information, that yield no return or whose services will be utilized only at a later time.

Having summarized the leading ideas of the chapter, we proceed to a more detailed and technical discussion of them. If at some point a reader should find the material too demanding of time, the more general argument may be picked up again on page 110.

Time-bound Information

Information Collected after Sudden Perception
of an Existing Investment Opportunity

The first problem to be considered involves the kind of information that can be developed only in lockstep with the passage of time. River flow data and climatological information are good examples, although certain aspects of past river behavior can be brought to light by a careful study of vegetation along streams and perhaps other objects on which river behavior can leave its mark.[2]

Similarly, certain climatic variables, notably precipitation, leave their marks on long-lasting vegetation, such as trees. Careful study of such phenomena can supplement and extend data collected in the ordinary fashion. In both cases, unsystematic historical records antedating a data collection program may yield useful information about some variables, for example, flood frequency and severity. And it may be possible to extend the record for certain locations by studying the relations between their data and that for other places with a longer record.[3] It is still the case, however, that stream data and climatological data are mainly dependent

[2] See, for example, U.S. Geological Survey, *Botanical Evidence of Floods and Flood-Plain Deposition*, Professional Paper 485-A (Washington: U.S. Government Printing Office, 1964).

[3] See, for example, United Nations, ECAFE, World Meteorological Organization, *Hydrologic Networks and Methods*, Flood Control Series No. 15 (Bangkok, 1960). (Transactions of Interregional Seminar on Hydrologic Networks and Methods, held at Bangkok, Thailand, July 14–27, 1959.)

in the first instance on records which are extended only as the phenomena unfold with the passage of time.

The other type of information can be developed more nearly independently of time; examples are forest inventories, the characteristics of a mineral deposit, a soil survey, or the physical characteristics of a dam site. The cost of gathering this information is less closely related to the passage of time, but it is not completely independent. Later it will become evident that the considerations involved in the time-bound information considered in the first type—e.g., river flow data—are of considerable relevance also for information whose connection with the passage of time is looser— e.g., soil surveys.

Now let us consider the task faced by, say, a large irrigation development agency of a government. It finds that it is repeatedly planning projects of a similar type involving similar sites that do not have uniform hydrology. We assume that each time such an investment opportunity is perceived, the agency finds that no flow data are available.[4]

We assume that there is only one way to develop flow data, namely, by waiting for the years to pass by while a record is being made of the flow. How many years should pass before construction of the project is undertaken? If this type of project is constructed only after a few years of data have been generated, average returns will be lowered. In many cases the structure(s) will be of the wrong size or scope with consequent losses from destruction or damage, failure to take advantage of economic potential, or excess capacity.

On the other hand, delay in construction means a delay in the start of the flow of net incomes that could otherwise be had. As we shall see, this is a very important factor in deciding how long to wait for data to accumulate.

To simplify exposition, we assume that the distribution of annual flow is normal and that its dispersion is known but that the mean flow, on which design of the project and payoff depend, is not known. It is further assumed that the demand for the product(s) of the project is constant through time. This demand had been there all the time, but only a certain number of projects are perceived each year.

In summary, the conditions assumed are:

1. Unchanging demand function.

2. Distribution of annual flow normal, variance known.

3. Payoff depends on unknown mean annual flow and design of structures.

---

[4] This is not an unusual situation. I have heard more than once the equivalent of, "There's the engineer who perceived x damsite."

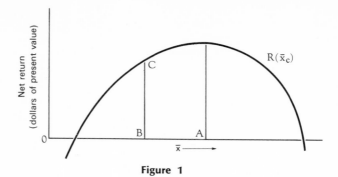

Figure 1

The steps to be followed in deciding how many years to wait for data to accumulate are the following:

1. To develop the relation, $R(\bar{x}_c)$, between net return and mean annual flow, $\bar{x}_c$, assumed to be known with certainty.

2. To develop the relation, $R(\bar{x}_e \mid \bar{x}^*)$ between net return and estimated mean annual flow, $\bar{x}_e$, given a specific actual mean flow, $\bar{x}^*$.

3. To develop the relation, $R(n)$, between expected net return and number of years of data available for calculating estimated mean flow, $\bar{x}_e$.

$R(\bar{x})$—*Relation between net return and mean flow known with certainty.* The site characteristics for one type of project will yield a maximum present value of the flow of revenues and outlays for one average flow. This is the flow best adapted to the site characteristics. Higher flows will reduce net return, say, because of higher structure costs to cope with the flow, whereas lower flows will reduce receipts. That is, lower mean flows simply would not exploit fully the characteristics of the site. For example, in Figure 1, in which $\bar{x}_c$ signifies $\bar{x}$ assumed to be known with certainty, a mean flow of OA would yield the maximum net return and most fully exploit the site characteristics. All other mean flows would yield a lower return. For example, if OB was known to be the mean flow, OC would be the net return for works best adapted to the site characteristics *and* the flow OB.[5]

[5] The form of the function will depend on the particular circumstances of the investment opportunity. For some types of bridge problems, $R(\bar{x}_c)$ might have no maximum.

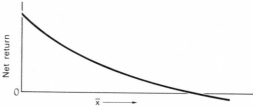

Suppose, for example, that a small flow would stop a certain flow of traffic. Then larger flows would simply necessitate a more costly structure and reduce the net return.

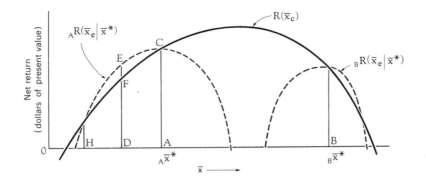

Figure 2

$R(\bar{x}_e \mid \bar{x}^*)$—*Net return with design based on erroneous flow estimate.* If mean flow must be estimated, realized net return will necessarily be less than for a project designed for the correct mean flow. How much less will depend on the size of the error in the estimate.

In Figure 2, suppose the true mean flow is OA and that the estimate is correct, i.e., $\bar{x}_e = {}_A\bar{x}^*$.[6] In this case net return is AC, that is $R(\bar{x}_e \mid \bar{x}^*) = R(\bar{x}_c)$. If the mean is estimated to be OD, however, net return is diminished from AC to DE. It is higher than the return, DF, corresponding to an actual mean flow of OD, although there is no reason why it couldn't be lower, as it is to the left of OH.

For $\bar{x}_e$ greater than OA, realized return is less than OC and is below $R(\bar{x}_c)$.

Case B, falling on the right-hand branch of $R(\bar{x}_c)$, illustrates the situation in which actual mean flow is greater than that best adapted to site characteristics.

Now let us return to case A. The frequency with which mean flow is estimated to be OD, with true flow equal to OA, clearly is going to depend on the number of years of data available. If five years of data are available, for example, a series of cases of this type would yield a distribution of $\bar{x}_e$'s centered at OA, the true mean $({}_A\bar{x}^*)$, but many estimates would be in error. There would be a normal distribution of $\bar{x}_e$'s, as illustrated by Figure 3, which reproduces case A and shows the corresponding frequency distribution of $\bar{x}_e$ around ${}_A\bar{x}^*$.

Consider the net return, DE, associated with the strip at OD. The relative frequency (the area under the whole frequency curve is equal to one) of DE is indicated by the strip DL.

---

[6] The subscript e indicates "estimated" and A indicates case A.

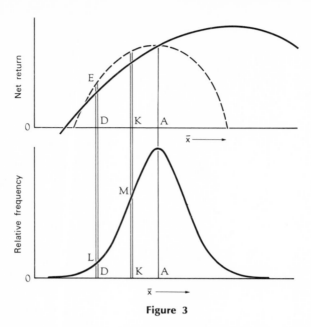

Figure 3

The net return for $\bar{x}_e$ closer to $OA = {}_A\bar{x}^*$ is more frequent, as indicated by OK and the strip KM in the frequency diagram.

If net return strips of this type are taken over the whole range of $\bar{x}_e$, the net return for each is multiplied by the corresponding probability strip in the lower diagram and all are summed, the result is expected net return, Exp (R), for cases in which five years of data are available.

Now consider how Figure 3 would be changed if sixteen years of data were available for each estimate of $\bar{x}_e$ in a series instead of four. The net return functions would be unchanged, but the relative frequency function would be less dispersed, poor estimates being less frequent. The two situations are compared in Figure 4. Thus an $\bar{x}_e = OD$ becomes less frequent whereas estimates close enough to OA become more frequent. Thus, the expected net return for $n = 16$ would be higher than for $n = 4$.

$V(n)$—*Expected net return as function of number of years of data.* Expected values of net return for different number of years of data available, n, can be combined into a function, $V(n)$, illustrated in Figure 5. This may be negative for small n. It will increase with n but at a decreasing rate as it approaches a maximum for large samples which yield almost correct estimates of $\bar{x}^*$.

Note that this function does not take into account the cost of generating information.

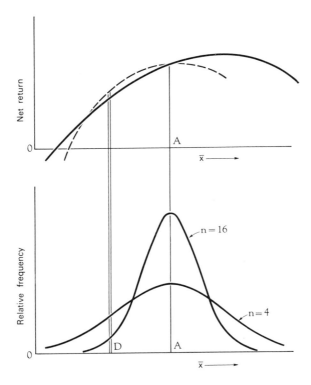

Figure 4

In this simple example, it is a consequence of the standard deviation of the estimated mean, $\sigma_{\bar{x}_e} = \dfrac{\sigma_{\bar{x}_i}}{\sqrt{n}}$, that the first units of information, measured by number of years of data, are very valuable indeed. The ratio of $\sigma^2_{\bar{x}_e}$ for samples of n and $(n + 1)$ is $\dfrac{n}{n + 1}$. This approaches one with what, for this problem, is considerable rapidity.

The effect of successive increases in sample size on expected annual return depends on the particular form of the return function, $R(\bar{x}_e \mid \bar{x}^*)$, of course. The more rapidly $R(\bar{x}_e \mid \bar{x}^*)$ falls off on either side of $\bar{x}^*$, the more pronounced will be the effect on expected return of a given decrease in $\sigma_{\bar{x}_e}$.

How many years of data should be developed? If no data are available at the time the investment opportunity is perceived, the optimum length of time to wait for data accumulation before starting construction will depend on expected net return, $V(n)$, the cost of collecting data, assumed

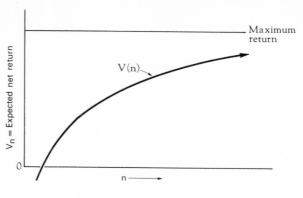

Figure 5

to be k per year, and the rate of discount. To avoid burdensome exposition, design and construction are assumed to be instantaneous and simultaneous.[7]

If "now" is viewed as $t = 0$ and construction takes place after waiting t years for data to accumulate, the present value of the net return, $V(n)$, *as of the date of construction*, can be increased by waiting another year for more data. A wait of another year postpones the whole stream of annual net revenues for one year, however.

The cost of this postponement is one year's interest on $V(t)$ (the present value of the stream of net receipts as of time t) or $rV(t)$. Thus $V(t)$ must be increased by at least this quantity to warrant waiting another year for more data. As more data accumulates, successive increases in $V(t)$ diminish. The optimum time to construct comes when the increase in $V(t)$, labelled $V'(t)$, is equal to interest on $V(t)$, assuming that the annual cost of data collection, k, is zero:

$$V'(t) = rV(t)$$

If the annual cost of data collection, k, is not zero, then the increase must be higher than this by k, and the above expression becomes:

$$V'(t) = rV(t) + k$$

---

[7] Our exposition will proceed on the assumption that the product of the structure is sold at a constant competitive price. Where the product of the structure confronts a sloping demand curve, the economist-adviser must be careful not to advise a design that will maximize total receipts less costs, for this is a monopoly solution. The project should maximize consumers' plus producer surplus, which requires equality between marginal consumer evaluations (indicated by price) and marginal cost. Errors in prediction must be evaluated by their effect on this surplus and not by their effect on net revenues.

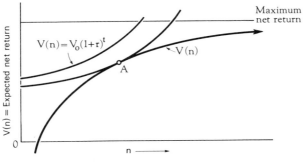

Figure 6

By dividing both sides of this equation by $V(t)$, we get the $\dfrac{\text{percentage}}{100}$ rate of increase in $V(t)$:

$$\frac{V'(t)}{V(t)} = r + \frac{k}{V(t)}.$$

Of course this maximum must be at a high enough level to cover the cost of collecting the data accumulated with interest to the same point in time.[8]

Thus if annual cost of data collection is small in relation to $V(n)$, it will pay to postpone construction almost to the point where $V(n)$ is increasing at the rate of interest or discount.

These relationships are illustrated in Figure 6. Along with $V(n)$ have been drawn two curves each of which has a given present value for all points on the curve satisfying the relation $V(n) = V_0(1 + r)^t$. That is, the curve increases at the rate of interest. The highest of these curves attainable, assuming $k = 0$, is that curve which touches $V(n)$ at only one point, i.e.,

---

[8] In general terms, if $V(n)$ = expected present value of streams of revenues and outlays at time of construction given that n years of data are available, then since $n = t$, viewing "now" as $t = 0$, we seek to maximize as of "now"

$$W = V(t)e^{-rt} - \int_0^{t_1} ke^{-rt}\, dt$$

$$\frac{dW}{dt} = V(t)e^{-rt}(-r) + e^{-rt}V'(t) - ke^{-rt} = 0,$$

or, $V'(t) = rV(t) + k.$

It is also necessary that total information costs be covered by $V(n)$ if the data are to be collected, that is,

$$V(t_1) \geq \int_0^{t_1} k\, e^{rt}\, dt$$

$$\geq \frac{k}{r}(e^{rt_1} - 1).$$

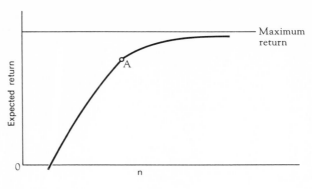

Figure 7

point A. At this point $V(n)$ is increasing at the rate of discount. If k is not equal to zero, then the optimum number of years will be less than that indicated by point A and $V(n)$ must be rising more rapidly than the rate of interest.

Note that it will never pay to wait for the "complete" information necessary to attain the maximum present value as of the date of construction, for this would entail waiting forever.

Is there a "minimum amount of information?" On the basis of the foregoing analysis of the basic information situation, it is possible to suggest a useful interpretation of an idea frequently encountered but rarely defined—that there is a "minimum necessary" quantity of information that should be available before committing funds to a whole project.

The notion of a "minimum necessary" amount of information might be represented by the case in which the expected annual return curve changes slope rapidly at a level close to the maximum return, as at point A in Figure 7. The increase in expected annual return as data increase is very rapid up to point A but then rapidly falls off.

Actually, there probably are many situations of this sort, but their proper solution is so obvious so far as the optimum quantity of information is concerned that we tend not to realize that they are particular cases of a more general problem. An extreme case in point is that of a tailor who is asked to make a pair of pants. Assuming the legs are to be of the same length, how long should they be? In terms of our model, the question is how much time (the analogue of n) should be devoted to getting some relevant information. One possibility is to make the legs the same length as those of the last pair he made. Another is to make them equal to the average length of legs of pants made in the the last year,

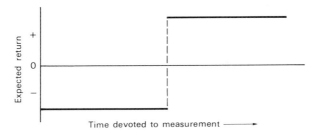

Figure 8

perhaps taking account of the secular change in the length of his customers' legs if he has pretensions to being a fancy estimator. Still a third option is to measure the customer's legs. The expected return function for this option is negative up to the amount of time required for measurement. Then it jumps to a positive level and stays there. Once the legs are measured, there is no point in repeating the exercise.

Many types of information can be looked at in more or less similar terms. There are some things that simply "must" be known before a dam is constructed, for example. One had better know the composition of the foundation and walls of the site, whether the reservoir will be leaky, whether the site is on a fault, and so on. The expected return is lowered so much by failing to collect these and other little pieces of information that there is hardly any choice—they *have* to be collected.

Size of project and optimum wait for data. There seems to be no necessary connection between size of project, as measured by construction cost, and the optimum number of years to wait for data to generate. All depends on the relation between size of project and the form and location of $V(n)$. In one special case the optimum number of years of data will be independent of size of project. Suppose annual costs and revenues in different projects for "similar" sites are related proportionally. After tracing all the steps to derive $V(n)$, we find that $V_i(n) = a_i V_0(n)$ where i stands for the ith project. If annual cost of data varies with size so that $k_i = a_i k_0$, then the condition for maximizing the present value of the investment opportunity becomes

$$V_i'(t) = a_i V_0'(t) = r a_i V_0(t) + a_i k_0$$

or

$$V_0'(t) = r V_0(t) + k_0$$

and the optimum wait for data is the same for all projects.

If size of project is associated with a uniform absolute vertical movement of $V(n)$ and is independent of k, then smaller projects would require a longer wait. Consider in Figure 9 the two $V(n)$ curves:

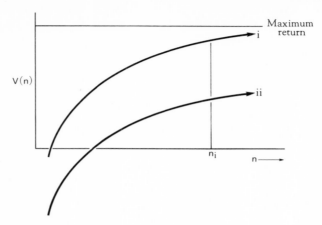

Figure 9

If n_i is the optimum number of years of data for curve i, then at n_i $V'_{ii} >$ $[r(V_i - C) + k]$ (where C is the vertical displacement) and the number of years of data must be increased to attain equality and the optimum position for curve ii. If k varies with size of project, the increase in the waiting period in moving from curve i to ii would be even greater since a decrease in k *raises* the optimum number of years of data. The lower the cost of information, the more it pays to spend on it. In many cases k probably varies directly with size of project. For example, large water projects are associated with larger streams on which annual costs of data collection are higher.

Note that it will not pay to spend anything for even one year of data if the necessary condition above is associated with a $V(n)$ less than the accumulated cost (with interest) of data collection up to that point in time.[9]

It should be remembered that some of the data necessary for project design are not time-bound. Given the general shape of their return curves, alluded to earlier, expenditure on these types of information obviously will vary with the physical size of the project.

Sudden Growth in Demand Foreseen

In the previous example demand was assumed constant but without perception of the investment opportunity until some arbitrary point in

[9] If $V(n_0)$ is equal to or less than the accumulated cost of information, $\frac{k}{r}(e^{rt} - 1)$, at the optimum, the opposite curvatures of these two functions (the second derivative is negative for $V(n)$ and positive for $\frac{k}{r}(e^{rt} - 1)$) insure that accumulated cost of information is greater than V for all n's other than n_0.

time. Now the problem is complicated by assuming that demand grows and that this growth is foreseen.

The simplest representation of a growth in demand is the sudden flowering of a regional demand from zero level. We assume that price and cost conditions are constant before and after the birth of the demand. While demands are not born as adults in the real world, this case is useful in analyzing the question of how many years before a project becomes feasible data collection should have been started. The proper time for *construction*, if data are available for design, obviously is the date of birth of the demand. The question then is how many years before this date the data program should be initiated.

In contrast with the preceding problem, one more year of data can now be had without postponing the series of annual surpluses from the project. Suppose the demand will be born in 1977 and that construction will take place then. The number of years of data can be increased from nine, say, to ten just by starting the data collection program in 1967 instead of 1968. The additional, or marginal, cost of doing this, with present value measured as of the date of construction, will be the annual cost of the data in 1967, k, accumulated to 1977 at the rate of discount r. Starting the data program earlier will increase the present value of the investment opportunity, $V(n)$, as of the date of construction at the birth of the demand. The start should be pushed back to the point where the increase in $V(n)$ is balanced by the cost of starting to collect data one year earlier, that is, where

$$\frac{dV(n)}{dn} = V'(n) = k(1 + r)^n.$$

In addition it is necessary that $V(n)$ exceed or equal the cumulated cost of the n years of data. Otherwise total costs of the project, including information costs, would not be covered.

Anticipation of the time when demand is born can not shorten the optimum number of years of data. If the birth of demand is not foreseen and it pays to wait for, say, ten years of data before constructing, it certainly will pay to start collecting data at least ten years before the birth of demand in the case where it is foreseen.[10]

---

[10] In the case where birth of demand is *not* foreseen, $V(n)$ must at least cover the cumulated cost of the n_1 years of data:

$$V(n_1) \geq \int_0^{n_1} k\, e^{rn_1}\, dn = \frac{k}{r}(e^{rn_1} - 1)$$

or, $$rV(n_1) + k \geq k\, e^{rn_1}$$

   That is, $$V'(n_1) \geq k\, e^{rn_1}.$$

But where the birth of demand is foreseen, the slope of $V(n_2)$ must be brought to *equality* with $k\, e^{rn_2}$ to attain optimum n. Since $V'(n)$ diminishes with increase in n, the required n_2 must be larger than n_1.

How much longer will be the optimum number of years of data if the birth of demand is foreseen? When it is not foreseen, postponement of the stream of net revenues imposes a definite limit on the period for data collection regardless of how low the annual cost of data may be. With anticipation of the birth of demand, there is no interest cost because of postponement of the project. Hence the optimum date for beginning the data program is earlier the lower the cost of a year's data, as is evident from $V'(n) = k(1 + r)^n$. If k is of appreciable size in relation to $V(n)$, however, the optimum length of data program diminishes rapidly.[11] One implication of this is that it doesn't pay to spend money on data collection over a long period just to squeeze a little more out of an anticipated poor project. There is no point in beating a dead horse.

The cost of failing to anticipate growth of demand. If the birth of demand in our example is not anticipated, clearly the whole investment opportunity, including data costs, must have a lower present value as of a given date (say, the date of birth of demand) than if the opportunity is foreseen. That there must be a loss (or no gain) by failing to anticipate is obvious, for when the opportunity is anticipated, all of the patterns of action open when there is failure to anticipate are still open and there are more, some of which may be better. Unfortunately, there is no simple general way to express this loss from failure to anticipate, even for the simple case being considered. The loss will be greater the more slowly the rise in $V(n)$ slows down with more data. It will be greater the smaller the annual cost of data.[12]

---

[11] Suppose, for example, that $r = .10$ and $\dfrac{k}{V(n_1)} = .01$. Then if birth of demand is not anticipated, $\dfrac{V'(n_1)}{V(n_1)} = r + \dfrac{k}{V(n_1)} = .11$. If we set $\dfrac{k}{(Vn_1)} e^{rn_3}$ equal to .11 and find n_3, this value will be larger than the correct n_2 in $\dfrac{V'(n_2)}{V(n_2)} = \dfrac{k}{V(n_2)} e^{rn_2}$. This is evident from the graphs of $V'(n)$ and $k e^{rn}$ and from the fact that $n_2 > n_1$, as shown in the preceding footnote. Even so, $n_3 = 24$.

If $r = .10$ and $\dfrac{k}{V(n_1)} = .02$, $n_3 = 17$.

If $r = .10$ and $\dfrac{k}{V(n_1)} = .03$, $n_3 = 13$.

If $r = .15$, the corresponding n_3's are 16, 11, and 9.

[12] The way things work out can be illustrated by an example containing some specific functions. Assume that: $V(n) = 100 - \dfrac{500}{n}$ (i.e., the maximum present value as of date of construction is 100 with complete information, that is, as $n \to \infty$. $V(n) < 0$ for $n < 5$).

The above discussion of the advantages of anticipating an investment opportunity is of some use in interpreting the view, often expressed, that a country that is trying desperately to develop must take more chances and start projects with a smaller number of years or quantity of data at hand than should a more developed country.

Assuming the appropriate rate of discount is the same in both countries, if the underdeveloped country has not anticipated possible projects by starting data programs ahead of time, it will be true that it should start projects with less data. But in the case where each country has less than the optimum number of years of data, the periods for collecting data before construction should be the same—assuming the rate of discount to be the same.

What some proponents of this view seem to have in mind is that the underdeveloped country is likely to be in a situation in which political stability will be seriously threatened unless the government comes up with something a good deal better than "expected" results. It must therefore "play the long shots." Apart from the notorious unreliability of evaluations of political instability, it ill befits a government to take unwarranted expectations as a given, for government is at least partly responsible for them. Its function ought to be the formation of a situation in which there

---

Cost of information accumulated to time of construction at the rate of discount,

r, is $K = \int_0^n k\, e^{rn}\, dn = \dfrac{k(e^{rn} - 1)}{r}$.

In the case of anticipation of the birth of demand, we seek to maximize $W_a = V(n_a) - K = 100 - \dfrac{500}{n_a} - \dfrac{.3(e^{.1 n_a} - 1)}{.10}$ where $k = .3$ per year and $r = .10$ per year.

Setting $\dfrac{dW_a}{dn} = 0$, the solution is found to be $n_a = 17.3$ years, with $W_a = 57.2$.

With more than 17.3 years, the increased cost of data outweighs the gain in $V(n)$. With fewer than 17.3 years, the cost of mistakes in design outweigh the savings in the cost of producing data.

In the case where the birth of demand is *not* anticipated, W_s (s for surprise) is given by the same expression $[V(n_s) - K]$, if valued as of the date of construction, but to compare the outcome with the other case it must be discounted back to the date of birth of demand. Accordingly, $W_s = \left[V(n_s) - \dfrac{k(e^{rn_s} - 1)}{r} \right] e^{-rn_s} = \left[100 - \dfrac{500}{n_s} - \dfrac{.3(e^{.1 n_s} - 1)}{.1} \right] e^{-.1 n_s}$. Setting $\dfrac{dW_s}{dn_s} = 0$, the length of the data program to maximize W_s is 9.80 years. W_s is 16.5, much lower than the 57.2 in the case where the birth of demand is anticipated. At the time of construction, W_s is much higher than the 16.5, being 44.2, but 9.8 years of real income from the project have been lost as compared with the other case. Hence 44.2 after discount is equivalent to only 16.5 since $e^{-.1(9.80)} = .38$.

can be realistic expectations of economic progress even though limited, as it inevitably must be. If "long shots" are played on too wide a scale, the result may be a major contribution to waste in a context where the effort should rather be the avoidance of possibilities of losses that are large relative to resources available.

Gradual Growth of Demand Foreseen

Determination of the best times to start data collection and to construct is more complex in more realistic cases in which demand grows from year to year. The easiest way to proceed now that electronic computers can shoulder the burden of calculation is to solve the following problem for *each* possible year of construction: By how many years should initiation of data collection precede construction?

For each of these problems there will be a maximum expected value (discounted to the date of construction) associated with a certain number of years of data. The maximum of these maxima, with all of these discounted to a common date, represents the best time for construction and will also indicate the time when the data program should be begun.

It should be possible to make estimates of this type, using either a long historical trace of data or generating synthetic traces. With all the elements of our model at hand, we should have a much better idea of the optimum length of time to begin collecting data before construction and would be in a position to make sensitivity analyses of the effect of different rates of discount and of different river regimens on the optimum number of years of data.[13]

But where do long series of data come from with which to experiment in this way? There are some long series, to be sure, but the behavior of different streams varies enormously, as is illustrated (in Table 13) by the

Table 13.   Characteristics of Annual Flow of Five Chilean Rivers

Characteristic	Name of river				
	Rapel	Choapa	Elqui	Aconcagua	Bío-Bío
Average annual flow (m³/sec.) = $\bar{x}$	222	12.4	11.1	41.7 ·	747
Median flow	200	10.0	8.55	38.1	807
Coefficient of variation = $\frac{\sigma}{\bar{x}}$	0.30	0.52	0.69	0.57	0.23
Asymmetry = $\frac{3(\bar{x} - \text{Med.})}{\sigma}$	0.94	1.1	1.0	0.79	−1.06

[13] A procedure for estimating dates of start of data program and construction for the case of rising demand is given in the Appendix to this chapter.

five rivers in Chile with the longest records of flow, ranging from eighteen to thirty-four years.

While it is quite possible to generate synthetic traces of any length whatsoever,[14] the difficulty comes in specifying the system that is used to generate the synthetic trace. The natural processes involved are so complex and so poorly understood that it is impossible—so far—to go directly from the natural process to the statistical characteristics of these aspects of river behavior that are of interest. And long historical series for rivers of the same type in essential respects are not available, partly, or mostly, because we don't know very well what are the essential respects. Certainly the situation is the same with respect to climatic data.

The suggestion of Ven Te Chow that the extreme values of these distributions may represent the results of a natural process different from that ordinarily at work seems especially disturbing, if only because of the rarity with which the one process apparently is operating.[15]

The gaps in our understanding of some of the aspects of hydrologic distributions are partly responsible for the desire to have long series of data available. But another element that works in the same direction is the assignment of a large penalty in the calculations of present values to structural failure.[16] There may be many reasons for assigning a large penalty, not the least of which is the fate of the construction agency before

---

[14] For a brief general discussion, see Ven Te Chow, "Sequential Generation of Hydrologic Information," in *Handbook of Applied Hydrology* (New York: McGraw-Hill, 1964), pp. 8–91. The nature of a synthetic trace can be understood by considering a simple (and inadequate) way to generate one. Prepare a deck of cards, each of which has one number on it representing annual flow (or the variable of interest), with the frequencies of different flows in conformity with desired characteristics of the distribution chosen. The cards could then be numbered in a sequence (the order would make no difference) and a table of random numbers used to select the sequence of flow values, it being permissible to use any card more than once. Use of a good table of random numbers in this way is equivalent to shuffling the deck with replacement of the card last drawn, except that the table is "more random."

[15] See Ven Te Chow, "Statistical and Probability Analysis of Hydrologic Data," in *ibid.*, pp. 8–33 to 8–37.

In the case of Chile, Luis Lliboutry suggests that the bimodal nature of the distribution of annual precipitation in Santiago may indicate that distinct natural processes are at work. See his *Nieves y Glaciares de Chile* (Santiago: Ediciones de la Universidad de Chile, 1956), p. 296.

For a general survey of statistical problems in hydrology, see Leo R. Beard, *Statistical Methods in Hydrology* (Sacramento: U.S. Army Corps of Engineers, January 1962).

A recent study dealing with hydrology simulation problems is Myron B Fiering, *Streamflow Synthesis* (Cambridge: Harvard University Press, 1967).

[16] Perhaps better characterized as a "judgment" than a calculation.

a legislative body if it has a record of structural failures—which failures conceivably might be economical in the absence of the large penalty assigned. After all, if a group of structures is designed so that the probability of failure in any given year is one thousandth and a stock of 100 such structures is maintained, there will be a failure once every ten years on the average. If this is more than legislators care to experience, knowledge about the right tail of a distribution becomes important. If it can't be had, the only out for the construction agency is obvious excess structural strength, although other features need not be in excess capacity.

There are two other means of partial accommodation to a paucity of data on, say, streamflow. In some cases there may be a possibility of designing the structure so as to be able to handle a wider range of the variable in question. Suppose the true value of the variable on which design depends is 100 (a purely arbitrary number). A structure designed for this may yield a net present value of 50, say.

Suppose, though, that the design variable is erroneously estimated to be 80 and a structure is designed specifically for this, anticipating a net rent of 45. The realized rent turns out to be, say, 20. However, it may have been possible to design the structure so that even though it works best if the design variable turns out to be 80, say, with a net rent of 35, it can accommodate itself to a level of 100 for the design variable with a net rent of 25 instead of 20.

The other type of accommodation possible in some cases is to design the structure so that expansion is possible. For example, certain types of dams can be increased in size, and irrigation projects do not have to be constructed all at once. This type of accommodation may be especially suitable where demand for the project's output is uncertain or must develop over time. Starting out on a smaller scale, where feasible, enables the earlier enjoyment of at least a part of the project's potential contribution to welfare.

Information That Is Not Time-Bound

All of the basic elements that were present in the preceding analysis— the quantity and cost of information, the timing of the expenditure on information, and the returns to information—are present in the case of information that is less rigidly connected with the passage of time. It is still the case that development of too much information will not improve returns sufficiently to cover the cumulated cost of the information and interest on the postponed stream of net inflows. It is still possible to start collecting information too early to be justified by the extra return produced.

Thus the same economizing logic as for the cases already discussed is applicable to all types of information about natural resources. In all cases, this logic impels us to ask the same questions: Is this information program being started too early? Should construction be begun even though information is not complete? Will this information have any pay-off or will its collection be waste motion?

Although the basic logic of economizing is the same for information that is not time-bound, quantification is far more difficult than for information whose quantity can be measured as number of observations, say as years of data. Still it is useful to distinguish two types of information not rigidly connected with time.

The first type is information connected with a particular localized project. Information on site characteristics for a construction project is an example. Here the total return curves probably tend to be of the step type mentioned earlier. That is, there tends to be a "necessary" quantity of information in the sense that nothing is gained if you have less than this quantity, and the return it can produce is not increased by going beyond this quantity. Other examples would be soil information to be used either in planning capital outlay (e.g., terracing) or in operation (e.g., planning a rotation).

Two characteristics of information connected with a particular project seem especially pertinent to its management. First, it tends to be generated near the time of its use in construction or current production. Second, the fact that the information is generated over a limited area has an effect on cost per unit area because some costs do not vary in proportion to area. For a given project, cost of information per unit area will depend on the rate at which information of a given quality is generated (e.g., number of acres per month) and on the total number of acres to be covered. If too low a rate is chosen, costs are raised for two reasons. First, reducing the rate of work does not reduce some costs proportionately, for example, super-visory cost, vehicle cost, storage and building costs, and others. Second, if the information is to be ready for use at a given date, a lower rate of production necessitates starting at an earlier time. Even if the lower rate of information production did not raise cost of information per acre at all, earlier outlays must bear interest for a longer period of time. Information production of the type under discussion ordinarily does not require a great deal of time, but even moderate extension in the period to cover a given area can increase cost significantly even with an alternative return on capital as low as, say, ten per cent. For example, suppose the optimum uniform rate of work for a certain area requires a certain outlay per year for one year. If the work period is started one year earlier but at a rate only half as large, cumulated cost at completion will be a little more than five per cent greater even though undiscounted cost per acre is increased minimally by the lower rate of production per unit time.[17]

The second type of information whose development is not rigidly bound up with time is typified by natural resource surveys that cover large areas only a part of which will receive further investment outlay. Geological surveys, timber surveys, etc., may be used as part of a sifting process. Here the problem of minimizing cost within the survey itself differs from the latter case in that there is greater freedom to go to higher rates of production (of survey output) in order to avoid interest cost on outlays made before the information is needed.

[17] Continuous compounding of interest is assumed. The undiscounted average time of outlay is pushed six months further back by the change in the period of production from one to two years.

In general terms, assuming the information is to be available at a given date, the optimum constant rate of production of information is determined as follows:

Undiscounted outlay per year, k, for producing information of a given type and quality will depend on the rate at which it is generated, measured as, say, acres covered per year, a, and the total area to be covered, N acres: $k = k(a,N)$. Marginal outlay per acre per year will fall with increases in a from small values because of economies of scale and possibly might rise with a large enough a, especially if N is small, for in this case a high rate of production will result in crowding on the small total area to be covered. Similarly, small projects are expensive, and marginal outlay with respect to a will fall rapidly when N is small but eventually might rise. The object is to minimize the present value of the costs at time of completion:

$$\text{Total cost at completion} = \int_0^{\frac{N}{a}} k\, e^{r\frac{n}{a}}\frac{dn}{a} = \int_0^N \frac{k}{a}\, e^{\frac{r}{a}n}\, dn$$

where r is the annual rate of interest or discount

$$= \frac{k}{r}(e^{r\frac{N}{a}} - 1).$$

$$\frac{dTC}{da} = \frac{-kN}{a^2}\, e^{r\frac{N}{a}} + k'_a\, \frac{(e^{r\frac{N}{a}} - 1)}{r} = 0.$$

The significance of these terms is as follows. Imagine that a period, $\frac{N}{a_0}$, is presently used. If a in each period is reduced by da, the second term represents the cumulated value of these savings at the date of completion. But the period, $\frac{N}{a_0}$, will have to be increased in order to cover N acres in all, and this will be done by extending the period of production backward. For each former year, output in this earlier period will have to be increased by da. The average cost per acre is $\frac{k}{a}$. Hence (average cost per acre) × (number of years) × (total amount taken from former years cumulated to termina-tion date) equals $\frac{k}{a} \cdot \frac{N}{a} \cdot e^{r\frac{N}{a}}\, da$, and this increase in cost must balance the gain from the other term to minimize cost.

In sifting type surveys, however, the question of whether to undertake the survey at all takes on an overwhelming importance as compared with, say, information for immediate construction purposes. The cost of undertaking sifting type surveys too early is increased, not by some percentage close to the annual rate of interest, but by a multiple of this. Ten years of prematurity will increase cost *by* about 160 per cent with annually compounded interest at 10 per cent. Assertions that prematurity need not cause concern because it is better to have too much than too little information in view of its "low" cost do not take into proper account the productivity of the alternative use of capital as reflected by the rate of interest, or discount.

There is no way to wish away the difficulties in forming judgments about the returns to this type of resource information. Still, quantitative efforts to do this have been very few, and the possibilities are far from exhausted. It is not necessary to wait on accurate numbers, however, to improve decisions. It is important that even approximate judgments be made on the basis of the correct logical framework. Merely to ask the right question is sometimes sufficient to get a useful answer.

Accumulation of Resource Information Viewed in the Large

In the early stages of development of the natural resources of an area, not very much is known about the characteristics of different pieces of land. The result is that investment in natural resources, whether for gaining more information or for production of a physical product, is subject to a considerable dispersion of returns. As investment proceeds, more and more is found out about the characteristics of different parcels of land. For example, land once thought to be usable for grazing may be found not to be. As a consequence, there is a constant reclassification of parcels of land in the minds and records of investors so far as characteristics bearing on productivity are concerned. Because of the increasingly accurate pigeonholing of parcels of land, the dispersion of returns to investment is lowered with the passage of time. But in a system in which technology is changing and in which demands and prices are free to move, these forces can restore economic life to parcels of land that have been temporarily laid on the shelf as not warranting further investment. Thus we find money being invested in mineral and agricultural lands which formerly were thought to have been of no value either because we have learned how to use them or because the prices of the products they can "grow" are higher. Eventually perhaps our knowledge of the investment prospects for the different types of land will be quite complete, but even "advanced" countries find it advisable to go over the same ground more than once.

New facts are needed which no one knew how to use before, and changing demands necessitate changed emphases on different types of information.

From the point of view of a country trying to "develop," the whole process of increasing and extending information on natural resources should add up to the exploitation of good opportunities for investment at *all* the stages of information so as to maintain a flow of natural resource investment projects which enter the stage of exploitation commensurate with the general range of investment opportunities open to the country. Of course it is not necessary to compare particular investment prospects against particular alternatives. There is no need, for example, to compare investment in a natural resource project with investment in industry of a certain type. Investment in *each* line should be adjusted to yield the same marginal return, which should reflect the decision the country has arrived at—no matter how—as to the division of potential output between investment and consumption. An adequate evaluation is made if the general rate of return to investment is used to determine whether a particular investment opportunity has a positive present value or not.

In practical terms, the attainment of a flow of natural resource investment in the later stages, where private enterprise may be the dominant form of organization, will necessitate some judicious efforts by government agencies to provide information about prospects for which returns are very uncertain. An important part of the problem is to avoid amassing information that has no economic significance or which pertains to land with zero value both before and after the investment in information.

The discussion in this chapter has been couched in abstract but simple economic terms, the purpose being to fix certain economic ideas which ought to form the mental model by which we think about the allocation of expenditure on natural resource information. With these ideas in mind and assisted by the discussion in earlier chapters of the physical aspects of natural resource information activities, we are prepared to look at some of the implications for actual decisions that have to be made when organizing and administering information programs.

A Procedure for Determining Optimum Date of Construction and Length of Data Program When Demand Is Growing

When demand grows over a period of years, earlier construction of a project will mean that the works are smaller than would be optimum with later construction. Hence, early construction will result in the inability to satisfy some demand at a later time or having to satisfy it with something poorer than the best plant. Later construction will be better adapted to satisfying the later and higher demands, but will sacrifice completely the net receipts that could have been enjoyed in the meanwhile. Clearly some one date is superior to others.

For certain types of projects it is not correct to think of investment outlays as being made approximately at a given point in time, for an early large investment for a main structure can be followed by additional investment to be made later as demand grows. An example would be a dam followed by a growing distribution network and investment in technical training in irrigation practices. The date of construction may still be thought of as a single date of construction, however. The possibility of spreading investment outlays over a period of time is allowed for in the subsequent discussion.

The basic idea in the sequence of steps that follows is to use a computer to simulate the outcomes of a large number of experiments with different numbers of years of data available. In this way we can estimate the expected effects on return of starting data collection five years before construction, ten years, and so on.

The steps are as follows:

1. Estimate the demand function for each year.

2. Derive the "true" trace of relevant data, e.g., flow. This "true" trace is to be used to calculate dollar returns to plants designed from *sample data series*. The true trace might be fifty years long, for example. A particular plant design would be calculated from a sample of, say, five years of date. The object is to find out what would happen if, in a series of projects, five-year data collection periods were the basis for design.

The "true" trace might be a long historical series if available or it might be generated from parameters derived from more limited historical data. For example, one might use the model $x_t = rx_{(t-1)} + (1 - r)\bar{x} +$

$S_x(1 - r^2)\epsilon$,[18] where x is annual flow, r is serial correlation, S_x is standard deviation of the x's, and ϵ is a random variable with mean zero and a specified distribution. The choice of this distribution is a very important element of the problem.

Number the values of the "true" trace from one to n.

3. Draw a sample of, say, five consecutive years from the "true" trace. *Use this sample* to estimate the constants of the equation in Step 2 (or of whatever generating equation is being used).

4. Generate a long trace, using constants estimated from five-year sample.

5. Using trace from Step 4, calculate optimum size plant for construction in each year around suspected optimum year by calculating present value of annual surpluses for various sizes of structure. For example, in year t the trace gives an annual flow x_t. This flow *and* a given size of structure will permit the sale of a certain quantity, q_t, of product (often in the same unit as x) which will be sold at a certain price dependent on the demand curve for that year. There will be costs of c_t incurred in this year in connection with the sale. Include outlays for information in costs.

Sum the present values of these annual surpluses, including cost of construction, incurred at $t = 0$, in the sum. The highest of these sums gives the tentative optimum size for the year in question.

6. Repeat Step 5 but move whole trace of Step 4 back one year. That is, the original year n in Step 4 is now $(n - 1)$.

7. Repeat Step 5 but move trace of Step 4 back two years. That is, the original year n in Step 4 is now $(n - 2)$.

8. Keep on moving trace of Step 4 back a year at a time.

As this is done, a new present value will be generated for each calendar year for which plant size is being determined.

For each calendar year, average these present values as the process proceeds.

Stop Step 8 when these averages stabilize.

9. Discount the average present value for each year to a common date. The maximum of these will indicate optimum plant size and date of construction as determined by the first sample of five years of data.

10. Evaluate the present value as of a given calendar date of the first five-year sample plant size and date of construction, *using flows from the "true" trace of Step 2.*

11. Repeat Step 10, moving the "true" trace back a year at a time. Each time this is done, we get an estimate of the present value of the opportunity associated with the first sample of five.

[18] See Ven Te Chow, "Sequential Generation of Hydrologic Information," in *Handbook of Applied Hydrology*, p. 8–94.

When the running average of these estimates stabilizes, we have the expected value of the opportunity for the first sample of five.

12. Repeat Steps 3 to 11 for a second sample of five.

13. When the average of the present values in Step 11 stabilizes, we have the expected value associated with samples of five.

14. Repeat steps 3 to 13 for samples of six, seven, etc.

15. Prepare table showing relation between starting date of data program and present value of investment opportunity.

VI: Some Guidelines for Organization and Administration of Information Activities

Our search for guidelines for the management of information activities rests on a general view about the role of information in economic decisions about natural resources. The goal is not the amassing of "complete" information, nor is it particularly advisable to move toward this goal as "rapidly as possible," for what sensible meaning could these goals have? In the most general terms, we want information that will permit suitable investment decisions in the years immediately ahead—suitable, that is, in view of the fact that information has a real cost and that the course of economic development is powerfully constrained by forces whose operation is not going to be upset by the generation of any quantity of information whatsoever. Not only may more of one type of information mean less of others, but we run the risk of accumulating information, not for the solution of an actual problem by use of a complete information model, but for the sake of information itself, that is, for the accumulation of information that may never be used. We can not collect all the information "necessary" to solve a specified list of problems, partly because the particular problems to be solved "now" depend on information gathered earlier and partly because it pays to have only enough information to reach an acceptable solution.

How can we proceed to our rules for economizing? A conceivable method would be to emulate the agricultural economist who, together with his technical brethren, may be able to tell us how to handle the application of a certain type of fertilizer. On the basis of experiment or by statistical analysis of (varied) non-experimental fertilizer applications, he can say that with soil of a certain type, a certain pattern of rotation, and with certain climatic conditions, it will pay to apply a certain quantity of fertilizer per acre per season with present costs and prices.

For obvious reasons, no procedure very close to this is now possible with natural resource information, nor does such a procedure seem feasible on a large scale in the future. The benefits flowing from natural resource information are often quite diffuse. Not only that, but much information activity must anticipate the time of its use. And, unlike the case of the fertilizer, it is not easy to specify the product of some types of information. Superficially, some types of information may seem less than valuable because their collection serves only to cull out losing prospects—prospects, however, which could have absorbed a lot of investment funds had they been continued.

However difficult it is to make numerical estimates of the value of a little more or a little less information, two procedures are within our power. First, it is possible to make some suggestions for economizing which, while they do not result in a fine adjustment of outlays in the light of product produced, can be of help in preventing some gross misallocations of funds. Also it should be recalled that in many situations it is possible to be reasonably sure that a certain increase in expenditure will result in a product whose value is greater—or less—than the outlay in question.

The second possibility for dealing with the allocation problem involves a search for forms of organization and types of relations among organizations that will facilitate the making of judgments about marginal changes in information and its benefits. Even though we can't estimate the value of information, we may be able to specify some of the features of an organization that will enable improved evaluation of marginal changes in the information programs as time goes along.

The suggestions that are made here have two general characteristics. First, they look toward specialization and a full use of the specialist in the execution of natural resource information programs. But the specialist must be constrained to operate within the system by which investment and operating decisions in the natural resource field are reached. He is the servant of this system.

Second, the goal should be a system in which information programs are adjusted to the needs and demands of the governmental agencies and private entities that use natural resource information. It is to be expected that the balance of the programs and their content will change as time goes on.[1]

---

[1] Two authors have written on these problems with an approach similar in some respects to the one in this document, although there are numerous divergencies.

See Estevam Strauss, "Algunos Aspectos de la Investigación y Explotación de Recursos Naturales en América Latina Relacionados con la Planificación Económica, Parte I," July 1965, mimeo.; and "Recursos Naturales y Planificación Económica en América Latina, Parte II," November 1965, mimeo. (Santiago: Instituto Latinoamericano de Planificación Económica y Social). Part I also is available in English.

See also Leon Laitman, "El Desarrollo de Datos Sobre Recursos Naturales para la Planificación Económica. Un Método Integral," in *Temas Geográficos-Económicos*, Proceedings of Unión Geográfica Internacional, Conferencia Regional Latinoamericana, Vol. II (Mexico City: Sociedad Mexicana de Geografía y Estadística, 1966), p. 19.

How Much Information?

Our first guideline is obvious and perhaps rather formal, but it needs to be pointed out and kept clearly in mind.

The quantity of information collected should be increased so long as the present value of the investment opportunity (or cost savings if this is the use to which the information is put) is increased by more than the cost of the information.

This problem has been discussed at considerable length in Chapter V. Here the discussion is simply a reminder of the main lines of the argument but can not very well be passed over, for the general orientation toward the management of information as a part of the process of maximizing the present social value of the investment opportunities undertaken is essential if we are to avoid uneconomic accumulation or failure to accumulate information.

Our analysis began by considering the simple case in which we suddenly become aware of an investment opportunity with constant demand and cost conditions after construction is completed. The proper size depends on one or more aspects of the behavior of a natural resource stochastic variable, for example, the flow of a stream. We can estimate the relevant characteristics of the behavior of this variable only on the basis of observed data. The problem is, how long can we afford to wait for data to accumulate before constructing?

The main problem here is the estimation of a function which relates expected present value of the investment opportunity at time t to the number of years of data available, where t is also the number of years of data available at the time of construction, t. We may think of $t = 0$ as "now," the moment in which the investment opportunity is perceived.

The expected value of the investment opportunity will be low with little data available, but will rise with more data available. With little data available, the structure often[2] would be too large (resulting in unused capacity) or too small (resulting in lost opportunity for product or structural failure), thus reducing the expected present value of the opportunity. For small enough quantities of data, the expected value will be negative.[3]

---

[2] We must imagine what would happen if many structures of this type were constructed with estimates based on the availability of, say, ten years of data. Then the same question must be asked for many cases of eleven years, and so on.

[3] Alberto Martinez has pointed out that in many parts of South America lack of climatological data makes it impossible to determine whether climate rules out the use of a foreign plant. He characterizes as innumerable the cases in which dams have been too large or too small, in the one case never filling and in the other in danger of failure. All types of works within reach of a river are frequently damaged because design has not been able to take into account the likely flows. They often are just not known. See his "Informe sobre Clima y Meteorologia de Sudamérica," (UNESCO/CASTALA/2.1.2 II.1), p. 13.

As the quantity of data increases, expected value (always as of time t) will rise but at a decreasing rate. With our assumption of constant price and cost conditions, expected value will approach a maximum as our estimates of the values of the relevant parameters of the distribution involved approach the true values.[4]

We can go immediately to the conclusion that construction should take place when the cost of getting one more year of information is equal to the resulting increase in expected present value. The cost of getting one more year of data is made up of two elements, the outlay during the year to get the data, k, and interest on the expected present value of the opportunity we would have experienced if we had not waited one more year. That is, if $V(t)$ is the basic function, we should wait until its rate of increase, $V'(t)$, is equal to $[rV(t) + k]$, where r is the rate of discount (the rate of return on investment).

Several conclusions are evident. First, it never will pay to wait for "complete" information. Second, an extremely important element of the problem is the cost coming from postponement of the stream of net revenues from the project. This factor means it does not pay to accumulate data until the increment in expected value is equal to the annual cost of the data. The $\frac{\text{percentage}}{100}$ rate of increase per year in expected value $\frac{V'(t)}{V(t)}$ must not be less than $\frac{rV(t) + k}{V(t)} = r + \frac{k}{V(t)}$.[5] This means the effect on expected value of one more year of data must be quite sizable to justify waiting.

Now let us change the problem to a form that corresponds better to the problem facing information agencies. Suppose we are aware of the existence of a possible investment opportunity which will become viable some day because demand is growing.

The simplest case of demand growth is very unrealistic but still instructive. Assume that demand explodes into existence full blown at a certain time. How many years ago should we have started collecting data? If we are free to choose the time for construction, it is obvious that this should be when the demand comes into existence. What we must compare is the cost of reaching *back* in time for one more year of data (accumulating this cost to the date of construction at the rate of discount) with the resulting increase in expected value. In this case, one more year of data does not require postponing the stream of net rents, but on the other hand we

---

[4] For example, the payoff may depend on the frequency of floods over a certain level, average annual flow, average flow during a certain part of the year, the dispersion of monthly flows, or other aspects of flow of the stream.

[5] Note that what is involved is the ratio of k to $V(t)$, not the ratio of k to the capital cost of the project.

incur an interest cost, which reflects real opportunities for investment that have been given up, on the funds spent on developing information.

For more realistic cases in which demands grow from year to year, the problem is more complex. We may think of the immediately preceding question—by how many years should the data program anticipate construction—as being analyzed separately for each possible date of construction. For each of these cases there will be a maximum expected value (discounted to the date of construction) associated with a certain number of years of data. The maximum of these maxima, with all of these discounted to a common date, represents the best time for construction and will also indicate the time when the data program should be begun. It should be possible to make estimates of this type, at least retrospectively.

Quantitative estimates of the sort required by these simple models are not feasible for many problems of information. In some cases there is difficulty in quantifying the information. In others the benefits are very diffuse or hard to measure. In all cases, however, the simple model poses the relevant questions. We should be trying to judge the product that will result from more information and should bear in mind the powerful role that should be played by the rate of discount in making these judgments. Postponement of a stream of net rents is very costly, as is also the premature assembly of information. These are not "merely financial considerations" but reflect the fact that capital goods have a return in real product.

What Areas Are Suitable?

For the most part, natural resource information programs should be concentrated in or near the areas already being exploited.

Although this suggestion may seem surprising, the considerations supporting it are quite compelling if expenditure on information is to be evaluated as a public investment. There are some partial exceptions, however.

First of all, as economic product and population grow in settled areas, it will pay to increase all the inputs that are used with natural resources, and for certain types of resources one of these inputs is information about the resource. One may think, for example, of soil and information about it. In this particular case, and in some others, too, the capacity of the owners or managers of natural resources to use information grows over time. The level of education may be rising, the extension service may have become more effective, or they simply may have learned how to put the available information to work and are now ready to use more detailed and more sophisticated information. Thus the need for information about natural resources does not vanish just because the natural resources of an area are being exploited. The emphasis may change as among resources and also the type of information may change, but the demand or need will remain.

But not only do there continue to be opportunities to invest in more information in areas already under exploitation. The very fact of the present locational pattern of economic activity implies that entrepreneurs have found the obstacles to the extension of economic activities to other areas to be insuperable, given the alternative investment opportunities available and the necessity of covering costs. In parts of some countries there are areas so disfavored that economic activity in them is not only sparse but nonexistent for all practical purposes.

Natural resource survey information is not likely to diminish the impact of the forces that have resulted in some areas having little or no productive activity in the natural resource industries. The extension of economic activity to very far distant or idle areas has two strikes against it, and in some cases more.

First of all, thanks to indivisibilities that are present in the construction of many types of infrastructure, it is certain that the cost of infrastructure services will be higher in areas with a low density of economic activity. It is not possible to construct a 100-mile highway for a flow of k ton-miles per year at one thousandth of the cost of a highway for a flow of $1,000\ k$ ton-miles per year. Nor can one family have one thousandth of a physician residing within walking distance of their plot in the newly exploited area.

Second, transportation is especially important in raising the cost of economic activity that is far distant from established centers, not only because of underutilization of capacity, the factor just discussed, but because of distance itself. For example, in the case of ore of various types, rail and port charges are sometimes 75 per cent of the cost of the ore delivered on board an oceangoing vessel.[6] In the case of the Pine Point lead-zinc development on the south side of Great Slave Lake in northern Canada, extension of the existing railway line accounted for two-thirds of a total investment of $128 million.[7] Or consider the prospects for a lumber operation on one of the Amazon tributaries. Assuming some reasonably homogeneous stands of marketable timber could be found, the transport handicap is simply gigantic, involving not only the handicap of distance but the obstacle posed by rapids and other hazards. What is more, it may be possible to exploit similar stands much farther down-

[6] Myles A. Walsh, "Development and Mechanization of Small Mines," in *Natural Resources*, Vol. II, U.S. Papers Prepared for the United Nations Conference on the Application of Science and Technology for the Benefit of the Less Developed Areas (Washington: U.S. Government Printing Office, 1963), p. 238.
[7] *Mining Journal*, August 27, 1965, p. 143.

stream where the transport problems are of a more routine nature and can be solved at a much lower cost.

There appears to be a strong tendency to suppose that programs to develop information about natural resources should involve extensive efforts in areas with little or no economic activity, if there are such areas in the country in question. Often the task seems to be conceived as one of filling in a *tabula rasa*. Actually a great deal is known about areas not now intensively exploited, granted that this may not amount to much in comparison with what could be known. But, more significant, the present pattern of economic activity and the present boundaries of economic activity imply the possession of a very useful type of information—that an important obstacle to the extension of economic activity has been encountered. This factor is strongly emphasized by the Paddock brothers in their recent study of agricultural development problems, and their viewpoint is buttressed by many examples from extensive experience.[8] Time and time again, someone has thought that he perceived a production opportunity that had been neglected, only to have his subsequent failure bring to his attention an unfavorable aspect of the opportunity that he either had not seen or had brushed aside as unimportant.

The possibility of colonizing new lands no doubt accounts in many cases for the pressure to survey natural resources in such areas. In Latin America, for instance, many countries have such rapid rates of population growth that the task of creating productive jobs for the growing numbers presents many difficulties. In this situation, the tremendous areas of Latin America that are not now exploited for crops or grazing seem often to be thought of as a fine opportunity for colonization. Only 5 per cent of the total area of Latin America is presently used as arable land, and only another 20 per cent is used for pasture.[9]

While there seems to have been remarkably little attempt to make comprehensive economic evaluations of past colonization projects, the verdict of those who have studied the question is that projects in recent decades have been marked by many failures. It seems fair to say that they do not view future colonization as an important outlet for future population.

For example, Christodoulou, in a general review of colonization problems, writes, "The high proportion of failures in colonization projects certainly would have been lower if a thorough evaluation of past experience had been made and if norms and directions for future programs had been

[8] William and Paul Paddock, *Hungry Nations* (Boston: Little, Brown, 1964).
[9] See Carlos Plaza V., "Los Recursos Naturales en la Integración Latinoamericana" (Santiago: Instituto Latinoamericano de Planificación Económica y Social, October 1966), mimeo., preliminary version, p. 20.

drawn from this evaluation."[10] Barraclough and Domike emphasize that colonization projects have incurred very high capital costs, sometimes more than twenty times the annual income of local small producers. This does not necessarily indicate economic failure, of course, for net income conceivably could be large enough to cover interest on investment and leave a net income for the producer. They seem to say this has not been the case, however. They judge projects with foreign colonists to have been more successful than those with domestic colonists because of better education and better social organization, among other factors. They do not view colonization as being able to take care of the "excess" population produced in rural areas.[11]

The argument for the development of survey type information on uninhabited areas would seem to rest on the presumption that without this information we are missing some valuable production opportunities that can be brought to light in no other way. Insofar as these areas are humid forest areas, the difficulty to be overcome does not appear to be one of locating rich areas exploitable with present techniques and large enough to stand the handicap of distance. Instead, so far as agricultural use of these areas is concerned, the problem appears to be one of developing methods for using these areas.

Many experts have examined the obstacles confronting exploitation of the hot humid areas and have found them to be very serious indeed. John Phillips, drawing on his experience in many countries, has emphasized three types of problems. First is an impressive array of health problems,

[10] D. Christodoulou, "La Colonización de Tierras: Algunos Aspectos Fundamentales que Suelen Descuidarse," *Boletín Mensual de Economía y Estadística Agrícolas* (FAO), Vol. 14, No. 10 (October 1965), p. 1 (my translation).

[11] Solon Barraclough and Arthur L. Domike, "La Estructura Agraria en Siete Paises de América Latina," *El Trimestre Económico*, Vol. XXXIII (2), No. 130 (April–June 1966). See especially pp. 261–63. See also the series of papers on colonization projects in various parts of Latin America presented at the 1966 meeting of the Unión Geográfica Internacional, Conferencia Regional Latinoamericana held in Mexico City, *La Geografía y los Problemas de Población*, Tomo I. The papers and proceedings were published by La Sociedad Mexicana de Geografía y Estadística (Mexico City, 1966). The following are of special interest:

Craig L. Dozier, "Problemas Para la Colonización Efectiva de Tierras Nuevas en América Latina: Algunos Ejemplos Actuales" (p. 229);

Alejandro Medina Valderrama, "El Estudio de Geografía Regional, Síntesis de la Colonización de la Selva Peruana" (p. 247);

Ulv Masing, "San Vito de Java: Análisis del éxito y fracaso de una colonia de agricultores inmigrantes en el bosque lluvioso de Costa Rica" (p. 267);

Gottfried Pfeifer, "Observaciones a lo Largo de las Nuevas Fronteras de Colonización en Paraná y Matto Grosso" (p. 267);

David E. Snyder, "Realidades Geográficas de la Colonización Fronteriza Contemporánea en América del Sur" (p. 329).

not necessarily insuperable but as of now serious in many areas, and the prospect for rapidly reducing them to tolerable levels is not bright. The severity of the health problems is closely connected with the second type of problem emphasized by Phillips—securing the adoption by colonists of "best practice," both with respect to matters bearing on health and in production activities. The third type of problem is perhaps most funda-mental, however, namely, the lack of understanding on a technical level of methods of exploitation which will yield enough to make settlement feasible. His assessment of the difficulties deserves quotation in full:

We are still ignorant about the technique and economy of the thinning or the complete removal of woody growth, for the purpose of utilizing the ground for the growing of annual and perennial crops. This is true for cocoa, coffee, pepper, banana and sundry food crops which may be grown in suitable association with indigeneous trees and shrubs left *in situ*, and for those like oil-palm, tea, rubber, cotton, sisal and plantation banana and annuals suitable for mechanized cultiva-tion requiring almost complete removal of the woody growth above and below ground.
The history of each and every larger-scaled enterprise, attempted on land where removal or thinning of woody growth has been a preliminary requirement, reveals how serious a problem is the effective clearing or thinning of such growth —compatible with satisfactory protection of the soil and the economy of invest-ment. Instructive examples of what not to do are seen in experiences gained in the wooded savanna of Tanganyika (East African Groundnuts Scheme), the jungle of the Dry Zone of Ceylon (Gal Oya Irrigation Scheme) and in the humid *selva* of Peru (*vide* the valiant efforts of a well-known and philanthropic Ameri-can, Mr. R. Letourneau . . . to clear land for pasturage). To these spectacular examples could be added many a small project by both governments and private enterprise from Latin America, through Africa to India and South-East Asia.[12]

Stamp places a similar emphasis on the technical difficulties of using the hot humid areas for agricultural purposes. While the growth of trees is indeed remarkable, the large excess of rainfall over evaporation results in rapid impoverishment by leaching of soil near the surface as soon as the tree cover is removed. He concludes, "By and large, if cleared, equa-torial forests would provide vast areas of poor or indifferent soils, liable to become still further impoverished, and further liable to marked soil erosion."[13] He observes that in the equatorial regions that have proved

[12] John Phillips, *The Development of Agriculture and Forestry in the Tropics* (London: Faber and Faber, 1961), p. 83.
[13] L. Dudley Stamp, *Our Developing World* (London: Faber and Faber, 1960), pp. 47–51.

to be productive, the soil and terrain conditions are often rather special (e.g., clay which can be worked into a water-holding layer for rice culture or a climate that is monsoonal).

It should also be noted that the transportation obstacle to the extension of economic activity by jumps from present activity, while it operates in all types of regions, becomes an even more important obstacle in the case of the hot humid areas, reaching its acme when excess water is combined with a rough terrain. Dozier's description of the 195-kilometer road from La Paz to the colonization project on the upper Beni River vividly illustrates the difficulties. The real trouble comes in the last 75 kilometers—a mere 47 miles. This stretch has an abundant rainfall, concentrated in half of the year but with plenty of rain in the so-called dry months, too. The road is constructed, not on a natural rock base, but on clay easily exposed on the mountainsides. Wherever natural drainage is insufficient, during and after rains the road becomes a quagmire of unbelievable proportions. For all practical purposes mobility stops, except for the most powerful road construction trucks and tractors. An ordinary four-wheel-drive vehicle can cover the 47 miles in a day—if it is lucky. In this particular case, the better quality of the first 120 kilometers from La Paz has resulted in spontaneous settlement on this stretch around Caranavi—with better economic success than is being enjoyed by the organized colonization project on the Beni.[14]

So far as agricultural and forest development products are concerned, then, the conclusion seems reasonable enough that viable investment opportunity is the more unlikely the bigger the jump (in economic terms) from present activity, and all the more unlikely if the jump is to the warm humid areas. This generalization seems applicable also to forest development projects. With little prospect for viable investment, natural resources information activity can well be concentrated in areas of present economic activity and those immediately adjoining. Note two particular implications. Where transportation routes are extended for non-economic reasons—for example, the development of a highway for military purposes—natural resources information activity immediately becomes appropriate, for one of the principal handicaps to investment, the cost of transportation, has been removed. In the evaluation of investment opportunities in such a case, the opportunity should be charged (or private investors should be charged) only with the additional transport costs occasioned by the investment. Secondly, the development of resource information for areas near those presently exploited will insure the development of information for areas

14 Dozier, *op. cit.*, pp. 238–39.

in which spontaneous settlement is taking place.[15] The monitoring and understanding of this process is of great importance for a variety of reasons. So far as natural resources are concerned, the settlement is often in areas susceptible to erosion damage from the methods of production used. Although the economic and social results of these settlements are of great importance to various governmental programs, for example, public works and governmental services of various types, the matter apparently is receiving little study.[16]

There are a couple of partial exceptions to the areal allocation guide suggested here, the first of which is minerals. The exception is only partial, because many minerals and mineral products have so low a value in relation to weight that they can stand long overland hauls only in settled areas or where the volume of mineral or mineral product to be shipped is big enough not to leave a large quantity of excess transport capacity. This suggests that the location of activity aimed at the search for minerals in unexploited areas should be guided by prior indications that the area is mineralized and by the transport possibilities, such as rivers or rail routes, over which construction costs will be low. Where a distant area appears very promising there may be a possibility of developing a mining district which would be able to support transport. Similarly, more valuable products, such as precious or exotic metals, can support air transport of the mineral or its final product. Thus the search for them can be more extensive. With a sufficiently great rate of production and large enough reserves, petroleum and natural gas can move quite long distances by pipeline. Accordingly the search for them may appropriately be more wide-ranging in some circumstances.

What these remarks on minerals seem to add up to is that quite general geologic studies of unsettled areas may be justified if existing information is not discouraging. A step-by-step procedure would also be desirable here if existing information points to some areas as being better prospects than others.

Another possible exception to our areal allocation guideline is hydrologic and meteorologic data. In each case the natural system in some aspect of which we have a current economic interest may extend into areas without

---

[15] In some cases, of course, the boundary between viable and non-viable areas is so sharp—Chile has many examples, e.g., her northern valleys and mountain barriers— that there is no reason to develop certain types of information beyond the barrier.

[16] This is the judgment of Ing. Augusto Eulacio of FAO (Santiago, Chile). See also Inter-American Committee for Agricultural Development, *Inventory of Information Basic to the Planning of Agricultural Development in Latin America, Regional Report* (Washington: Pan American Union, 1963), p. 38.

economic activity. The weather systems of the west coast of South America are cases in point.

Here, fortunately, there is a good possibility that satellite photos may be able to substitute in part for conventional weather data from the ocean area, which could be developed only at much cost. As for water, the fact that it can be transported downhill, either in a river or a pipe, may mean that hydraulic information from quite remote areas will have a present use. In these cases, however, costs of collecting reliable data in remote areas on a regular basis may be very high. The personnel available may make it difficult to secure reliable management and reading of even simple instruments, and the various possibilities for automatic recording or radio sending equipment bring with them another set of personnel and maintenance problems.

Some Suggestions for Managing Certain
Types of Information Activities

The remarks that follow do not purport to be a systematic account of how to manage information activities of specific types, for they are far too brief and sketchy. Instead, they are in part the incidental product, on a less general level, of my attempt to relate the problems of the several information fields to economic development.

The incompleteness of these remarks is attributable partly to the fact that the problems of economization in each field must be worked out by the experts in that field working in conjunction with those who will use the information. Just as important, however: the problems of individual countries are so varied and the quality of the agencies that produce and use this information is also so varied that any analysis of general applicability ends up being rather platitudinous and empty of specific content. Hence, the following are simply particular points that have impressed me as important or likely to be neglected.

Aerial Photography

Since photographs are a tool to develop specific types of information, the photography program should depend on these other programs, remembering, of course, that there is a non-governmental demand for the photos themselves, wanted for a wide variety of uses. Would it therefore be desirable to have stereo pairs available for the whole country, just to be sure the photos are available if needed? Much depends on the circumstances.

First of all, if no use is going to be made of the photos in the fairly near future, why spend prematurely when there are urgent needs for capital? Furthermore, costs of photography go down and the quality of images or the variety of images available improves as time goes on. Nor do all uses require photos of the same scale or stereo pairs with the same angle of view.[17] In addition, cultural information deteriorates with age, although the old photo will still be of value where the change from the old to the new photo is itself of interest. This consideration suggests the desirability of trying to anticipate the various cases in which it is desired to measure change over time by use of air photos. The areas involved should be included in the early photography. Perhaps inclusion on a sampling basis would be sufficient.

On the other hand, if information derived from air photos is to form the basis of a land tax of the type that Chile is now using, photos are required for all of the area to be included in the system. The whole country may not have to be covered, however, as was the case with Chile.

General Purpose Maps

It should be relatively easy to get a feel for the demand for general purpose maps. The cost of making certain types of maps, especially plani-metric, will be substantially lower once satellite photos are available. There will be little reason not to map a whole country.

Topographic maps, much more expensive, should be developed as demand dictates. This will mean priority for areas in which there is pros-pective construction activity, including private construction, public works, and highways. Areas of expanding activity will be favored by this criterion. In some cases, topographic maps will be wanted as a base for geologic maps. Some of these areas may be distant from presently expanding areas of economic activity, as may be true if the geologic information is wanted for mineral search.

Geological Data

In our discussion of the guideline suggesting that activities generating information about natural resources should be concentrated in or near areas already being exploited, information useful to the search for minerals was mentioned as a partial exception. We now examine the nature of this exception more closely to see what guidelines can be suggested for geo-logical investigations.

---

[17] For expert opinion along these lines, see W. Schermerhorn, "Planning of Aerial Sur-veys for the Over-all Development of the Natural Resources of a Country," in *Proceed-ings of United Nations Seminar on Aerial Survey Methods and Equipment*, Mineral Re-sources Development Series No. 12, Bangkok, 1960, p. 68; and A. P. A. Vink, "Aerial Photographs and the Soil Sciences," paper presented at the 1964 Toulouse Conference (UNESCO/NS/90, Paris, February 28, 1964), p. 21.

The demand for that part of the activities of a geological organization that is derived from the programs of other governmental agencies presents few problems. There will be demands for help on engineering geology in connection with the many types of structures involved in various government programs—highways, bridges, port facilities, dams, canals, buildings, airports, etc. The water development agencies will want various types of geological studies made as a part of river basin planning work. Groundwater problems will have to be studied as a part of the programs of agencies concerned with water supply for cities and industry or for irrigation.

The satisfaction of these demands from governmental agencies will account for a substantial part of the expenditure of a government for geological information, but there are no especially difficult problems in anticipating the demand or in organizing to satisfy it. So far as the financing of such studies is concerned, it would be desirable that the requesting agency reimburse the geological agency for the work done. A reimbursement procedure will insure that when an agency requests funds for a project the amount will include the cost of geological studies and will not be deceptively low. In addition, the necessity of reimbursement may stimulate the agency demanding the service to compare the price asked by the geological agency with the price asked by a private consulting firm. There may well be circumstances in which it is more economical to buy routine geological service from private firms specializing in it rather than from a governmental unit.

The more difficult problem in providing geological information relates to the search for minerals and petroleum. A full dress analysis of the problem of mineral search is so large and so difficult a problem as to require a separate volume. However, a few general observations may be helpful in preventing useless expenditure.

It is my belief that the general orientation of a geological agency is an important factor in attaining the kind of program that will most benefit a country so far as its mineral resources are concerned. It is assumed in this discussion that a government is interested in the economic return to be had from geological investigations and not in amassing information for its own sake. Geological surveys, like all other activities involving a recognized discipline, are subject to the tendency to orient the agency's activities toward "professional" objectives that may be in conflict with economic objectives. Obviously this does not mean that studies oriented toward the economic objective of providing information which will eventuate in the discovery and exploitation of deposits must be *un*professional. It does mean, however, that the tendency to set too stringent standards of various types must be avoided, and that efforts to attain complete coverage of large areas with maps of certain scales must always be regarded as instrumental rather than goals. That is, complete coverage of an area can be a proper goal only if it is estimated that complete coverage will be productive in economic terms.

At all points in the programming of geological information activities the question must be asked: Will this pay off or not? If the attitude toward commitment of personnel and equipment is not of a persistently questioning nature, distortions in the program may easily become so great that it will be clear to impartial examination that money is being wasted. In particular, the problem of program determination cannot be solved by dwelling upon the "basic" nature of the data being generated. To claim that some one type of data is "basic" is the equivalent of sweeping the problem under the rug and ignoring it. Indeed, if good estimates of the productivity of all types of information could be made, the conclusion would be that they are all equally basic in the sense that another dollar spent on any one of them would produce the same gain—namely, one dollar's worth of gain.

Let us suppose that those who determine the program of the geological agency do in fact possess this questioning attitude, seeking always to eliminate programs that will not contribute to economic product and to expand to proper size those that do. Are there any general guiding considerations to be borne in mind?

In my opinion we must recognize that the problem of devising programs for the early stages of the exploration process, usually determined by and financed by government, is one about which views are far from unanimous. The reasons for this state of affairs are not hard to find, for evaluation of different programs is complicated first of all by the fact that the physical environments of countries are certainly different—unfortunately in ways that are hard to quantify. Thus it may be hard to see that a program suitable for one country may not be at all useful for another. Not only do the physical attributes of countries differ in many subtle ways, but so also do the institutions and organizations available to exploit the information generated. Second, it is difficult to measure the product of activities in these earlier stages. If we think in terms of a sifting process in which techniques that cost little per unit area are used to sift out smaller areas for more intensive study by more costly methods, how many targets are mistakenly rejected by the early siftings? This problem is not completely intractable and can be studied, but there certainly is no good solution as yet. Equally difficult is the probability of estimating the number of targets that eventually will be discovered.

While the quantitative study of the programming of exploration activities is in a rather rudimentary state, the common view of the desirable program involves a succession of siftings, with the more expensive activities reserved for the later stages so that they need be applied only to a smaller area.

Having in mind this sifting idea, the program planner has in front of him not simply a large area about which nothing is known but ordinarily an array of areas, each with a different body of information bearing on minerals and, just as important, with different characteristics that will influence the value of any minerals that are present in the area. Furthermore, he has at his disposal not simply regional geological investigation, geochemical investigation, etc., but each of these coupled with the possibility of using it at different levels of intensity. What are some of the characteristics of the program he should come up with? Is there anything that should be avoided?

First, to reiterate, complete coverage for its own sake by any activity is to be avoided. The aim is, instead, to reject areas as unprofitable prospects for investigation by more expensive techniques—at least until cheaper methods are available.

Second, there are likely to be possibilities for further study in areas in which there has been or is mineral production or in which minerals are known to be present. The nature and level of detail of the additional studies will depend on the information already available. Such areas deserve consideration for further study for two reasons: (1) Where some targets have already been found, more are likely to be present, unless, of course, the area has already been thoroughly investigated. (2) A deposit found in an already producing area is likely to be more valuable than its physical twin in a non-producing area, for processing and transport capacity may already be available.

What about large areas about which very little is known? Here there is a case for small-scale geological studies to obtain an idea of the gross geologic picture. Satellite photos, supplementing other investigation, may turn out to be particularly useful because of the excellent synoptic view they can give. It may turn out that exploratory magnetic surveys at a considerable altitude are a useful interpretative aid, as may also be geochemical surveys with a low density to hold cost down. The object of such small-scale investigation, using conventional air photos, too, is to develop an understanding of the geology of the area to enable the identification of areas worthy of more intensive investigation, if not of metallogenic provinces.[18]

If a country has a large area that is unknown geologically, should small-scale information be developed for the whole area right away or for only a part of it? Here two guides already discussed come into play. By limiting

[18] See Sherwin F. Kelly, "The Pillars of Our Prosperity and the Impending Drain on Mineral Resources" (reprinted from *Western Miner and Oil Review*, October 1960, by Western Miner Press, Vancouver, B.C., Canada), for a discussion of literature bearing on the identification of metallogenic provinces by using information that can be developed on a small scale.

initial efforts to the more easily accessible parts of the whole area, it will
be possible to get deposits to the production stage sooner, thus advancing
the time when they begin to yield a return to the country. In view of
interest (the productivity of investment), this is an exceedingly important
gain. It also enables postponement of the cost of small-scale geologic
investigation in areas in which deposits would be developed only later.
Of course, if geologic ignorance is not spread uniformly over the whole
area, a presently inaccessible area with information suggesting the likelihood of rich deposits may well be worth investigating more intensively.

In general, the decision procedure should emphasize flexibility, in that
the status of the different possible areas for investigation should constantly
be reassessed in the light of information that has been added to that already
available, in the light of new techniques or changes in the cost of using
known techniques and changes in prices, or any other factors affecting the
value of deposits that may be found.

While the process of search may be thought of as a sifting process,
all rejections for further investigation should be regarded as tentative.
A change in any one of the circumstances just mentioned may make it
advisable to resume study of an area. As one of my critics has emphasized
so strongly and correctly, regional geology may be studied on many levels
of precision and detail, with strong emphasis on some aspects of the area's
geology and less on others, depending on the interests toward which the
investigation is directed and on the characteristics of the region.[19] Thus
as time goes on and more knowledge is accumulated about the mineral
resources of a country, we should expect less and less reliance on the
extensive survey and more reliance on intensive studies concentrated on
smaller areas.

The preceding discussion is relevant to a country of some size. In the
case of a small country, the same considerations would suggest the desirability of considering extensive investigations simultaneously for the small
country and a neighboring country (or countries), which may also be small,
of course.

Hydrologic and Meteorologic Data

As was emphasized in Chapter V, data on a natural flow variable or a
changing state of nature can be gathered only with the passage of time or
by the usually difficult reconstruction of the past. The frequency with
which we wish to observe the variable or state will depend on the rapidity
and amplitude of variation in the variable or on the rate at which the state
of nature in question is changing. Thus, geological maps do not have to be

---

[19] Vincent E. McKelvey of the U.S. Geological Survey, letter of June 22, 1967.

redone because of changes in the rocks, although they have to be for other reasons. The progress of dunes, changes in vegetation, or the progress of erosion can be studied by readings taken at intervals of years.

Hydraulic and meteorologic variables, on the other hand, exhibit great variability over much shorter periods of time. What is more, we have a strong interest in what may be almost momentary values of the variables— for example, floods and temperatures below freezing. To capture them, a continuously operating program must be set up. Meteorological data are wanted not only for the economically important activity of weather forecasting but also for establishing climatological characteristics so important for agriculture. The agriculturist, especially the innovator, can make good use of the knowledge of some aspect or aspects of the distributions of length of growing season, date of first frost, date of last frost, diurnal and monthly temperature distributions, rainfall, snow, and other characteristics.

Hydrologic data are clearly necessary if hydraulic works of any kind are to be erected, although, as we shall see, the data have been most rudimentary or nonexistent in many cases.

A group of technical experts in the field of hydro-meteorological networks recently suggested thirty to forty years of data for base gauging stations.[20] Where there is extreme variation in precipitation and runoff this minimum period might be extended to as much as seventy or eighty years. It is not at all clear what was meant by "minimum requirement." In my estimation, postponement of viable projects for at least thirty to forty years would almost surely be productive of a net loss because of the sacrifice of net rents involved, but perhaps they were not thinking of postponement. Perhaps the suggested minimum number of years represents the number needed before the technicians feel quite certain about the nature of the distribution in question and some of its parameters. The economic goal, however, is the maximization of the present value of the net rents of the resources involved and not the minimization of the discomfort of the hydrologists and meteorologists who are called on to advise on a project. With "insufficient" data, some projects will be designed incorrectly, but the average gain on these may be substantial even though part of the potential gain is lost.

The United Nations *Manual of Standards and Criteria for Planning Water Resource Projects*[21] suggests that records of stream discharge "should be continuous for a period of time which will be typical of the

---

[20] *Nature and Resources*, UNESCO, Vol. I, No. 4 (December 1965). The symposium on design of hydro-meteorological networks was held in June 1965 in Quebec, Canada.
[21] United Nations, New York, 1964, p. 8.

conditions to be anticipated in operating the project." While this suggestion seems at first glance unexceptionable—and probably not very helpful—I believe it to be fundamentally wrong. The primary social object is *not* to discover the "typical conditions" of the streams of the country, but to maximize the present values of the net rents on a *series* of projects. For a country with no historical streamflow data, this may justify or require the construction of projects before data sufficient to represent *typical* conditions have been generated, and this is even more likely in those cases where projects can be constructed and put into operation in smaller pieces.

It is important to understand that the failure of a particular project or number of projects to attain "maximum" return because of insufficient streamflow data at the time of design is not necessarily an indication of poor planning. Rather, a record showing that failure to attain maximum return was never attributable to insufficient streamflow data might well indicate mismanagement. But does it constitute mismanagement not to have enough data available to maximize the present value of the opportunity? The verdict certainly is yes, but the extenuating circumstances may be quite compelling, too.[22]

How far should a country go, then, in trying to anticipate—by many years—the need for these types of data? One possibility is to use the density[23] of gauging stations in developed countries as a guide. A number of such studies have been made, although never with the explicit recommendation that the practice in wealthy countries should guide the others. The practice of the wealthy countries is not the right guide, of course. For one thing, the density of their stations may be wrong even for their circumstances, but, more important, their circumstances are different. The question of payoff from the data can not be avoided, no matter how inexact the answer. And there are areas in some countries where the cost of developing a gauging capability would be very high.

Perhaps some partial guides are possible, reflecting the general view that as the demand for water increases more and more data on streamflow and other water characteristics are needed for proper economizing decisions. The following suggestions are directed to hydrologic data:

[22] We note in passing that the manual, *Feasibility Studies, Economic and Technical Soundness Analysis, Capital Projects* (Washington: U.S. Department of State, Agency for International Development, Office of Engineering, October 1, 1964) says nothing of the problem under discussion. Although the problem is alluded to in a few places in Ven Te Chow (ed.), *Handbook of Applied Hydrology* (New York: McGraw-Hill, 1964), most of the discussions are based on the presumption, of which the authors are aware, that relevant parameters of the distributions are known. There is no attempt to estimate the value of the marginal product of hydrologic data.

[23] Various measures have been discussed, for example, stations per unit area, stations per capita.

1. In areas in which there is potential irrigable land and the possibility of developing water supply, collection of streamflow data should be begun "immediately." Gauging stations are not established overnight, of course, but there is an important difference between a vague intention to institute measurement at some indefinite time in the future and a program that is working systematically to put a network of stations in operation. Needless to say, the designation of such areas must be based on at least a rough judgment that there is a chance of developing economically feasible projects. The location of stations must be related properly to structure sites, relations among streams, and the suitability of the site itself for measurement; and the variables to be measured must be chosen with an eye to the potential projects. Competent technical advice is essential and is easy to obtain if needed.

Similarly, data collection should be begun for potential hydropower sites with possibilities for development.

2. Measurement is needed in flood problem areas. The data are needed not only for the design of storage structures but for the protection of structures susceptible to flood damage and for the design of programs to control flood plain use.

3. In areas where municipal and industrial water supply are beginning to be thought of as problems, stream measurement and ground-water investigation are called for, bearing in mind that the year-to-year solution of such problems does not rest solely on supply adjustment but on demand adjustment as well.

It is likely that the above criteria would result in the establishment of stations on the principal streams of a country and a part of the tributaries, the number depending on the size of the main streams (that is, on their order, in the technical sense) and the characteristics of the terrain through which the streams go. The requirement that the area currently has economic activity or that there be a possibility of viable water projects implies that in some countries uninhabited areas may not have much stream measurement. This is fortunate, for some of these areas present difficult measurement problems, which may even be beyond solution for the countries concerned for some time to come.

Although hydrologic and meteorological data serve purposes that are different in part, the geographic areas of most interest are often the same, and there often will be economies in establishing joint stations. A unified administration of the activities deserves careful consideration.

In Chile and the western United States, there has been no postponement of dam construction to wait for the accumulation of more data.[24] In many cases dams have been constructed before any streamflow data have been

---

[24] See tables on streamflow data, Appendix B to this chapter.

available for the stream in question. In other cases a gauge has been established on a stream only years after a dam's construction. The dam itself serves as a gauge, of course, but in the case of Chile the organizations taking possession of a dam sometimes have not reported flow data to the responsible governmental unit; consequently, the date of installation of the first gauge after construction of a dam has some significance for the public records.

Let us consider the case of dams constructed in the western United States and take into account only gauges close to the dam[25] and for which data on the area drained by the dam are available. Taking for each dam the longest record for gauges close to the dam, the information shown in Table 14 is obtained.

Table 14.   Years of Data Available at Time of Start of Construction of 27 Dams in Western United States

Years	Frequency
0–	6
10–	11
20–	6
30–40	4

The simple average for the twenty-seven dams is 17.2 years.

Data for areas of drainage were not available for eight other dams.[26] If we include the maximum number of years of any station on these streams no matter how far from the dam, the simple average for the whole group of dams rises to 21.9 years.

If similar simple averages are calculated for gauges that are near the dam but not downstream of it, some gauges of long record are eliminated and the averages are lowered to 9.1 years for the twenty-seven dams and to 15.4 for the thirty-five dams.[27]

A similar but not exactly comparable tabulation can be made for Chile. Here it was necessary to take the data for the station that was closest to

[25] In Appendix B to this chapter, Table 18, gauges are classified by the ratio
$$\frac{\text{area drained by gauge}}{\text{area drained by dam}}.$$
Gauges with this ratio between .76 and 1.25 are defined as close. If the ratio is less than one, the gauge is upstream of the dams; if over one, it is downstream.

[26] See Appendix B to this chapter, Table 19.

[27] If a gauge was not installed in the reach above the dam until after construction was started, there was zero years of data available at date of start of construction.

the dam, yielding an average number of years of data of 6.3. In some cases the data available did not indicate this definitely.

If this had been done with the U.S. dams, the average number of years of data available would have been considerably lower—8.1 years as compared with the 17.2 years obtained for the 27 "close" stations above or below the dam. Precipitation data were the basis for design of nine other Chilean dams.

Table 15.   Years of Streamflow Data Available at Start of Construction of Dams in Chile for Station Nearest Dam

Years	Frequency
0	10[1]
1–4	3
5–	4
10–	2
15–	0
20–	0
25–	0
30–	1
35–	1
40–	0
	—
	21

[1] Lago Pullingue and Lago Puyehue have been assigned zero years although the precise dates of start of construction were not available.

How is it possible to design a dam with little or no flow data? First it may be noted that the need for flow data is less pressing if planned withdrawals are rather clearly small relative to the relevant aspect of the stream's flow. However, data are potentially productive even in cases of this type because a structure is involved that is exposed to the forces of high flows and must be designed to withstand them.

Apart from this, precipitation data may be available and can be made use of, especially if they can be related to flow data of adjacent basins or to flow data for a part of the basin in question. People living in the locality may be able to give useful estimates of extreme stages and frequencies. And the period of construction will provide at least one year of data, with modifications of design possible at least during the first part of the period of construction. In Chile's case, these possibilities were not sufficient to prevent some notable cases of overcapacity, especially for a group of dams constructed around the 1920's. These dams, together with costs (in escudos of 1964 value), are listed in Table 16.

Table 16. Seven Dams in Chile Constructed Without Streamflow Data, 1919–35

Dam	Cost (*million escudos, 1964*)	Construction initiated in:
Lautaro	7.0	1928
Huechún	9.4	1929
Recoleta	13.0	1929
Cogotí	21.0	1935
Casablanca	5.0	1929
Cerrillos	.2	1931
Laguna de Planchón	1.3[1]	1919

[1] 1962 escudos.

Lautaro has been empty 90 per cent of the time. Cogotí has had water for only 40 per cent of the planned irrigated acreage. Recoleta had to have a feeder canal to supply water from another stream. The Casablanca reservoirs are underutilized. At Culimo, the flow has been 30 per cent below that estimated.[28]

In some of the Chilean cases it probably would have paid to postpone construction simply in order to accumulate more data. After all, if the expected present value of net rents with little or no data is zero,[29] the improvement from one more year of data need be only as great as the cost of the station for a year, and that is not very much in most cases, but it would have been better still if collection of flow data had begun earlier. In terms of the present example, even with a discount rate of 10 per cent per year the present value of the net rents need improve only by 2.6 times the cost of another year's data to justify starting the collection ten years before construction rather than nine.[30]

Soil Surveys and Related Studies

One way to approach the problem of the rate at which soil surveys and related studies should be pursued is to take a look at an effort to develop such information rapidly and on an extensive scale and see what happened. In the Chilean aerophotogrammetric project,[31] one of the immediate objectives was the institution of a new land tax system, under which the

[28] See René Villarroel and Heinrich Horn, *Rentabilidad de las Obras de Regadío en Explotación Construidas por el Estado* (Santiago: Dirección de Planeamiento del Ministerio de Obras Públicas, 1963), p. 16.

[29] I do not assert that it must be zero without formal data. Casual observation may permit the design of a structure and plan with a positive present value.

[30] If k is the cost of the 10th year's data, $(1.10)^{10} k = 2.6 k$, which is the amount by which the present value of the opportunity must increase to justify the expenditure.

[31] Hereinafter called "the project" if the reference is clear from the context.

value on which the proportional tax would be based would depend on the land capability class to which the project assigned the parcel in question and on the "price" or unit hectare value assigned to land of this class.[32]

Accordingly, the project first located property boundaries on controlled photomosaics, a task that required extensive field work to locate the property boundaries. It should be noted that this property line identification was only for tax purposes. In addition, plots were classified according to present use, using, for example, a classification with seven categories for lands with extensive cultivation.[33] In addition, soils were classified (350 soil series were classified) with underlying information on weathering, drainage, texture, density, stoniness, slope and other characteristics indicated on photomosaics. Finally the plots were assigned to land capability classes.[34]

The property boundaries and land capability assignments coming out of these procedures seem to have functioned satisfactorily so far as land taxation is concerned and the classifications developed have also served to give an excellent portrayal—for fairly large areas—of the various classifications made.

But are the data sufficiently accurate to be relied on in the evaluation of, say, an irrigation project? Are they sufficiently accurate to be useful to the person managing a farm, assuming he would be willing and able to use the data?

The answers to these questions, so far as data coming directly out of the project are concerned (that is, with no reworking or additional field sampling), are probably no. A soil sample was taken, on the average, for every 29 square kilometers, or every 11 square miles. More important, however, is the fact that Chile is undertaking a $2.5 million soils survey project[35] that will work largely in areas already covered by the aero-photogrammetric project. It appears that one of the important tasks of the project is to provide soils data detailed enough for use by the Corporación de la Reforma Agraria (CORA) in the management of the properties it has or will take over. That is to say, the data of the aero project were not adequate for this purpose.[36]

---

[32] The unit value also varies according to the province and the distance from market in the case of Chile.

[33] Accuracy of classification prior to field check is said to have been 84 per cent. See Luis Vera, *Agricultural Land Inventory Techniques* (Washington: Pan American Union, 1964), p. 67.

[34] *Ibid.*, pp. 7 and 78.

[35] Financed partly by the UN Special Fund. FAO is the executing agency. See Chapter IV, Table 12.

[36] I hasten to add that to my knowledge no official of the Chilean government or of the Organization of American States has ever claimed they were.

So far as more detailed soil surveys are concerned, the first priority is irrigation and colonization projects if more preliminary investigations have not served to eliminate the project from consideration. Beyond these needs, a soil survey program should not be permitted to get ahead of the capacity to use the data. If the detailed information is going to have an impact on production, it must be put into use by the persons who are making the management decisions for *individual fields*, whether these people are owner-operators, managers of privately owned lands, or bureaucrats managing lands in the hands of the government. It is not difficult to see the overwhelming importance of the system by which technical data on natural resource characteristics and production responses thereto are brought to bear on decisions that affect agricultural productivity.

If a country is not going to adopt a land tax of the Chilean type, how valuable would be information of the same type? A project could derive information on size of farm, land use, soils characteristics, and land capability estimates, all of a level of precision suitable for "regional" studies.[37]

But are soil survey data essential to progress in productivity? In the case of the United States, it is interesting to observe that after sixty years of effort about a half of the farmland has been covered by soil surveys detailed enough for conservation planning.[38] This, however, does not warrant the conclusion that productivity rises very nicely without information on soils. Apart from the fact that proper use of soil information is but one factor in productivity, a comprehensive extension system was in operation, as well as other ways of disseminating information, which made it possible for farmers to develop a good deal of soil information on their own account even though their ground was not yet included in a soil map. A soil survey does not start from a level of no information.

Certainly data on farm size and current land use[39] can be developed more easily from photomosaics and air photos than by any all-ground method. The same is no doubt true of soil information, subject to the limitations of precision in a large and rapid survey mentioned above.

These types of data would be extremely useful no matter what type of planning is done for the agricultural sector. Even in a system in which agricultural production decisions are made entirely by private operators

[37] In the case of land use statistics, the experience and difficulties of the United States may contain some valuable lessons for countries that are expanding their land use data programs. The subject is discussed comprehensively in Marion Clawson with Charles L. Stewart, *Land Use Information* (Washington: Resources for the Future, 1965).

[38] *Ibid.*, p. 214.

[39] But there are important limitations on the types and detail of information that can be developed without extensive ground checking.

responding to market prices, a government could make use of such data, especially for size of farm and land use, since they may be relevant to possible government programs. Perhaps soil information of the regional type would be less valuable to such a government, but the possibility of checking on the progress of erosion would be of value in some countries. In areas of very low income, however, my opinion—and it is only that—is that other opportunities for investment would yield a higher return, having in mind principally education of both young and adults on many fronts.

It should be noted that the types of information just discussed provide a picture of only certain parts of the agricultural system. To understand how it functions, other methods would have to be used to obtain data on output and yield by crop and location, inputs and outputs in physical and value terms for different types of farms by location, and so on. Although such information is not within the scope of this study, gathering of data by aerial methods is effective in some cases because it is a means by which a comparatively small group of well-trained professionals and subprofessionals can do the whole job without having to rely on an administrative machine and personnel whose principal objectives are in directions quite different from the production of reliable data. If the economic series on inputs and outputs of farm enterprises are gathered by a sampling program rather than by attempts at complete coverage, a similar advantage can be gained, namely, the use of trained and disciplined personnel. Sampling is not the answer to all data needs, but it should be evaluated as a possibility for all types of data.[40]

Should Studies of Natural Resources be Integrated?

An "integrated study of natural resources" is commonly taken to mean the simultaneous study of all the resources in an area. Such a study necessarily will involve specialists from several disciplines. The advantage is thought to be a better and more useful description and evaluation of the area's resources than if one type of specialist studied all aspects of the resources or if the specialists worked in isolation from each other. "Simultaneous study of resources" can mean different things, however, in that different experts studying a given area at the same time may pursue their work rather independently, with collaboration taking place only at the administrative level, or they may collaborate closely at the substantive level. In the former case, simultaneous work will reduce cost but will have little effect

---

[40] Even aerial methods, which in a sense make or seem to make complete coverage possible, are better looked on in many cases as a means of increasing the efficiency of ground sampling, or, what is the same thing, a means of reducing the number of field samples required to attain a given level of precision.

on the products of the study. The Chilean aerophotogrammetric project, although often cited as an integrated project, is not regarded by some experts familiar with its operation as involving a close interdisciplinary co-operation at the substantive level. On the other hand, some of the studies of the Peruvian general resource agency, Oficina Nacional de Evaluación de Recursos Naturales, do exhibit a close collaboration between the specialists, as does also the preliminary study of the Guayas basin prepared by the Organization of American States.[41]

The arguments for substantively integrated studies generally seem to stress what might be called the unity of nature. That is, natural phenomena of many different types, although often investigated in separate compartments, frequently are closely interrelated. One may think, for example, of climate, geomorphology, and vegetation; of climatic history and mineral deposition; or of man's simplification of the biologic environment by cultivation practices and the rise of "pests." As the argument goes, in all cases we are dealing with a complex system that is in a moving equilibrium with respect to the natural and man-made forces for change that are acting on it. If we propose to alter the balance of these forces, for example, by developing a natural resource, the whole system must be considered if we are to predict and evaluate the outcome. The following is a good and typical statement of the point:

> Experience acquired in the last twenty years in the evaluation of natural resources demonstrates that different methods must be combined to obtain optimum results.
> The first of these is to adopt . . . an ecological point of view. That is, we must constantly remind ourselves of the interactions between living things and their physical and biological environment. With this point of view it is possible to work with nature instead of against it. This point of view is particularly necessary in regions in which the environment is relatively little known, and it can help to avoid failures attributable to the incorrect use of agricultural or industrial methods which might give good results in other ecological conditions. In the most general sense, this ecological focus embraces sociological considerations, which all too frequently are not taken into account.
> The second method, which of course is not independent of the first, is the integration of studies of the environment since the various elements are interrelated. . . . The use of aerial methods can facilitate the making of those combined studies a great deal. . . . Moreover, in regions not well known and to which access is difficult, integrated studies offer the additional advantage of being done together, which definitely is less costly than a series of individual studies.

[41] The Peruvian studies are cited and discussed in Chapter VII, p. 182; the Guayas basin study is referred to in Chapter III, p. 67.

Finally, . . . a "conservation focus" should be adopted, . . . which means to give attention not only to the possible ways of utilizing the resources and mechanisms of nature, but also to the basic disturbances and irreversible processes which human intervention can unchain and leave as the actual net result.[42]

Surely there is much force to these views, a force which should have been evident to educated people in western countries at least since Marsh wrote his classic, *Man and Nature*, more than a hundred years ago.[43] Since his time many more cases of unnecessary waste and destruction of natural resources have accumulated, resulting from a failure to perceive or take into account important changes flowing from the exploitation of natural resources.

But the fact that the repercussions flowing from human intervention in natural systems are sometimes hard to perceive soon enough to avoid them does not point to the desirability of doing all studies of natural resources in an integrated fashion. It does point to the desirability of organizing things in such a way that specialized knowledge has the opportunity to point out effects that are likely to go unnoticed without its help, but this does not require simultaneous study. It may be more convenient and more responsive to demand for information if the different specialists study an area at different times. Once again, the idea of a *tabula rasa* seems to be lurking behind the argument for integrated studies, but in reality our knowledge of an area often will be sufficient to enable the conclusion that one of a few specialties is of dominant importance in the study of an area. In such circumstances, a too thoroughgoing insistence on an integrated study will result in a pro forma and sterile participation of the specialists who have little to contribute. There will be a tendency for studies to take on a purely technical orientation to the neglect of economic objectives which in my view should be orienting from the very beginning those natural resource studies that are a part of an economic development program. The specialized personnel required for integrated studies are so scarce that great care must be taken to use them where they are most needed.

In some circumstances partly or wholly integrated studies are desirable, however. That is, there are occasions on which two or more specialties should be united in the simultaneous study of an area.

[42] UNESCO, Department of Natural Sciences, Division of Scientific Research on Natural Resources, "Aspectos Principales del Tema Recursos Naturales y su Utilización" (UNESCO/CASTALA/2.1.1., Paris, September 8, 1965), p. 4. (My translation from the Spanish version.)
[43] George Perkins Marsh, *Man and Nature, or, Physical Geography as Modified by Human Action* (Cambridge: Harvard University Press, 1965). This is essentially a republication of the original edition, published by Charles Scribner in 1864.

One of the circumstances in which an integrated study is desirable is the case of areas with only minor or no economic activity which are thought to present some possibilities for development. These might be, for example, "new lands" adjacent to already exploited areas or brought close to them by the possibility of cheap transportation. Here all aspects of the area must be appraised if only to evaluate investment for transportation and other investment of the public utility type which may service a variety of economic activities.

A second situation calling for a more or less integrated study is when comprehensive use of the hydraulic resources of a river basin is being considered. Here a number of resources may be affected if only by being covered up with water, and all of these must be evaluated both to design and evaluate the final proposal.

Even in these two cases there is a question of which specialists should participate and to what extent. Having in mind the objective of avoiding failures that the specialist's study or knowledge could have helped avoid, it is necessary that they be consulted in what might be called a "touch-base" procedure at two stages. The first is at the stage when the (potentially) integrated study is being designed. Taking into account the knowledge he already possesses of the area in question, the specialist should be able to suggest at this stage how intensive should be the participation of his specialty. Later when the report of the study is under preparation, those specialists who did not participate very actively in the study should be given the opportunity to criticize the proposals formulated, perhaps when they are at the draft stage. Care is required at this point, for as projects develop in the minds of their designers they tend to acquire a momentum of their own. The intervention or criticism of the specialist must not come so late in the process that his critical remarks have no influence.

The idea here is that the specialist many times will be able to say, on the basis of knowledge that already exists, "this is all very well, but you have failed to take into account a certain factor which will reduce returns by x per cent." Or he may be able to remind the enthusiasts that a similar project was undertaken elsewhere under similar circumstances, with disastrous results.

We conclude, then, that the reasons usually adduced for integrated studies are cogent so far as the participation of different disciplines are concerned, but that the question of simultaneous study of an area must be decided case by case. In some circumstances it will be advantageous.

What are Some of the Organizational Problems?

The extent to which the basic objectives of natural resource information programs are achieved will depend in part on the organization of the different types of agencies involved and on the relations between them.

The fact that the information programs develop physical data on natural resources but that these data are used by agencies whose main concern is of an economic nature gives the problem of organization a special importance. The following discussion is confined largely to governmental questions, having in mind principally the problems faced by a country of substantial size. Those of smaller countries constitute a special and more difficult situation, discussed in Chapter VII.

The basic premise to keep in mind in considering organizational problems is that information activities should provide data and help contribute to the formation of a steady flow of investment projects in the industries concerned, or contribute to a reduction in the cost of managing and using certain natural resources.

The various governmental functions that impinge on these questions of organization are the following:

1. Economic planning.
2. Determination of the allocation of the governmental budget. Our interest is in the budget allocations to the agencies that produce natural resource information.
3. The making of investment and operating decisions for resources administered in whole or in part by the government. Here are included agencies that "administer" a certain type of resource—e.g., a ministry of agriculture, a department of irrigation, a forest service, or an air pollution control agency.
4. Dissemination of information to be used by private users of resources in investment and operating decisions.
5. Generation of natural resource information. The usual pattern is one of several agencies, some of them independent. This is often true of the cartographic service (frequently named a "Military Geographic Service" or something similar because of the military's interest in maps) and the geological survey organization. But some natural resource information agencies are attached to the executing ministries that use the information. For example, soil survey units may be attached to a ministry of agriculture which also contains the extension service function (not necessarily with that title) by which information is put into the hands of farm managers.

So far as Latin American governments are concerned, the first function, planning, is not performed in a very thoroughgoing manner in some of the governments, because the planning function is somewhat divorced from the agencies that control the government's investment decisions. The budgetary function may nominally be located in a single agency, perhaps a treasury ministry, but the budgetary process is always far more complicated than this, the power of budgetary decision in fact being often dispersed among a number of centers of power.

Although all of the above functions are involved in the problem of organizing the natural resource information agencies, our interest is principally in these agencies themselves. There are two main questions to be discussed:

First, should the natural resource information activities be administered together in a single agency or not?

Second, whether these activities are together in a single agency or not, what should be their relations with agencies performing the other functions listed above?

A Single Agency Containing All Natural Resource Information Agencies

There are several possible variants of the single agency for all types of natural resource information. Each of the variants discussed here has serious weaknesses.

One possibility is a single agency that works exclusively on the basis of integrated surveys. While this might be attractive to someone who can see only the interrelations of resources, the reality is that a strong demand for one type of information in a certain location often arises entirely independently of demands for other types of information for the same place. There is no reason to think that demands for resource information are always to spring into existence simultaneously for the same location. It would be surprising if this were to happen, for at any given moment certain types of information pertaining to a particular geographical area may be further developed than are other types. Why redo the same task just to be working in an integrated manner? And, as noted earlier, at a particular point in time the type of project in view, being quite specialized, may need only one or a few types of information.

Another type of single agency would be what might be labelled a natural resources institute, that is, an institute located at the side of the mainstream of governmental activity and which would possess a substantial degree of autonomy, but which in all probability could not get along without substantial financial support from the government.

Support for the institute type of organization perhaps arises from the idea that since the activities that generate information are technical, or sometimes scientific, they ought to be off at the side where the continuity of their work will not be disrupted by the constant revisions of programs necessary to meet the unco-ordinated demands of the public and the various governmental agencies concerned with the administration of natural resources. This argument rests on a mistaken view of the main function of these agencies, which is to supply information to meet the information demands of public and private economic units. While the activities of information agencies may contribute to the development of science, this contribution should be ancillary to the main purpose. Furthermore, the separated institute form of organization makes it difficult to develop needed close working relations between the natural resource information personnel and the users of the information. For example, some of the personnel of the information agencies ought to play a part in the process of project conception and elaboration. Effective channels of communication are needed between the information agencies and those that use the information, both in order to make effective use of the information and also to make the information programs responsive to the demands for information.

A single agency which was not off at the side as a separate institute would avoid its disadvantages, for it now would be easier to develop responsiveness to demands for information and arrangements that would make for more effective use of the information. But if all the organizations that produce natural resource information are contained in this agency, it probably will contain too much. The work of some natural resource information is so closely bound up with executive departments or ministries on the one hand, or with public enterprises on the other, that their work is far more useful if the information organization is a part of the using agency. This seems to be the case with soil units, which are more effectively used if they are in the agency which is concerned with putting the information to use in the management decisions made by farm operators. The same type of argument applies to the activity that develops data on forests. Here a part of the "inventory" capability may well be directed very closely to operational needs (especially preparation of operation plans), or for private operators who may not have effective access to private capabilities of this sort. Another case in point is that of the government petroleum operation. If the exploration function is performed by the government rather than by contract or a concessionaire, an operation of any size would probably wish to develop its own geological capability to take advantage of the specialization that has developed within this field and to secure a better co-ordination between the exploration work and operations plans.

There is no neat solution to the problem of where to put information organizations requiring close connections with the using agencies. If there are demands for information from multiple sources, economies of large-scale operation probably would indicate the desirability of only one organization, perhaps located in the appropriate executive department. If demands are large enough, multiple information units are feasible so far as economies of scale are concerned, since the higher costs associated with excessively small units can be avoided, but problems of co-ordinating their work remain.

A Small General Resource Information Agency

Can resource information be organized in a way that will leave certain units in executive departments where such a course seems to be justified, but will still achieve an effective response to widely differing demands for information? Let us examine the following organization scheme with this question in mind.

Those information units that require a close relation with an operating program would be located in the appropriate executive department. The others would function as separate, specialized units, but their activities would be "co-ordinated" in various ways by a small general agency for resource information. The information units not in executive departments could exist as independent agencies with the general agency also existing as a separate agency, or, perhaps preferably if tradition and bureaucratic politics permitted, they could be brought into a single resource information unit.

In the latter case, however, the separate information producing activities should continue to function in a substantially independent manner. There are solid reasons for the specializations of function that have developed. These involve substantial independence of programs, specialization of personnel and equipment, professional esprit de corps, and so on. This independence would not be complete, however, for the general resource information agency would perform certain functions which would impinge on the specialized resource information units.

A general resource agency with the usual specialized information activities organized as separate agencies is now used in Chile and Peru. However, the functions of the general resource information agencies differ one from the other, and in both cases they differ from the functions of such an agency as is envisioned here.

What should be the tasks of the small general resource information agency? Six are suggested here.

1. It would be the appropriate agency to conduct such integrated surveys of natural resources as are made. It would not be necessary that the agency have sufficient personnel of its own to staff such studies completely, for personnel could be borrowed from the specialized information units such as a geological or mapping organization. It would be preferable that these adjust their programs to the temporary loan of personnel rather than that the general agency be forced to embark on specialized studies to keep a large staff busy. The agency should have some capability in economic analysis on its staff, considerably more than the more specialized agencies. As a part of this task, it might take the lead or at least participate strongly in such assessments of regional economic potential as are made. Such assessments, which presumably are to help

potential investors, both governmental and private, often seem to ignore information on the quality and quantity of various resources.

2. Studies of the various natural resources in any one country are numerous, but many of the reports are hard to locate. The general resource information agency would be well advised not only to keep up to date some type of "inventory" record of all this information, but also to summarize or present in useful form the various types of extant information. This stock of information represents the present understanding of the country's resources; consequently it is important that it be available to many people in forms easily understood so that investment plans can be based on the best information available at the time. As a part of this task, the general agency would necessarily be conversant with the current programs of the specialized information units. Even quite general information about natural resources has an important influence on the investment process because it is an important determinant of the allocation of efforts to conceive and develop specific investment opportunities.

In the case of Chile, the Instituto de Investigación de Recursos Naturales (hereinafter called IREN) has compiled a bibliography of studies of the natural resources of Chile, indicating where each publication can be found. In the case of Peru, the Oficina Nacional de Evaluación de Recursos Naturales (hereinafter called ONERN) has published several volumes on different aspects of natural resources which summarize and organize the available information.

3. The need for natural resource agencies to adjust their programs to the demands of the users of the data has received a great deal of emphasis. But how are these agencies to know what the demands are? In those cases where information is sold—as may be the case with maps, photographs, and photomosaics, for example—the volume of sales provides indication of the behavior of demand and can be used to give something of an indication of changes in demand, for example, as between localities. Nor is there any reason why maps, etc., should not be sold rather than given to governmental agencies. In the case of certain types of special projects, it would be entirely reasonable to do such studies for a fee to be paid by the agency requesting the study. Not only is this a salutary way to avoid idle requests for more and more studies, but it provides for financing of the service agency on a meaningful basis.

Unfortunately, however, such devices can not be applied on so large a scale that all the finance problems of these service agencies are taken care of. The problem lies in the diffuseness of the benefits that flow from the different types of studies. If we can presume that users understand the value of the information, then we can say that at a minimum they should be charged a price equal to the cost of providing one more copy of the results, but in those cases where there is a problem of getting potential users to acquire and learn to use the information, perhaps a price below even this level would be justified, for a time at least.

Apart from such solid evidences of demand as sales receipts provide, the general resource information agency could well be assembling other information which, while far less definitive than sales receipts or fees, is still useful. For one thing, the agency should be examining the programs of the agencies using resource information to see what is implied for the activities of the agencies that have to provide the information. The task is more complicated than merely examining the work program, because the lead time required for many types of information is considerable. Consequently, a special effort must be made to obtain careful estimates of the nature and location of activities which require resource information for their planning rather far into the future.

The tasks suggested here and under point 2, above, can be as simple or as complex as one cares to make them. Strauss has suggested that the relevant facts might be summarized in a series of tables. This information could provide the basis for further investigation and deliberation to the extent desirable in the context of a particular country.[44]

In Strauss's scheme, information would be presented in a series of five tables, as follows:[45]

Table I would indicate the various resource information agencies operating in the country, the size and nature of their programs, and their source of money.

Table II would summarize the present state of knowledge of natural resources for each discipline or resource.

Table III would summarize the type of information needed for programs or projects needing resource information.

Table IV would present, for each project or program, the types of information needed at each stage of the project, information available, and additional investigation needed, together with date when needed, cost, and source of funds.

Table V would take the information in Table IV and classify it by discipline and type of study demanded. The annual cost of making the studies would be estimated. Present capacity would be compared with capacity required to produce the studies demanded.

The tables may seem to suggest that the determination of the demand for resource information and next year's information program is simpler

---

[44] See Estevam Strauss, "Recursos Naturales y Planificación Económica en América Latina, Parte II" (Santiago: Instituto Latinoamericano de Planificación Económica y Social; November 1965, mimeo.).

[45] Appendix A to this chapter contains the row and column headings of these tables.

and more mechanistic than it actually can be. While one should not think that a mechanistic determination of the demand for information or next year's program can be made by looking at projects and making a few calculations, a good part of the information in these tables constitutes an indispensable point of departure for making adjustments in information programs so that demands will be met more effectively. Some of the information required for the tables exists either in information producing units or in user agencies. Its assembly in one place would provide a better basis for budget decisions and for co-ordination of the programs of different information units, recognizing, at the same time, that most countries would have much difficulty in assembling the data for the whole group of tables and in keeping them up to date.

A study of the demand by governmental agencies for natural resources information has been made for Nicaragua by the Natural Resources Division of the Inter American Geodetic Survey with the assistance of the Oficina de Planificación de Nicaragua, by means of a questionnaire and interviews.[46] The study was made as part of the preparation for the tax improvement and natural resources inventory project, but many aspects of the study are applicable to the continuing problem of determining the size and content of a resource information program and can be adapted to it. The information gathered differs from that asked for in Strauss's tables in several respects, mainly in that the types of information are specified in much greater detail. The Nicaragua report is perhaps less mechanistic. While a good deal of this detail is a breakdown of material customarily contained in, say, a geological or soils study, it is interesting to observe differences in agency response as to their need for each detailed category.

The availability of a completed study of user agency demands for resource data makes quite clear the uncertainty surrounding many of the demands. Nor can one take negative responses ("No, I don't use that type of data and don't want it.") at their face value. Perhaps the data are used elsewhere or perhaps they should be used.

4. The general resource information agency could perform an important function of co-ordination. Although the programs of the specialized information units can and should be pursued in substantial independence, there are several points at which they are related either to each other or to user agencies. In the first place, the general agency, which will have a rather comprehensive view of the demand for the different types of infor-

---

[46] *Survey of Data Needs of User Agencies*, U.S. Army, Inter American Geodetic Survey, Natural Resources Division, Fort Clayton, Canal Zone, April 1966. The study was prepared for the Oficina de Planificación de Nicaragua and the USAID Mission to Nicaragua.

mation, should be consulted by the specialized information agencies in preparing their annual budgets and work programs. Secondly, in many countries there are several agencies collecting similar types of data. In this case, some agency ought to have the authority to harmonize certain aspects of their activity, such as types of data to be collected, location of stations, method of presentation, and standards of precision.

Although the work programs of the specialized information units are independent to a substantial degree, it may be possible to arrange work schedules so as to reap some savings. By consolidating demands for aerial photography, it may be possible to let larger contracts at some saving. An examination of work schedules by location may also reveal opportunities for different information units to work simultaneously in the same areas, not to make an integrated study but to reap the savings that are possible by simultaneous field operations or by consecutive field operations which can keep some capital facilities in more continuous operation. These considerations perhaps are not too important in thickly populated areas where facilities of all types are readily available, but in sparsely settled or remote areas they have a much greater importance.

5. As a result of having compiled information on demands for information and on the work programs of the specialized information units, the general resource information agency would be in a position to give valuable advice to the budget authority on the programs of these agencies and to make suggestions for changes in budget. It would be possible, and perhaps desirable, to make the specialized information units subordinate to the general agency for budget purposes, although such subordination need not involve any change in administrative autonomy within each specialized agency.

The problem dealt with here is a delicate one from the point of view of interagency relationships. The established specialized information agencies are likely to cherish their present autonomy, if they have it. While a new general agency conceivably could establish a satisfactory co-ordination of information activities by persuasion over a period of years, the task of getting the general agency to function in the manner envisioned here would be facilitated if the general agency had budgetary power. Such power would in fact change the programs of the specialized agencies only in those cases where the agency had been pursuing a program that ignored changing demands or the related activities of other information agencies.

6. The final function suggested for the general agency is to arrange and stimulate the participation of resource information specialists in project formation and evaluation within the government. More generally, the task of the agency is to act as an intermediary between the information specialist and those involved in the investment decision process, outside as well as within the government.

Within the government, the goal certainly should not be the participation of all resource information people in project formulation and evaluation, but a sufficient number should participate so as to work toward twin goals: (a) to get economists and engineers in the "planning commission," if there is one, and in the executive departments (where natural resource projects often are formulated) to understand the significance of resource information for their work, and (b) to get resource information people better acquainted with the uses to which their product is put and the way in which it is used.

As a part of this task, the general resource agency would administer the "touch-base" system mentioned earlier, whereby a project that has taken form in a preliminary or working document would be subjected to the rapid scrutiny of various resource experts for the purpose of detecting places where important information has not been used.

Clearly, one aspect of this task is to show potential users how to use resource data. The general agency could well supplement the already existing efforts of this type of activity by the specialized information agencies. This work should be directed to private as well as governmental users.[47]

Implications of Orienting Resource Information to the Investment Decision Process

The desirability of close relations between natural resource information agencies and user agencies, with an eye to improving investment decisions, has been stressed throughout this study and in this section in particular. There are important advantages to be gained from an economic orientation at all stages of the process of assembling natural resource information. While one can not but agree with Christian's and Stewart's view that premature assessment of economic feasibility may lead to error that may perpetuate itself, the neglect of an economic orientation can result in the collection of data that will never have any economic significance. It should be possible for the units in a decision structure to learn to discriminate between estimates of feasibility based on different quantities of data and to understand that assumptions are not data. If we can't get this far, the outlook for the quality of government investment decisions is rather bleak.[48]

[47] For example, ONERN in Peru has given courses in photo interpretation of natural resources to employees of various government agencies. IREN in Chile views education in the use of its materials as an important task.

[48] The discussion of this point is on p. 128 of the authoritative paper by C. S. Christian and G. A. Stewart, "Methodology of Integrated Surveys," UNESCO/NS/NR/94, Paris, April 17, 1964. (Paper given at 1964 Toulouse Conference on Principles and Methods of Integrating Aerial Survey Studies of Natural Resources for Potential Development.)

Our emphasis on viewing the management of natural resource information as a part of the process of making investment and operating decisions within government has lead inexorably to a consideration of the procedures and the people who will be using the data. In order to promote better use of data as well as to shape data programs to conform to demands, the general resource information agency has been viewed as the vehicle through which these goals can be approached, not immediately, but more closely with the passage of time. On the other hand, it should be noted that there has been no suggestion of centralizing the process by which natural resource investment projects are conceived and evaluated. To do so would be to run the risk that a point of view resting on inappropriate objectives would unduly influence investment decisions. Capture of the process by those who can see only the productivity of the type of investment with which they are familiar—whether that be roads, dams, or whatever—is to be avoided. To avoid this, the necessity for having different types of specialists participate and confront each other has been emphasized, as has also the desirability of buttressing evaluations with relevant data.

The view that development of resource information should be closely related to the process by which investment and operating decisions are made casts doubt on the advisability of large and rapid survey projects designed to produce a great deal of resource data quickly. Rather than develop information far ahead of the capability of using it, which is likely to result in the development of information not well adapted to demands, we should examine the advisability of information projects that continue for longer periods of time. Instead of confining the projects largely to the development of technical information, they might better put a substantial part of their effort on developing capacity to use resource data. It is perhaps more important to develop economic and engineering personnel who can use technical resource data in project or program design and evaluation than it is to train technicians to develop the technical resource information. Although I am not arguing that a country should not train its own technical resource information personnel, it is true that the international market for some technical services and investigations in the natural resource field is quite well developed. Not only is it possible to write rather definite specifications for many of these jobs, but the country buying the services is protected by a substantial degree of competition. For example, aerial photography certainly can be purchased, as can also the making of topographic maps, and so on down the list. But a country can not or dare not purchase the making of investment decisions. It really has no choice here but to develop its own nationals. It is not necessary that they be used at all points in the decision process, but nationals with a high level of competence are needed for at least the higher ranks, and it is much better if they clearly dominate all parts of the data using agencies.

Benefits and Costs—Going Beyond Natural Resource Information

The final guideline is that a program to improve the quality of natural resource data and its use must develop the economic data required to put resource data to use. Resource data by themselves are useless for investment or operating decisions. The only way to assess the economic potential of an investment opportunity involving a natural resource is to feed the physical data into a calculation of benefits and costs, using relationships between the cost of inputs and the value of outputs derived from actual experience or which are closely related to actual experience.

This means that the past record of experience is of overwhelming importance, for only by analyzing it can we make plans for the future. Records of inputs and outputs are needed in both physical and value terms, and the inputs from natural resources need to be expressed in quantitative terms of some sort that constitute a description of the quality or qualities of the natural resource. This means that the task of improving census data and of making studies of the operations of industries and separate firms is of great importance. For some types of activity it is possible to use relationships from foreign experience, but the relevance of such experience is always less than complete and in many cases it is positively misleading and not pertinent in any way whatsoever.

Within a government, all types of agencies operating in the natural resources fields, including both information agencies and user agencies, need a strong post-audit program for their activities. The questions are easy to put and hard to answer. How has colonization project X actually turned out? Can we summarize all of its benefits and all of its costs in proper economic terms? Or, why did we decide to develop information on a certain area that has been used by nobody?

Any program of post-audit needs all the help it can get. Consequently, efforts by persons outside the government (even from foreign countries) to evaluate experience should be encouraged and facilitated rather than discouraged, as is so often the case. There is an equally great need for studies of private enterprise in these fields, for in many cases it is the private operator who is managing the natural resource in whose development the government may have had a part.

In situations where our evaluations of past experience are inadequate to provide reliable estimates of the viability of a natural resource project, what can be done? For example, if a project involves the use of resources different from those heretofore used or contemplates the use of new methods of production or new modes of organization, past experience, even though it has been recorded and analyzed, will be to some extent an inadequate basis for estimation. This is likely to be the situation whenever an attempt is made to extend production to unused land, for the very fact that it is idle suggests that it differs from occupied land in important respects. Some of the difficulties may be surmountable, but others perhaps not.

In situations in which the past provides an inadequate basis for evaluation, there is no choice but to accumulate experience, but this need not require an indefinite wait before investment can begin. One possibility is to make extensive use of trial runs or research in the very location in which investment is proposed. With this procedure, at least some of the factors relevant to success or failure will be put to actual test. Usually it will not be possible to put all of them to test, because it will rarely be possible to duplicate completely the situation that will exist after investment is completed. For example, the employees of an agricultural research organization doing a test run on the suitability of an area for colonization will differ in important ways from the colonists who will come later on. There will be significant differences in education, health level, training, work habits, and so on.

It would be easy to assemble an impressive list of authorities who are united in this view. The strong words of John Phillips, writing from an extensive experience in many countries, are typical.

Only by careful study, *in situ*, supported by well-planned and ably conducted pilot projects, would it be possible to offer sound and firmly based guidance about the prospective viability of the numerous propositions which today are advocated by politicians and very senior officials responsible for so-called agricultural and associated development. The highly imaginative and grandiose schemes usually are dismissable because of their not being based on the elements of either agricultural or common sense.[49]

Still another way to accumulate experience before investing large sums is to try to design projects that are divisible, that is, to design them in such a way that a small commitment of funds will provide actual results (not only experimental) before investing the next increment. The example, par excellence, of this strategy is the gradual extension of settlement in small steps. Here there is opportunity for a rather complete test, including some elements of infrastructure. Where divisible projects are possible, and they often are not, they almost become self-evaluating with the consequent elimination of the threat of large-scale failure.

[49] John Phillips, *The Development of Agriculture and Forestry in the Tropics* (London: Faber and Faber, 1961), p. 175.

Perhaps the classic illustration of the points we have been making is provided by the post World War II scheme to grow peanuts on huge plantations in East and Central Africa, using ground cleared from uninhabited bush country. This scheme, with a planned capital cost of £24 million, was to be the largest single agricultural development ever undertaken.[50] All possible important mistakes seem to have been made. First, the advice of competent agricultural specialists was ignored. They had forecast failure on the ground that the rainfall regimen (single season rainfall of 25–30 inches) was basically unsuited to agriculture.[51] Second, although extensive research activities were envisaged on all aspects of resources that had anything to do with success, investment was started before research rather than the other way around.[52] Third, large sums ($65 million) were committed when it would have been possible to proceed in steps small enough to verify that lack of water was a serious problem, that compact and gritty soil caused rapid runoff and rapid wear on implements in one area, that soil nutrients were deficient in another, that in another area monsoon-type rainfall created an erosion problem, and that tsetse fly was a problem as well as other pests and insects.[53] As for cost estimates, ground clearing ran ten times anticipated levels and monthly labor turnover was 10 per cent.[54]

This failure is not attributable to "bad administration," as is sometimes alleged, for no amount of good administration would have brought success. Instead, it is an example of a whole decision process gone wrong. The lessons for such gigantic projects as the Carretera Marginal de la Selva and colonizing the Amazon basin are clear. If these projects are in fact not viable, we should proceed so as to find this out without wasting enormous sums that could have been put to good use elsewhere.

[50] Olive Holmes, *Peoples, Politics, and Peanuts in Eastern Africa*, Foreign Policy Reports (New York: Foreign Policy Association, December 1, 1950), p. 159. See also *A Plan for the Mechanized Production of Groundnuts in East and Central Africa*, presented by the Minister of Food to Parliament by Command of His Majesty, February 1947 (London: HMSO, Cmd. 7030); and *East African Groundnuts Scheme, Review of Progress to the end of November, 1947*, presented by the Minister of Food to Parliament by Command of His Majesty, January 1948 (London: HMSO, Cmd. 7314).

[51] See Leslie H. Brown, "An Assessment of Some Development Schemes in Africa in the Light of Human Needs and the Environment," in *The Ecology of Man in the Tropical Environment* (Morges, Switzerland, 1964), p. 284. This volume contains the proceedings and papers of the Ninth Technical Meeting of the International Union for the Conservation of Nature and Natural Resources, held at Nairobi, Kenya, September 1963.

[52] Edith Tilton Penrose, "A Great African Project," *Scientific Monthly*, Vol. LXVI, No. 4 (April 1948), p. 325.

[53] Holmes, pp. 159–60.

[54] *Nation*, December 3, 1949, p. 542; and Holmes, *ibid*.

Row and Column Headings of Tables on the Status of Resource Information in Latin America[55]

TABLE I

STRUCTURE OF THE SYSTEM OF INVESTIGATION
FOR NATURAL RESOURCES

Column headings:

a) Code

b) Name of administrative body

c) Place in administrative hierarchy

d) Disciplines in which the agency operates

e) Personnel

       Technical-scientific

       Technical aid

       Administrative

f) Capital

       Land and buildings

       Equipment

g) Budget for year

h) Sources of finance

TABLE II

STRUCTURE OF THE PRESENT SUPPLY OF KNOWLEDGE
OF NATURAL RESOURCES

Row headings are disciplines and resources, as follows:

1) Cartography

2) Aerial photography

3) Integrated photo interpretation and geomorphology

4) Geology

5) Meteorology and hydrology

6) Hydrology

7) Hydrogeology

8) Mineral resources

[55] Taken from Estevam Strauss, "Recursos Naturales y Planificación Económica en América Latina, Parte II" (Santiago: Instituto Latinoamericano de Planificación Económica y Social, November 1965, mimeo.).

9) Fossil fuels
10) Seismology
11) Soils
12) Natural pastures
13) Forests
14) Hunting and fishing (non-oceanic)
15) Oceanography and biological resources of the sea
16) General ecology

Columnar headings are as follows:
a) Activities
      Basic data survey
      Laboratory analysis
      Data processing
      Basic research
      Technological research
      Resource administration
      Data distribution
      Distribution of studies
b) Present state of knowledge
      Unit of measure
      Exploratory-scale or precision
      Reconnaissance-scale or precision
      Semi-detailed-scale or precision
      Detailed-scale or precision
c) Present annual capacity
      Reconnaissance-scale or precision
      Semi-detailed-scale or precision
      Detailed-scale or precision
d) Present average unit cost and time required per unit of study with the scale or precision indicated
      Reconnaissance
      Semi-detailed
      Detailed

TABLE III

PRIMARY DEMAND FOR NATURAL RESOURCE INFORMATION[56]

Column headings:
a) Programs or projects
b) Agency responsible

[56] In the particular case of Peru, for which the tables were originally prepared, the words are added, "for perfecting and putting into operation the national plan for economic and social development."

c) Stages and date of decision at each stage
d) Natural resources involved in project
e) Location of project (sheets of national map)
f) Estimated total cost
g) Estimated cost of resource investigations
h) Financial sources

TABLE IV

DEMAND FOR NATURAL RESOURCE STUDIES FOR THE DEVELOPMENT OR PROJECTS OR PROGRAMS

(*One for each project or program*)

Project or program
Agency responsible
Location of project

Column headings:

a) Objective
b) Stages of project
c) Disciplines involved
d) Unit of measurement and scale or precision of data
e) Information necessary (in units)
f) Information available (in units)
g) Studies necessary (in units)
h) Period available for studies—completion date
i) Agency conducting studies
j) Cost of studies
k) Source of funds

TABLE V

TOTAL DEMAND FOR NATURAL RESOURCE STUDIES

Column headings:

a) Discipline
b) Studies required
  i) within a short period (detailed studies)
    number of projects
    unit of measurement and quantity
    period available
  ii) within a period of medium length (semi-detailed studies)
    number of projects
    unit of measurement and quantity
    period available

    iii) within a long period (reconnaissance)
        unit of measurement and quantity
        period available
c) Average annual expenditure for studies
        detailed
        semi-detailed
        reconnaissance
d) Present capacity for studies (measured over the period available) as a percentage of the demand for studies
        detailed
        semi-detailed
        reconnaissance

Streamflow Data for Chile and the Western United States

Table 17. Availability of Streamflow Data at Time of Construction of Dams in Chile

Name of the reservoir	River basin	Name of gauge	Date of installation of gauge[1]	Construction period	Capacity $10^6 m^3$	Period between initiation of data series and construction[2] (years)
Caritaya	Camarones	Conanorca	1958	1930–35	42	−28
Lautaro	Copiapó	La Puerta	1927–30–1947	1928–42	37	1
Lagunas del Huasco	Huasco	Algodones	1928–30–1948	1901–04	7	−27
La Laguna	Elqui	Algarrobal	1916–30–1946	1927–37	40	9
Recoleta	Limarí	Hurtado (entrada embalse Recoleta)	1928–31–1959	1929–34	100	1
Tutuvén	Maule	Tutuvén	1945–49	1944–53	16	−1
Cogotí	Limarí	Dieciocho	1941–46–1955	1935–40	150	−6
Laguna de Planchón	Mataquito	Claro en los Queñes	1929	1919–28	40	−10
Rungue	Rungue	Precipitation data		1959–60	2.28	—
De Casablanca						
Pitama	Estero Pitama			1929–31	2.1	—
Lo Orozco	Estero La Playa			1929–31	5.5	—
Lo Ovalle	Estero Lo Ovalle	Precipitation data		1929–32	13.5	—
Perales de T.	Estero Perales			1930–32	11.6	—
Purísima	Estero El Membrillo			1929–31	2.3	—
Huechún	Estero Chacabuco	Polpaico	1943	1929–32	30	−14
Huelehueico	Bío-Bío			1929–30	5.2	—
Cerrillos	Estero Leyla	Precipitation data		1931–32	3.4	—
Lolol	Estero Lolol			1929–38	6.4	—

Culimo	Quilimarí	Cóndores	1964	1929–35	10	−35
Laguna Invernada	Maule	Cipreses en des.	1941	1954–57	120	13
		Laguna Invernada				
Laguna del Maule	Maule	Laguna del Maule	1952	1946–60	1,430	−6
Lago Laja	Bío-Bío	Laja en Tucapel	1916	1952–54	4,500	36
Lago Pullinque	Valdivia	Uanehue en des.	1961	na–62	4.8	−[0]
		Lago Calafquén				
Lago Puyehue	Bueno	Pilmaiquén bajo	1942	na–1944	0.5	−[0]
		El Salto				
La Paloma	Limarí	Grande en Paloma	1927	1959–67	740	32
Ancoa	Maule	Morro	1953	1955–	103.5	2
Digua	Maule	Cato en Digua	1947	1954–	220	7
Yaso	Maipo	San Gabriel	1929	1953–	250	14
Rapel	Rapel	Corneche	1953	1961–	680	8
Bullileo	Maule	Sta. Filomena	1931	1938–48	60	7

1 Three dates indicate date of beginning, termination, and resumption of collection of data. Two dates indicate date of beginning and termination of collection of data.

2 A negative number indicates that data collection began after construction of the dam was initiated.

Sources: *Rentabilidad de las Obras de Regadío en Explotación Construidas por el Estado*, Ministry of Public Works, Planning Department, June 1963; *Inventario de recursos hidrológicos superficiales de Chile*, Ministry of Public Works, Planning Department, May 1963: *Estudio de la Disponibilidad de Recursos Hidráulicos en Chile*, University of Chile, Planning Center, June 1965; *Anuario Hidrológico de Chile, 1962–1963*, Hydrometeorological Project, United Nations—Government of Chile; *Los Recursos Hidráulicos de Chile*, UN Economic Commission for Latin America, Mexico, 1960. Also consulted for certain data were Enrique García, Chief, Water Resources Section, Irrigation Department, Luis Larroucau, Chief, Development Section, Irrigation Department, Luis Larenas of the same Section, and Andrés Arriagada from Water Resources Section, Empresa Nacional de Electricidad, S.A.

Table 18. Availability of Streamflow Data by Gauge at Time of Construction of Dams in Western United States[1]

Dam and construction period	Area drained by gauge / Area drained by dam						Area of drainage of dam (miles^2)
	1.25	1.25–1.01	1–.76	.75–.51	.50–.26	.25–0	
Elephant Butte 1912–16		23 (1889)	−3 (1915); −4 (1916)		17 (1895)		28,900
Marshall Ford 1937–42		39 (1898)	−3 (1940); 20[2] (1915)				38,130
Caballo 1936–38		−2 (1938)	−2 (1938); 12 (1924)	11 (1925)	36[2] (1896)		30,200
Conchas –40	15 (1909[2]); 5 (1905[2])	2 (1938); 2 (1938)	14 (1915[2]); 17 (1912[2])				7,409
Cascade 1946–48	7 (1922); 37 (1906)		−2 (1948); 5 (1941); 7 (1912[2])			36 (1908[2])	650
Owyhee 1928–32		24 (1890[2])	−1 (1929); −4 (1932)			2 (1926); 9 (1917[2]); 10 (1913[2])	11,160
Anderson Ranch 1944–50	19 (1896[2])	30 (1911)	−4 (1945); −2 (1943)				980
Arrowrock 1911–15		13 (1896[2])	−6 (1945); 0 (1917)			−4 (1915)	2,210
Jackson Lake 1910–11	7 (1903); 0 (1910)		1 (1909); 7 (1903)		0 (1911)		824
American Falls 1925–27		15[2] (1895)	−1 (1926); 19 (1906); 15 (1910)				13,580
Clear Lake 1908–10	4 (1904); 1 (1907)		4 (1904)		−1 (1909)		550
Link River 1921–	17 (1904)		−2 (1923)				3,810
Cle Elum 1931–33	25 (1906)		28 (1903)				203

Table. Stream gauges near selected Bureau of Reclamation dams. (Values shown are the number of years of record relative to the start of dam construction and the year data collection began; superscript 2 indicates interruption in data.)

Dam	Construction period	Gauge records (years relative to construction / year begun)	Area drained by dam (mi²)
(continuation)	1933–42	1938; 1913	—
North and Dry Falls	1949–51; 1946–49	9 / 1938; 34 / 1913	74,100
O'Sullivan	1947–49	11 / 1909²	4,150
Shasta	1938–45	46 / 1892; 0 / 1938; −4 / 1942; 13 / 1925; 18 / 1910; 11 / 1910	6,665
Friant	1939–42	32 / 1907; −2 / 1941	1,633
Granby	1941–50	37 / 1904; 12 / 1907²; −9 / 1950; 22 / 1904	311
Hoover	1931–36	29 / 1902; 14 / 1917; −4 / 1935; −2 / 1933; 9 / 1922	167,800
Theodore Roosevelt	1903–11	−7 / 1910; 5 / 1895²; 15 / 1888	5,830
Davis	1942–50	25 / 1917; 9 / 1933; −8 / 1950; 2 / 1905²	169,300
Buffalo Bill	1905–10	1 / 1897²; 3 / 1902; −5 / 1910; 1 / 1903²	7,340
Seminole	1936–39	31 / 1905; 23 / 1913; −3 / 1939; 29 / 1903²; −3 / 1939	7,340
Pathfinder	1905–9	4 / 1901; 1 / 1904; 2 / 1891²; 4 / 1895; −4 / 1909; 0 / 1905; 2 / 1903	10,700
Lake Tahoe	1909–13	10 / 1895²	519
Lahontan	1911–15	8 / 1899²; 4 / 1907; 0 / 1911; 12 / 1895²	1,450

[1] Gauges are classified by the ratio $\dfrac{\text{area drained by gauge}}{\text{area drained by dam}}$. Gauges with this ratio between 0.76 and 1.25 are defined as close. If the ratio is less than 1, the gauge is upstream of the dam; if over 1, it is downstream. In the case of the Elephant Butte dam, for example, there is a gauge downstream from the dam (the ratio is between 1.01 and 1.25). Twenty-three years of data were available at the time construction of the dam was initiated. Data collection at this gauge was started in 1889. For the same dam, two gauges are at the dam or immediately upstream. Data collection was initiated in 1915 and 1916, three and four years after construction was started on the dam. Data for this table and Table B-3 were compiled by Elizabeth Vogely from U.S. Geological streamflow records and U.S. Bureau of Reclamation reports.

[2] Indicates interruption in data.

Table 19. Availability of Streamflow Data at the Time of Construction in Western United States, for Dams without Data on Areas of Drainage

Dam	Location of gauge	Construction period	Number of years of data available at initiation of construction; and first year of data	Active capacity (1,000 acre-feet)
Boysen	Bighorn River at Thermopolis, 20 miles from Boysen dam	1947–52	42; 1900[1]	560
Tiber	Marias River at Shelby, upstream from reservoir	1952–56	45; 1902[1]	762
	Marias River at Brenkman, about the same distance downstream from Tiber Dam site		29; 1921[1]	
Trinity	Klamath River at mouth	1957–		2,160
	Trinity River at Hooper		26; 1921[1]	
	Trinity River near Lewiston			
Webster	Solomon at Webster	1952–56	28; 1920[1]	259
Hungry Horse	(?) 2 miles above the confluence of the South Fork with the Flathead	1948–53	19; 1929	
Kirwin[2]	Northfork of Solomon River of Kirwin	1952–55	29; 1919[1]	308
	Northfork of Solomon River near Downs		27; 1920[1]	
	Solomon River at Beloit		35; 1895[1]	
	Solomon River at Niles		?; 1897	
Canyon Ferry	?	1949–54	68; 1881	1,615
	?		26; 1923	
	?		11; 1938	
Foss	Foss Dam site[3]	1958–	12; 1936[1]	421
	Washita River at Anadarko		6; 1902[1]	
	Derwood		30; 1928	

[1] Indicates interruption in data.

[2] Indicates data were estimated by correlation with data for nearby streams.

[3] For 1936–48 the flow at the Foss Dam site was estimated as the difference between the measured flow at Clinton gauge and the estimated inflow between Clinton gauge and Foss Dam site.

VII: The Experience of Peru and Chile, and Some Problems of Small Countries

Having in mind the guidelines for managing resource information programs suggested in the preceding chapter, an examination of the experience of Chile and Peru can be instructive. It is always easier to formulate suggestions than to apply them; nevertheless, this examination may help to indicate at least some of the difficulties that may be encountered when a country initiates a program of this type in the expectation that it will stimulate economic development. A final section of the chapter deals with the special problems of small countries.

In the cases of Chile and Peru, our principal interests are in the circumstances in which the two general natural resource information agencies—Instituto de Investigación de Recursos Naturales (IREN) and Oficina Nacional de Evaluación de Recursos Naturales (ONERN)—were born, these agencies' conceptions of their functions, and their accomplishments to date. In each case, the new agency represented an addition to the family of resource information agencies; no agencies were abolished or consolidated to accommodate the new unit. And in each case, the establishment of the new unit was more or less closely associated in time with attempts to institute a more elaborate and institutionalized planning process in the government.

The Experience of Chile

The Project

In May of 1960 Chile was hit by a series of earthquakes, and the Organization of American States sent a mission to study the problem of reconstruction. Out of this study came a recommendation to use aerial photographs and related techniques to map the affected cities and to gather data needed for reconstruction. In 1961 the scope of the project was enlarged to include an elaborate group of studies of the Central Valley and the transverse valleys of the North. The total cost of the project, including the value of contributions in kind by the Chilean government, was about $5.5 million, with $2.5 million of this from Chile, $2.1 million from a twelve-year loan from the International Bank for Reconstruction and

Development, $0.6 million from the OAS, and $0.4 million from Empresa Nacional de Petróleo (ENAP), the Chilean government petroleum organization. The project covered 128,000 square kilometers at an average cost of $43 per square kilometer.

After the conclusion of the project in April 1964, all the materials of the project were delivered to the Corporación de Fomento de la Producción (CORFO). These were taken over by IREN as soon as it was formed a few months later. The Instituto has an advisory committee with members from its parent organization, CORFO, and from the government ministries, the universities, and the private sector.[1]

The economist who has little acquaintance with the disciplines involved may be misled by the technical terms used to describe the product of the Project. It would be easy for him to get the impression that the Project resulted in regional geologic studies of the Central Valley or that it resulted in a soils survey whose results could be used in improving agricultural practice on individual farm properties. It has already been pointed out that this is not the case so far as soils are concerned, and this is indicated by the fact that a large soils survey project is being initiated in the area already covered by the Project. The limited scope of the geological work done is similarly indicated by the fact that the Instituto de Investigaciones Geológicas (the Chilean geological survey) has a project to do a study of the regional geology of the area between Valdivia and Concepción, also included in the Project area.

It is quite difficult to characterize the product of the Project in a way that can convey to the economist something of its limitations as well as its potential uses.[2] We can start by indicating some parts of the Project which are easy to characterize. First are the photos, stereo pairs. The area between Concepción and Chiloé was covered at a scale of 1:50,000 from the ocean to the Argentine border. The Central Valley was covered at 1:20,000 and the transverse valleys at 1:30,000. The eight heavily damaged cities were covered at a scale of 1:10,000.

The photos and the mosaics made from them (1:20,000 in the case of the Central Valley) are available to the public. Large-scale topographic maps (1:2,000) were prepared for the damaged cities. Canals were mapped (i.e. the irrigation network; it can be transferred from overlays to, say, mosaics). Property boundaries were checked, mapped on mosaics, and

[1] See the pamphlet, *Información Básica para el Desarrollo Económico y la Planificación Regional* (IREN, December, 1964).
[2] The *Final Report* of the Project deserves criticism on one other score. It contains almost no cost information. It would be very helpful to all countries if public contracting or lending agencies would require the inclusion of detailed and informative cost data in the final reports of similar projects undertaken in the future.

measured. The 1954 declarations on water rights made to Impuestos Internos were copied onto forms for each district. Flow probability curves were calculated on the basis of available data for nine Central Valley basins for months in the irrigation season. Hydrologic and meteorological stations were located on small-scale maps. Existing climatological and meteorological data were used to produce a number of things, including a map of annual isohyets (1:250,000). A climatic map was prepared (1:1,000,000). Typical cultivation practices, together with periods of vegetation growth, were depicted in five circular graphs for each of five zones in the project area. Finally, a reconnaissance aeromagnetic survey of 70,000 square kilometers was made for ENAP with 1:50,000 isomagnetic maps and some other materials to provide information on the extent of the sedimentary basin, depth of basement, and indications of structures of interest to the searcher for petroleum. The survey was flown at 300 to 500 meters with four kilometer flight lines.

Apart from these products which can be described easily,[3] the soil and geologic work appears to me to have been directed to the goal of classifying land according to its capacity, with this classification to be used in the new system of land taxation. Thus the emphasis was on geomorphology with heavy emphasis on factors directly usable in appraising capacity (e.g., slope) or which would be useful to the soils men (e.g., landform) in attempting to determine soils boundaries. So far as physical information for natural resource development is concerned, the Project did not provide this on a detailed or even semi-detailed level.[4] The characterization often given to the data is that they are useful for a "regional" picture of the resources under study, which means that the data will often be found incorrect for small areas even though they are adequate for larger areas "on the average."

Two important parts of the product of the Project were the delineation on overlays[5] of the land use pattern and the classification of land by capacity. The picture of land use developed in the Project no doubt constituted an improvement over anything that previously had been available.

---

[3] The above list does not pretend to complete coverage, however. It is not completely clear when an item deserves mention as a separate product.

[4] The *Final Report* characterizes its land use maps as "semi-detailed in character," however. See *Final Report of the Proyecto Aerofotogramétrico, OEA/Chile* submitted by the Proyecto Aerofotogramétrico–Chile (made up of four contractors: Aero Service Corp., Fairchild Aerial Surveys, Geotechnics and Resources, and Hunting Survey Corp.) to the OEA, p. 118. Covering letter dated April 2, 1964. Obtainable from Organization of American States, Washington.

[5] An overlay is a transparent sheet of plastic on which are inked the feature(s) in question. The overlay can be superimposed on, say a photomosaic, and a copy made of the combination.

Nevertheless, determination of land use from photographs is difficult if the classification used is detailed, and while one might infer from some of the writings about this and similar projects that almost perfect accuracy can be achieved, a careful reading of the *Final Report* of the Chile Project shows this to be impossible. Indeed, it shows that no estimate of the final accuracy of the assignments to land use classes was made.

The question of accuracy warrants some discussion, in view of its importance to future projects of this type. The *Final Report* indicates that the following steps were used in assessing accuracy:[6]

1. Land use unit areas were assigned to use classes by photo interpretation.[7]

2. A field traverse on roads of about 33 kilometers per mosaic was made on 78 per cent of the mosaics. This distance was about equal to the length plus the width of the land covered by the mosaic.[8]

A check was made along this traverse. The report does not indicate the area that was actually checked, but this area was necessarily much less than the total area covered by the mosaic. A count was made of units initially classified correctly and those incorrectly. The percentage of units correct was the measure of accuracy. This was 84.3 per cent for the entire group checked.

3. Units verified to be classified incorrectly were corrected on the overlays.

What are the implications for the accuracy of the assignments as finally presented on the overlays? The best we can do is to use some illustrative calculations. Assume that a mosaic covers an area 18 × 12 kilometers. A check traverse is made straight down the middle in each direction. Assume that the accuracy of assignment to land use classes can be verified for a distance of one kilometer on each side of the road. Assume that *for the area checked* the percentage of correct assignments is 84.3 per cent, the average for the Project. Assume all errors are detected in the area checked and that they are corrected on the overlays. What percentage of accuracy will the overlay finally have?

If we assume the number of use units per square kilometer is the same in the area of the mosaic not checked as in the area checked and that the original accuracy of assignment was the same in all parts of the mosaic, the answer is that the whole mosaic will have a weighted average accuracy of $c(1.00) + (1 - c)p$ where c is the percentage/100 of the area of the

<hr>

[6] *Final Report*, p. 31.

[7] There was an average of 529 units per mosaic. Mosaics of scale 1:20,000 had 623 units. Mosaics of 1:50,000 and 1:60,000 had 359 units. These are sample averages. See *Final Report*, p. 42.

[8] *Final Report*, p. 39.

mosaic checked and p is the original percentage/100 of accuracy. With our illustrative numbers, c is $\dfrac{2(18 + 12 - 2)}{18 \times 12} = .26$. The final accuracy then .26(1.00) + .74(.843) = .88 for the mosaics checked (78 per cent of the mosaics), but accuracy remains at 84 per cent for those not checked. This provides some indication of what is meant when the data are said to be useful for "regional" purposes, for the original errors remain on $100(1 - c)$ per cent of the area covered by the Project. Twenty-seven per cent of the use units checked had an accuracy below 80 per cent.[9]

According to Ruiz-Tagle P.,[10] a helicopter was used in part of the checking. This would increase the portion of the mosaic checked considerably beyond the 26 per cent of the illustrative calculation and would increase the average of the mosaics checked above the 88 per cent.

The accuracy of the soils investigations was not studied in a similar manner. The problem is considerably more complex, of course. The soils investigations have been characterized by some Chilean experts as of a reconnaissance nature.

The classification of land according to its capacity, as distinguished from present use, made use of the types of information discussed in previous chapters, especially the soils and geomorphological information, with the resulting maps characterized as semi-detailed. Land was classified into eight groups ranging from land suited to cultivation with few limitations on use (Class I) through lands suitable for cultivation but with severe limitations, e.g., susceptibility to erosion or frequent crop damage (Class III), and lands not suitable to cultivation (Classes V to VIII).

The principal use to which the land capacity assignments have been put is in determining the assessed value of land, which is involved mainly in the land tax. Formerly, the assessed value was determined by assessors, with assessments among different owners to be proportional to market value. Under the new system, the quantity of land of a property in each land use category is determined, taking account of irrigation status. The quantity in each class is multiplied by an assigned value per hectare, which values differ from province to province and within a province from *comuna* to *comuna*,[11] although the value for a given class is often the same for a number of *comunas* in a province. The sum of the values thus ob-

[9] Some unknown part of the recorded inaccuracy is apparent rather than real, however, because of changes in land use in the period between the original assignment of a parcel and the check. I should think this would be unimportant. I am indebted to Donald MacPhail, professor of geography at the University of Colorado, for pointing out this possibility.
[10] Executive Director of IREN. Interview of April 18, 1968.
[11] In Chile, a *comuna* is a subdivision of a province.

tained is reduced by percentages which vary with the distance of the property from market and the type of road.[12] The result is intended to be an approximation to market value or at least a constant percentage thereof.

While it is too early for a thorough comparison of the old and new systems to have been made, some things are reasonably clear. First, I have found no Chilean who shows any enthusiasm for the revenue producing adequacy or interpersonal equity of the old system. All the same, it is interesting to note that two experts believe that assessed values have risen to about the same extent for large properties as for small.[13] Note, however, that this is consistent with very different increases for different properties.

The final Project report indicates that the old system functioned reasonably well in several respects:

1. There was good agreement among property owners on the location of property lines.[14]

2. The Project total of agricultural land area was only 3 per cent over that of owner declaration. But note that even if the total of owner declarations of area were correct, individual declarations could still be in substantial error, some too high and some too low, as is the case with the sample page from the Property Register reproduced on page 25 of the *Final Report*.

The scope for complaint by the property owner under the new system is limited to items over which disputes can easily be resolved. He may not complain (i.e. not with the expectation of receiving a personal adjustment) about the unit area value assigned to the different classes of land capacity. He may complain, and has to the extent of a good many thousand, about the area calculated and about misclassification of the capacity of his land. The many complaints in the first year were quite easily resolved, however. Thus, a number of experts[15] feel that taxpayer acceptance of the new

[12] A brief description is contained in Luis Vera, *Agricultural Land Inventory Techniques* (Washington: Pan American Union, 1964). pp. 104 ff.

[13] I am indebted to Srta. Milka Casanegra and Sr. Sergio González for discussions of the Chilean land tax situation.

[14] See p. 26 of *Final Report*. I am somewhat puzzled by the apparent contradiction between this finding and the two sample property sketch maps (one is a pre-Project sketch map of Impuestos Internos and the other a sketch map for the same area prepared during the Project) on p. 51 of Vera. The sketch maps show enormous differences. But these differences between the sketch maps do not necessitate similar differences in declared areas or in assessed values. They may indicate only that the pre-Project sketch maps were badly drawn.

[15] Including the two mentioned in fn. 13 and also Miguel Ruiz-Tagle P., Executive Director of IREN.

system is very good. This is so in spite of the fact that land tax collections in escudos of constant value have risen tremendously. The initial increase appears to have been enough to pay for the total cost of the Project. But some unknown portion of the observed increase could have been obtained without a Project by a major effort to reform property tax administration.

The significance of the apparent taxpayer acceptance of the new system is somewhat clouded by the fact that under the new Agrarian Reform Act, passed July 28, 1967, compensation for expropriated land is set at certain fractions (depending on a complex of circumstances peculiar to each property) of the assessed value. Given this feature of the agrarian reform law, perhaps it would have been possible to have obtained acceptance of a similar increase in assessed values under the old system.

The general outlines of the problem of evaluating a system of land taxation like Chile's may be put in this way. Suppose that there is a consensus that assessed values based on market value will secure interpersonal equity among landholders and that if interpersonal equity is secured, the community will be able to impose tax rates on property which, viewed as part of the whole tax system, will properly express the consensus on the taxation of landholders as compared with others. If the system of direct assessment functions poorly enough, resulting in sizable inequities among landholders,[16] and if the possible rate of improvement in the direct assessment system is low enough, there is a possibility that a system based on a well-executed land capability classification system will come so much closer to a true market value assessment that it will be regarded as producing more equitable assessments among different property holders.

A good test would be possible in Chile if very accurate sales prices could be obtained for a sample of properties. There are difficult problems involved, but they do not appear to be insurmountable. For example, many divisions of properties have taken place recently in Chile in anticipation of possible expropriation. Prices paid in these divisions could be compared with the assessed values for the different parcels.[17]

The result of such a test would be useful to all countries contemplating a similar change in their land tax systems. But the hardest problem is to compare the results of the *actual* direct assessment system against market prices. Since the direct system no longer is in operation in Chile, the comparison will become more and more difficult as time goes on.

---

[16] According to the *Final Report*, p. 27, 2 per cent of the landowners had never paid taxes.
[17] Ruiz-Tagle P. states that he and others who have been in a position to observe these divisions at close hand find the correspondence between assessed values and parcel prices to be quite close (interview of April 18, 1968).

In summary, if the spatial density of reliable transactions prices is not great enough or if other aspects of the direct assessment system are deficient, a system based on land classification may well yield better results on the basis of the market value criterion even though departing substantially from it.

It should be understood, of course, that a well-functioning system of direct assessment could utilize information of the type used in making assignments to the land capability classes of the Project. A good assessment system would start out with a network of actual sales prices and would then use all types of pertinent information on soils, geomorphology, etc. to interpolate or estimate market values for properties that have not changed hands recently. The present Chilean system differs in that sales prices, which are difficult to find out about, are used to determine provincial and *comunal* values rather than as base figures between which values are interpolated for other properties, as in a system of direct assessment.

Although the main application of the results of the Project probably has been to land taxation, the materials have had a variety of other applications, including the planning and programming of agrarian reform activities and of the work of the Instituto de Desarrollo Agropecuario (INDAP) with small farm operators. The land capability and other materials were useful in selecting the location for a sugar beet plant. The mosaics were useful in routing a series of microwave stations, high tension lines, and a pipeline. The property identification data, retrievable from tapes, facilitated the property acquisition work in connection with the high tension lines and pipeline. The customers of IREN have been extremely varied.

IREN

A few months after submission of the *Final Report* of the Project in April 1964, IREN was formed. The basic functions entrusted to it were (1) custody and administration of the product and equipment of the Project; (2) to keep up to date the information gathered by the Project and to assemble similar information for areas of the country not covered by the Project; (3) to present the Project information put on mosaics and overlays in a manner directly usable in preparing "projects of economic development"; and (4) to foster investigations of basic resources and to co-ordinate the work in this field of the various governmental organizations involved.

Since its formation, the work of IREN has indeed fallen under one or other of these functions. With respect to the functions suggested in

Chapter VI for a general resource information agency, IREN's program has a somewhat different emphasis.

In part it is fulfilling these functions. It has compiled a bibliography of extant information on resources. Much of its work is a continuation of analysis and work with the products of the Project such as measurement and tabulation of information present on the overlays, evaluation of susceptibility to erosion, and an inventory of dunes. It has made a preliminary "integrated" study of the natural resources of the provinces of Aysén and Magallanes with an eye to mapping out future study possibilities.[18]

But with respect to two themes emphasized in Chapter VI—the integration of some of the natural resource information personnel into the planning and investment decision process and the co-ordination of natural resource information programs—IREN's emphasis is rather different. Although IREN has made a number of studies at the request of agencies whose duty it is to conceive and design investment projects, the relation of IREN personnel to such activities does not appear to be close. Rather, it appears to conceive its role as one of supplying physical information about natural resources on a less than detailed level, giving assistance in using it, with the using agency proceeding to use it as it sees fit. IREN is, of course, maintaining the cadastral master sheets up to date for Impuestos Internos, which administers the land tax. Recently it has collaborated with the census agency in the preparation of maps showing the distribution of population, and the feasibility of preparing an economic atlas is being discussed with several agencies.

Co-ordination of the natural resource information programs of the different governmental agencies has received little emphasis in IREN's program, but an attempt has been made to assemble information on the different programs.

In describing these aspects of IREN's program, which are well known in Chile but which may be of interest to the governments of other countries, there is no intention of suggesting that IREN's program up to this date should have been different. Indeed, in view of IREN's origin, it was natural that its initial efforts would concentrate on work with the Project materials, an emphasis reflected both in its basic directives and its activities. After all, the agency was only two years old in August 1966, when I was studying its program, and the planning agency (Oficina de Planificación, or ODEPLAN) is even younger than that.

---

[18] A complete list of publications and a description of the work program is available from IREN.

The Experience of Peru

ONERN

Peru's "general natural resource information agency," ONERN, is about the same size as Chile's IREN, each agency employing roughly thirty-five people in a professional or technical capacity. With respect to origin and the nature of their programs, however, the two agencies differ considerably.

ONERN dates from 1962, and was formed in order to keep alive the capability to study natural resources that had been developed in the natural resources program (established in 1961) of El Servicio Cooperativo Interamericano de Fomento. Although ONERN began as part of the Instituto Nacional de Planificación, it has been an independent agency since January 1965.

The focus of ONERN's activities reflects its origin. Its principal function appears to be conceived as the making of integrated studies of natural resources as a part of the process of project development. A number of the studies completed to date had as their purpose the assessment or the development of information relevant to the evaluation of areas for colonization. The elaborate study of a part of the Puno area had a different focus, however, in that the area was already populated.[19]

The studies made by ONERN increasingly have been carried to the point of economic evaluation, and it appears likely that its own capability in economic analysis will become stronger as time goes on.[20]

Those of ONERN's assigned functions that go beyond making integrated studies are quite similar to the functions of its sister agency in Chile:[21]

a) To centralize, complete, maintain up to date, and to disseminate natural resource information.[22]

b) To establish a methodology that will permit feasibility comparisons in different areas of the country.

---

[19] *Programa de Inventario y Evaluación de los Recursos Naturales del Departamento de Puno, Sector de Prioridad I*; ONERN and Corporación de Desarrollo y Promoción Social y Económica del Departamento de Puno (Lima, 1965).

[20] For a recent example of its colonization studies, see *Inventario, Evaluación e Integración de los Recursos Naturales de la Zona del Río Pachitea*, ONERN (Lima, 1966).

[21] While the assigned functions of the two agencies are similar, the origins of the agencies are different. As we have seen, ONERN grew out of integrated survey activities rather closely connected with the development of particular projects. IREN, on the other hand, grew out of the large-scale survey following the 1960 earthquake.

[22] See *Programa . . . de Puno*, p. 15. This source contains a rather complete description of ONERN's program (which I have not tried to describe in full) as does also *Oficina Nacional de Evaluación de Recursos Naturales* (March, 1965), a bulletin of ONERN describing its activities. ONERN's director is José Lizárraga R.

c) To prepare basic documents for use in national planning.
d) To produce information and documents necessary for a rational use of natural resources.
e) To make specific resource studies where needed.[23]

ONERN is also charged with co-ordinating the different types of resource information activity being undertaken in the various parts of the Peruvian government. However, the rather high degree of co-ordination outlined in Chapter VI is not yet being performed, as is also the case with the Chilean agency, IREN.

With respect to the integration of information activities in the planning and investment decision process, ONERN's emphasis on integrated studies aimed at colonization has taken it some distance in this direction, and it appears to have developed working ties with various governmental agencies concerned with natural resource development.

.   .   .   .

Each of the two agencies examined is quite young and has concentrated, in different degrees, on the provision of physical information. Each of them has acted to a large extent as another natural resource agency, albeit of a "general" nature. While their respective modes of operation have, no doubt, been appropriate to their first years of existence, perhaps the future will show the advisability and feasibility of adding the functions discussed earlier and developing closer working ties with user agencies, including both planning agencies and the executive departments. In any case, the experience of these two agencies has provided and will continue to provide many worthwhile lessons for other countries.

Some Reflections on the Problems of Small Countries

Small countries are plagued by many problems that flow directly from the fact of their size, and the field of natural resource information is no exception. The basic problem involves economies of scale in all of its many aspects.

A small country may well find that it is very costly to develop the separate specialized resource information agencies that appear to be desirable in a larger country. In such a case, there are several possible adjustments to be considered. For example, some of the high costs of small-scale operation can be avoided by consolidating some or all of the information activities in one agency. There will be some facilities that can be used in common, and some of the personnel should be able to work in two or even more fields.

[23] Inventories of studies and information available have been prepared for three fields, soils, forests, and geology.

Where a technical capability is needed that goes beyond what the country has been able to develop, several paths are open. One possibility is to purchase the service desired—a satisfactory solution where types of services are involved for which definite specifications can be drawn. Or several countries might consolidate their information activities, using central facilities. This could be done on a permanent basis either through an existing organization or through a new organization more specialized to these purposes. The Common Market organization of Central America is an obvious possibility of the first type.

On a temporary basis, countries, whether they are small or large, would gain from a joint resource information effort where an opportunity for investment involves two or more countries. There should be some saving in cost and a gain in the compatibility of information if some of the technical information activities are jointly planned and jointly carried out.

Another possibility is to use the technical services provided by international organizations, which may find it advisable to devise projects of investigation that will involve more than one nation.

But the availability of these methods for coping with the problem of size still leaves small countries with a serious problem. For so long as a nation is independent, it and nobody else is responsible for its national budget; this is an inescapable implication of independence.

The consequence is that even the small country can not escape asking itself what natural resource information is needed and how it should be used. If the country is to contribute directly to the support of a joint information activity, the necessity of answers to these questions is obvious. From the point of view of the budget officer, the fact that the technical work may not be done by a national agency, but is purchased, is a mere difference of detail.

Even in the case where a resource survey is more or less a gift of another country or of an international agency, these questions retain their importance for the small country. It must still decide what kind of gift it is willing to receive. In most cases it will be able to exert a considerable influence on the type of gift offered—if it is able to articulate its needs effectively.

Although the small country can receive valuable advice in planning resource information activities from the Organization of American States, the Inter American Geodetic Survey, or from the technical aid programs of several large countries, it seems unlikely that outsiders can do better than a competent national in perceiving which projects can develop natural resource information adapted to the country's needs. If the country lacks competent help among its own people, it may end up as the victim of well-intentioned projects that are ill-adapted to its needs. In short, even with the best of advice from outside the country, technically competent nationals are required to set the terms of reference for the advisers and to put the information as finally developed to effective use.

The implication of the foregoing is clear. It is important that a small country develop a small but highly competent capability in the natural resource fields. The people concerned should not be highly specialized but should have a rather broad experience. A few well-trained, competent people are more important to the country than a large number of technicians with lower levels of training and competence. With such a capability, a small country is in a much better position to buy or arrange for outside help.

The need for continuity of service is especially great, a fact that probably reinforces the idea we have been pursuing that foreign personnel can not fulfill this type of function, where the decisions made are close to the mainstream of the governmental process. Yet there is a considerable body of experience that tends to show the feasibility of using foreigners as *advisers* at rather high levels, provided they are willing to make a long-term commitment to the job. The effectiveness of a small number of competent nationals can be increased considerably in this way.

VIII: Summary

This is a study of the problems involved in managing governmental programs that generate information about natural resources. Throughout, these problems are considered in relation to the more general problem of promoting economic development. While natural resource information programs present similar problems in all developing countries, and developed countries as well, they have been considered in a Latin American context. Some lessons are drawn from the experience of particular countries.

To appreciate the nature of the problems under study, let us examine a hypothetical version of a frequently encountered set of views on how to attain rapid economic development of a country's natural resources and, indeed, of the whole country.

In the past, the exploitation of our natural resources has been haphazard, a matter of trial and error. One might even characterize the process as irrational, for is it not obvious that we must know what we are dealing with before the right course of action can be chosen?

Fortunately for us, modern techniques enable us to gather information about natural resources easily and cheaply. There no longer is any excuse for planning the exploitation of resources on the basis of anything less than full information. Therefore, the first item on the agenda is to make a complete and comprehensive inventory of our physical resources.

This advice, superficially so attractive, is impossible to follow, for a complete resource inventory literally cannot be taken. Furthermore, nothing approaching a complete inventory is needed in order to make quite acceptable decisions for the development of natural resources. It might be noted that the Chilean aerophotogrammetric project of a few years ago did not provide anything like the complete information implied in some of the writing about it.

Still, some information is needed. The hard questions are: What types of information? In what areas? In what detail?

Of equal importance is a question that is commonly neglected: How should information-generating and other agencies be organized to work out acceptable answers to these questions and to achieve effective use of natural resource information, once it is available?

Information Is a Type of Investment

If unthinking emphasis on the accumulation of information makes no sense, what view does? Since we are asking how much should be spent on information of various types, and since this outlay yields no immediate flow of satisfaction to consumers but will be used in the production of other goods that do yield satisfaction, it is clear that from the point of view of economic analysis we are dealing with capital. For purposes of economic analysis, natural resources and information about them should be viewed as part of the capital stock of a country. The fact that they are initially a gift of nature and have not been produced makes no difference. Very often a natural resource is not ready to yield productive services, however, until additional work has been done on it, such as ascertaining its characteristics. The natural resource is entirely similar, then, to an unfinished capital good.

Thus the stock of information about natural resources, too, is a part of the stock of capital. Our problem can be described as one of providing some principles or guides for managing this part of the stock of capital we call natural resources: How should the size and composition of this stock of capital be determined? How can the best use of this stock of capital be achieved?

There is nothing novel about viewing information as a type of capital, but non-economists sometimes seem reluctant to do so. Insistence that information is capital points the way to the proper approach to managing natural resource information, namely, to organize natural resource information agencies and activities so that they fit properly into the process by which final investment decisions by government and private businesses are made.

Types of Information

Factual information on natural resources should be distinguished from new information on *how* to produce. It is important to understand what kind of information we are dealing with.

In the theory of production, a production function is thought of as a relation between outputs and inputs. That is, the production function shows how much output per unit time can be had if a certain quantity of inputs per unit time are put together *in a certain way*. Decision on which particular combination of inputs to use requires information on the prices of both outputs and inputs as well as the engineering or technical knowledge expressed in the production function. The firm or producing unit will try to adjust things so as to maximize profits—that is, the value of product minus cost.

It is important to note that a production function reflects a certain *state* of information about production processes. Technological progress consists in a *change* in the stock of this type of information so that for a given set of inputs it becomes possible to get more output. As it is said, the state of the arts has improved. Research, the objective of which is to change the production function in this way, might well be called "high-powered" activity in the sense that all producers will be able to use this information—subject to patent restrictions.

In contrast, it is important to note that outlays on natural resource information derived from survey or inventory activity are *not* outlays that alter the nature of the production function. They do not change the state of the art of "producing" a "finished" natural resource ready to yield productive services. Instead, if we think of the production function for "producing" a copper deposit, outlays in information (geophysical work, drilling, etc.) are simply an input on the same footing as any other. Although the natural resource scientist or technologist may call his information-generating activity "research," it is "low-powered" activity in the sense that the information has significance only for one production unit or a limited area. Research on *new methods* for finding mineral deposits or on new methods of farming has the objective of *changing* production functions, but expenditure on this type of activity is not expenditure to generate natural resource information in the sense used in this study.

The types of information activity with which this study is concerned are of the "survey" type, that is, repeated activities that tend to be performed by specialized agencies. Thus we are concerned with hydrologic and meteorologic data programs, geological mapping and activities related to mineral search, soil surveys, land capability surveys, forest inventories, and the like.

While it is not the purpose of this study to examine techniques or make technical suggestions for the conduct of each of these types of surveys, it is necessary to be aware of the fact that methods of gathering information have changed greatly in recent decades, especially since World War II. In general, the improved methods are associated with a much greater use of aviation, principally through aerial photography, but in some fields through the ability to carry light and sensitive instruments to measure variables which before World War II could be measured only on the ground with heavy and often delicate instrumentation and at great expense.

The availability of these improved methods of gathering information has reduced costs substantially, and in some cases so much so that it is now possible to do things which before were out of reach. The fact that it is *possible* now to gather so much information is in large part the source of the problem we are considering in this study. The possibilities for mis-management—both in allocation of funds and personnel whose produc-tivity may be much greater than is indicated by their salaries—are so great that a careful look at the field is imperative. We need to be clear on what information can be gathered, its significance for economic development, and on how it can best be used to raise income.

Costs

Statements about the cost of generating information are plagued with imprecision. The main difficulty comes in specifying the product, for phrases that sound the same can in fact refer to very different products. For example, a soil map 1:20,000 may refer to a study replete with field operations or to a study with hardly any field check of the guesses of an interpreter of the aerial photographs.

In the cases discussed, the number of factors that affect costs is very large, and they differ greatly from place to place. Consequently, the data represent only a rough impression drawn from an examination of "typical" cost in available estimates.

Aerial Photography

The cost of stereo pairs depends on scale and the size and location of the area to be covered. For the United States, 1:20,000 photography for a sizable area (say 500 square miles) appears to run, say, from $2.50 to $5 or so. An estimate for northern Canada runs a little higher. Costs for Latin America are somewhat higher, perhaps $6–$8 per square mile.

Topographic Mapping

Here, too, cost depends on scale, area to be covered, and type of terrain. 1:20,000 maps might run from $100 to $300 per square mile. 1:250,000 is far less costly, once estimated by FAO at $18–$26 per square mile, in-cluding the cost of ground control. Planimetric maps cost only about a tenth of this.

Regional Geological Studies

There are quite good data for northern Canada, where many thousands of square miles have been surveyed, using helicopter and planes, at field costs (not including staff salaries) ranging from $2 to $3 per square mile for studies on a scale of 1:500,000. Non-field costs ran from 30 per cent to 80 per cent of field costs.

Another reliable source suggests, again for Canada, $2–$4 per square mile for broad geological reconnaissance. Reconnaissance at a scale of 1:250,000 would run $5–$7, not too far out of line with the other Canadian source.

The effect of scale is very great. The same authority suggests that a 1:50,000 geological map would cost $30–$117 per square mile in Canada, a very favorable environment so far as cost is concerned.

Geophysical Surveys

These surveys commonly are flown over only selected portions of larger areas. Magnetic surveys by plane run, say, $6–$20 per linear mile. Electromagnetic surveys are more expensive, running $10–$20 per linear mile by plane. Radioactivity surveys alone cost about the same as magnetic surveys, but are often run simultaneously with other surveys at a quite low additional cost.

Soil Maps

The significance of the scale of a soil map particularly needs clarification. Two dividing lines that seem quite significant are these: Are the data detailed enough and accurate enough to be used for project evaluation? Can the data be used to aid in improving practice on a farm management unit?

One authority estimates that a semi-detailed soil *map*, reported at 1:25,000 and adequate for project evaluation, costs perhaps 40¢ per acre, but a complete survey might be almost a dollar an acre (equal to $640 per square mile).

The same authority suggests that reconnaissance surveys might run around $20 per square mile. A survey at 1:500,000 or 1:1,000,000, showing only broad physiographic terrain units, would be substantially less than this.

Integrated Surveys

A project for the Guayas basin in Ecuador, which is to yield data usable for project planning, estimates cost at $170 per square mile for the whole area initially studied.

The Chilean project mentioned earlier cost about $70 per square mile, but was considerably more in the direction of a reconnaissance survey than the Guayas survey.

Thus, if one thinks of a reconnaissance level survey at 1:250,000, involving photos, topographic maps, regional geology, and soils, the cost might be somewhere around $60 per square mile. A more detailed survey would cost much more.

Principles and Guidelines

Clearly there are no standards that will tell us that so many dollars per acre should be spent on each of the different types of information or that a certain percentage of a country's gross investment should be so spent. But are there any principles that can guide a country in working out the answers to the questions that were posed at the beginning of this chapter? Are there any guidelines? How should activities be organized to generate enough but not too much information?

In general, the suggestions made involve two main points:

1. Make full use of the specialist. He must be constrained, however, to operate effectively within the system by which investment decisions are reached.

2. The goal should be a system in which information programs are continually adjusted in response to the needs and demands of the agencies and private entities that use natural resource information. The extreme to be avoided is investment without information. It is to be expected that the balance of the programs and their content will change as time goes on. There is no point in generating information that is not or can not be used. Hence, information programs must be considered in the context in which the data will be used.

How Much Information?

Consider, first of all, data that develop only with the passage of time, such as hydrologic or climatic data. The basic idea here can be explained best by a very simple model. Suppose it is suddenly realized that an opportunity exists to construct a dam in a certain place. It is assumed that the course of annual revenues and non-construction costs will be the same for all possible dates of construction. If the dam and auxiliary works are made too big, there will be underutilized capacity. If they are too small, then there will be lost opportunity for payoff and, in some circumstances, danger of structural failure and consequent damage. With more data on water availability, a better estimate of optimum size can be made. The question is, how long should construction of the dam be postponed while more data on river flow are being accumulated with the passage of time?

The proper size of the dam depends on the distribution of the annual flow of the river, let us say, on the mean and the dispersion of values for individual years around the mean. If a series of such projects is designed on the basis of samples of, say, three years of data on river flow, in many cases the estimates of the true river flow will be widely off the mark, and the average present value (as of the date of construction) of the whole series of annual receipts minus outlays will be very low, possibly negative.

If each of the series of projects had been planned on the basis of samples of four years of data instead of three, the estimates of the true flow characteristics would be more accurate and the dam and auxiliary facilities would be better adapted to the potentialities of the site. Samples of five years of data would give still better results, and so on.

Suppose samples of eight years will yield an average present value of receipts (or benefits) minus outlays of 100. If construction were postponed another year so that samples of nine can be used, average present value of the investment opportunities would be, say, 114.

To decide whether or not to postpone construction for a year, the increase in present value of 14 must be balanced against the costs associated with postponement. There are two costs. First, there is interest for one year on the 100 that we would have had without postponement. If capital earns 10 per cent per year, this cost will be 10. Second, it costs money to collect data. If this is 3 per year, then the two costs together are 13, less than the increase of 14 in the present value of the opportunity. It would pay to wait for a year.

As soon as the gain from waiting for more data does not exceed the cost associated with postponement, further postponement is undesirable.

It is easy to see that postponing a start is a costly business if the project is very good. It will never pay to wait for "full" information.

Suppose, however, that awareness of the possibility of a project did not strike us like a bolt from the blue. When should we have started collecting data? If demand for the project product has always existed, then the answer clearly is that we should have started collecting data in the remote past and should have constructed the project long ago.

In the real world, however, demand grows, and often from a level at which production does not pay. The simplest case is that in which demand is non-existent up to a certain point in time and then at a certain time comes into being without further growth.

Obviously, the optimum time for construction is at the birth of demand. How many years earlier should the collection of data be begun?

In the former case, one more year of data entailed not only the cost of producing the data but also postponement of the stream of net rents by one year. But here, one more year of data does not cause postponement of the annual series of net receipts, because we are reaching backward to get more data. The only added cost of another year's data is the cost of collecting it, but this cost must be cumulated at the appropriate rate of interest to the date of construction. The gain in present value of the investment opportunity must be balanced against this cost.

Interest cost can be substantial. For example, if the rate of interest is 10 per cent per year, the appropriate multiplicative factor for ten years is $(1 + .10)^{10} = 2.59$.

Where demand is growing through time and the investment opportunity is perceived early enough, both the date of construction and the date at which data collection is started may be chosen freely. The conditions balancing additional gain versus cost in each of the problems just discussed must be met simultaneously.

The development of some types of natural resource data is not rigidly connected with the passage of time. Still, the considerations relevant to problems involving data whose development is time-bound are relevant here, including the cost of data, the period and starting date of data generation, and the date of the start of the project. Data connected with a particular site, e.g., site characteristics needed for detailed design, do not present much of a problem, although project delay remains very important and interest cost is far from negligible even for short periods. Other data may not be connected with a particular production site in that the main use of the data is to eliminate certain areas as not warranting further attention—at the moment. Mineral search data are an example of this. Here the timing of data collection is a matter of great importance, for data collection precedes final production (e.g., in a mine) by many years and must bear interest cost. Selection of area also is of great importance, for without an early test of the wisdom of the selection made, it is all too easy to make unproductive choices.

Data for What Areas?

The emphasis on payoff in the general formulation just discussed implies that additional information on natural resources should be developed for those areas and those resources where there appears to be some prospect of it contributing to the development of viable investment projects. A practical implication for countries that have extensive areas without economic activity is, I believe, that *natural resource information programs should be directed mainly at areas already under exploitation or in bordering unexploited areas.* Although this conclusion may seem surprising, the considerations that support it are quite compelling.

There is a tendency to consider the problem of natural resource information as if there were no information to start with. The task is conceived as one of filling in a *tabula rasa*, after which those parts that are to be studied more intensively are to be chosen from the whole area. We tend to be the victims of an erroneous reconstruction of economic history, evidently supposing that this is the way new lands were developed or that this is the way they ought to be developed. Both these views are wrong.

The context in which the areal allocation of information activity in this day and age is considered is never one of a *tabula rasa*. Instead, the present areal distribution of activity in the natural resource industries is the end result of many years of attempts to extend economic activity to new areas. The fact that present boundaries of economic activity are where they are should remind us that producers, up to this point at least, have encountered an insuperable obstacle to its expansion. Thus, when extension of activity to new regions is being considered, the attitude ought always to be one of skepticism—there probably is something wrong with the area.

Mere distance itself, which receives economic expression as transport cost, insures that the extension of *any* type of economic activity becomes increasingly undesirable the further away it is. For example, rail and port charges sometimes constitute as much as 75 per cent of the cost of ore delivered on board a ship. In the case of the Pine Point lead-zinc development on the south side of Great Slave Lake in Canada, two-thirds of the investment went for transportation.

The advantages flowing from the gradual extension of economic activity embrace more than transport considerations. Gradual extension permits a more intensive use of infrastructure, whereas leapfrogging tends strongly to promote excess capacity.

There are some partial exceptions to this line of argument. Minerals may be valuable enough to stand transport over fairly long distances, but this is not enough to justify indiscriminate search for minerals regardless of locational considerations. The further away the potential area, the better ought to be the preliminary indications.

Hydrologic and meteorologic data programs constitute a partial exception to the generalization that information gathering as well as economic development should proceed step by step. The reason is that data from remote areas, especially in the case of meteorology, may be needed in order to understand—for economic purposes—natural processes that involve large areas and that do not respect man-made frontiers of economic activity. Still, it will be advisable to have a greater density of stations in areas of existing economic activity.

Hydrologic and Meteorologic Data

Stations for hydrologic and meteorologic data should be established well in advance of actual need for the data. The reason for this is obvious, for these data are time-bound. We can have instant coffee and tea, but not instant data in these two fields.

Some extension of hydrologic records by precipitation records or by correlation with nearby stream records is possible, but there must be some actual observations to start with. Some locations for stations will have a much wider significance than others. Their selection will depend on technical considerations and on an assessment of regional economic possibilities.

Integrated Natural Resource Information Studies

To what extent should resource information studies be integrated, that is, several types of data collected simultaneously? The comprehensive inventory idea has already been disposed of as impractical and undesirable, if not impossible. Presumably any attempt at a comprehensive inventory would be an integrated study. But the question remains: What are the circumstances other than a comprehensive inventory in which integrated natural resource studies are desirable?

There are a number of examples of more or less integrated natural resource surveys, the larger ones usually of a more or less reconnaissance nature and the smaller ones sometimes considerably more detailed. Chile, Pakistan, the Walawe Ganga basin in Ceylon, Panama, Nicaragua, the Guayas basin in Ecuador (proposed), and Australia provide examples of such studies.

Advocates of integrated studies stress different reasons for their desirability. Some stress what might be called the unity of nature. That is, natural phenomena of many different types, although they are often investigated in separate compartments, are in fact interrelated. One may think of climate, geomorphology, and vegetation, or of climatic history and mineral deposition. As the argument goes, in all cases we are dealing with a complex system that is in a changing equilibrium with respect to the natural and man-made forces for change that are acting on it. If we propose to alter the balance of these forces, the whole system must be considered if we are to predict and evaluate the outcome. There is undoubtedly something to this argument—at least there are some occasions on which it has much force.

There are some circumstances in which an integrated survey rather clearly would be desirable, meaning by this a survey in which two or more aspects of the natural resources in question are investigated simultaneously. The general principle that seems to cover these cases is that where a project or action is contemplated that will result in a large change from the present pattern of economic activity, the more likely is an integrated study to be desirable.

For example, suppose that the potential investment is lumpy. Or, suppose it has a particular type of lumpiness in that it will have important locational effects on future economic activity. In these cases comprehensive evaluations of the complex investment opportunity are called for, and this means that attention must be paid to the whole gamut of natural resource possibilities.

The development of new lands is one of these cases where evaluation of the investment opportunity requires an across-the-board look at natural resources because all aspects or parts of the opportunity must be evaluated.

Similarly, evaluation of a dam of some size usually will require attention to several aspects of the natural resources involved or affected. There is no necessity to try to decide in advance how much information activity should be devoted to integrated studies. The decision can be made on a case by case basis.

Too much insistence on integrated studies runs the risk of using the time of valuable specialized personnel in integrated studies which could well be of narrower scope. There is no point in integrated studies per se, but only when there are advantages to be gained.

In many cases a project indeed will have aspects that involve several specialties. It does not necessarily follow that an integrated study is necessary, for a "touch-base" or "veto" system may be adequate. That is, a writeup of a proposed project can be circulated to representatives of specialties that are involved only in a minor way. It may be entirely adequate if they are able to say that they do or do not see reason for objection on the basis of available data. An examination of fiascos in the field of natural resource projects probably would reveal many cases where a specialist could have predicted failure on the basis of information already available to him—if he had been consulted and listened to.

Organization of Natural Resource Information Agencies

Should information-gathering units be combined in one large agency? Or should they be attached to agencies that use the data generated? Our main concern is not with the internal organization of each agency but with the effects of organizational structure on relations between agencies and on their performance.

The functions that are involved in this problem, having in mind quite a number of Latin American countries, are these:
   a) a governmental planning unit;
   b) determination of allocation of governmental budget;
   c) determination of the pattern of government investment involving natural resources;
   d) generation of natural resource information.

One organizational option has already been eliminated, namely, a single agency with strong emphasis on integrated surveys. In addition, however, it is the case that certain parts of the natural resource information program are substantially independent of others. This, plus the rather clear advantages of compact professional specialization for most of the information functions, argues for units that are specialized at least to some degree.

One organizational option that certainly would be undesirable would be natural resource information placed off at the side of the mainstream of governmental activity, say in the form of an institute, for without intimate contact with the machinery by which investment decisions are made, the programs of the natural resource agencies will not reflect actual demand for their services nor will effective use be made of the information generated.

Another type of single agency would be that in which essentially separate units, such as topographic mapping, geological survey, etc. are brought within a single agency with only a loose co-ordination or intermingling of activities. If all these units are included, a serious disadvantage is incurred in that certain information-producing activities, notably soil and forest survey, are so intimately connected with operating programs that their location within the operating department is highly desirable. The question is the degree of separability between data generation and data use. For detailed soil and forest survey, the need for close relationship is compelling. For soil survey at the reconnaissance level, the need is far less pressing, as is true also of hydrologic data. Indeed, in a large government there are so many operating agencies eager to generate their own hydrologic data that a separate data agency might be useful simply to impose a desirable unity on the collection of this type of data.

Another option would be to maintain separate information agencies, such as geological survey and topographic mapping, but to place soil and forest survey in the operating department. There might still be a place, however, for a small general natural resources agency. Two South American countries, Chile and Peru, have agencies that fit this description.

What functions might be performed by such an agency? First, it could be the executing agency for such integrated surveys as are undertaken, using either its own personnel or personnel borrowed from the specialized information agencies. Included here would be participation in studies having as their purpose the increasingly accurate assessment of regional potential and demands, so far as natural resources are concerned. Second, it could perform certain tasks of co-ordination. Where more than one agency is generating the same type of data, there may be a number of aspects of their work that need to be harmonized, such as station locations, standards of accuracy, types of data to be collected, and so on. So far as agencies producing *different* kinds of data are concerned, their programs may involve operations in approximately the same areas even though not part of an integrated survey. There may be significant opportunities for saving from joint operation in such places, especially if access to the area is difficult.

Third, the agency could act as a collecting point for information pointing to the coming demands for natural resource information and as the keeper of an inventory of what information is presently available. That is, it would have to be privy to the program plans of executing agencies and the past and current programs of the information agencies, attempting to derive from them implications for new information programs.

With this information at its command and the understanding gained in the process of putting it together, the agency would be in a position to perform a fourth function, namely, of advising the budget authority on the budget and programs of the information-generating agencies. This is a function that surely would be approached very gingerly by a relatively new agency.

Finally, a general natural resource agency could take the lead in arranging the participation of certain individuals from its own ranks and those of specialized information agencies in formulating particular projects or in participating in their evaluation. The goal is not to have every natural resource technician participating in the development of every natural resource project proposal. The goal should be, however, to attain face-to-face contact among some of the members of the three types of agencies, the planning commission, the executing agency, and the resource information agency.

In the case of Latin American countries, the type and scope of planning that will turn out eventually to be useful is still in the process of development and will be for many years to come. However things develop in a particular country, investment decisions involving natural resources will be improved if at least some of the planning personnel have a close and face-to-face working relation with personnel in the operating and the natural resource information agencies. In turn, the programs of these agencies will be better adapted to data demands. The achievement of these goals requires an orientation in all three types of agencies to investment possibilities, which will often be in the form of government projects. What is needed is a flow of project proposals, some very preliminary, some very advanced, but always with estimates of costs and benefits which can serve as the basis for later criticism and reformation. Revision should be the normal expectation, and evaluation by persons outside the government should be encouraged.

Our emphasis on the necessity of integrating the activities of natural resource information agencies into the process by which investment decisions are reached brings with it a couple of corollaries. It tends to call into question the advantages of a large and rapid survey program in a country that does not have the personnel or the procedures to put the data to work. Natural resource data do not make investment decisions by themselves, but require personnel, procedures, and other types of data. While a properly organized, large, short-term project will result in the training of domestic personnel in some of the technical information specialties, it will not train people in the use of these data nor promote the development of a system to do so.

Economic Data

The final guideline is that natural resource data do not speak by themselves but must be joined with other data before they are useful for investment decisions. Just as personnel to use resource data should be developed along with the capabilities of the resource information agencies, so also must the related economic data be developed.

The only way the economic potential of a natural resource can be assessed is to feed the physical data into a calculation of benefits and costs, using relationships between inputs and outputs derived from actual experience or which are closely related thereto. This means that the record of past economic activity is of overwhelming importance, for only by analyzing it can plans be made for the future. Records of inputs and outputs are needed, both in physical and economic terms. The work of improving census data and of making sample studies of the many types of operations in the natural resource industries is of great importance. All types of agencies operating in the natural resources fields, including both information and user agencies, need to make and encourage outsiders to make post-evaluations of their projects. There is an equally great need for studies of private enterprise in these fields, for in many cases it is the private operator who is managing the natural resource in whose development the government may have had a part. Unfortunately, the urge to push ahead on new and bigger projects is so strong that efforts to evaluate the past and to extract its lessons get neglected.

In situations where evaluations of past experience are inadequate to provide reliable predictions of the viability of natural resource projects, what should be done? If reliable evaluations are not at hand, there is no alternative to the accumulation of experience, but this need not mean an indefinite wait. One possibility is to make extensive use of an *in situ* research or trial runs. For example, the record of colonization projects in South America is said to be strewn with failures, although the extent of the failures and the reasons therefor usually are not known for lack of proper post-evaluation. Certainly, a part of these failures could have been avoided by *in situ* research designed to verify the feasibility of the type of production planned in that particular location. It is easy to assemble an impressive list of authorities who are united in this view.

Not all *fracasos* can be avoided in this manner, however. The reason is that in many cases the conditions under which a pilot run is made differ significantly from those under which the project will operate. For example, the employees of an agricultural research organization, doing a test run on the suitability of an area for colonization, may differ in important ways from the colonist who will come later with respect to general education, technical training, work habits, and so on.

There is still another possible aid, however, namely, to try to design projects that are divisible. In this way, a small commitment of funds can be made and the results evaluated before proceeding to larger commitments. If divisible projects can be designed, they almost become self-evaluating. The risk of large-scale failure poses no threat where this course of action is possible and where it is followed.

Would the history of the groundnuts scheme in East Africa have been different if this procedure had been followed? Almost certainly. The application of this strategy to such gigantic projects as the Carretera Marginal de la Selva on the east side of the Andes and "settling the Amazon basin" is clear.

Selected Bibliography

American Society of Photogrammetry. *Manual of Photogrammetry*. Washington, 1952.
———. *Manual of Photographic Interpretation*. Washington, 1960.
Beard, Leo R. *Statistical Methods in Hydrology*. Sacramento: U.S. Army Corps of Engineers, January 1962.
Brown, Leslie H. "An Assessment of Some Development Schemes in Africa in the Light of Human Needs and the Environment," in *The Ecology of Man in the Tropical Environment*. Morges, Switzerland, 1964.
Canada, Geological Survey of. Department of Mines and Technical Survey. *Helicopter Operations of the Geological Survey of Canada*, Bulletin 54. Ottawa: Queen's Printer, 1959.
Chow, Ven Te. "Sequential Generation of Hydrologic Information," in *Handbook of Applied Hydrology*. New York: McGraw-Hill, 1964.
———. "Statistical and Probability Analysis of Hydrologic Data," in *ibid.*
Clawson, Marion, with Charles L. Stewart. *Land Use Information*. Washington: Resources for the Future, Inc., 1965.
Davidson, D. M. *Economics of Geologic Exploration*. Preprint No. 5819A3. New York: American Institute of Mining and Metallurgical Engineers.
Economic Commission for Latin America. "Los Recursos Hidroeléctricos en América Latina: Su Medición y Aprovechamiento," *Boletín Económico de América Latina*. Santiago, February 1962.
———. *Los Recursos Naturales de América Latina: Parte I, Los Recursos Minerales y parte V, Los Suelos*. Santiago, 1963, mimeo.
———. *Los Recursos Naturales en América Latina, Su Conocimiento Actual e Investigaciones Necesarias en Este Campo*. General E/CN.12/670. Conference at Mar del Plata, Argentina, April 20, 1963. Santiago.
———. "Los Recursos Hidraúlicos del Perú." Santiago, December 1965.
Fahr, Samuel. *The Use of Aerial Photographs in Land Title Registration in Peru*. Misión Iowa. Ames: Iowa State University, August 6, 1965, hectograph.
Fiering, Myron B. *Streamflow Synthesis*. Cambridge: Harvard University Press, 1967.
Giret, Raoul, and Leon Bouvier. *L'Inventaire des Ressources Minerales; Methodes Permettant de le Realiser*. Paris: Compagnie Général de Géophysique, apparently 1960.

Holmes, Olive. *Peoples, Politics, and Peanuts in Eastern Africa.* New York: Foreign Policy Association, December 1, 1950.

Instituto Latinoamericano de Planificación Económica y Social. *Algunos Aspectos de la Investigación y Explotación de Recursos Naturales en América Latina Relacionados con la Planificación Económica, Parte I,* by Estevam Strauss (July 1965), mimeo. (also in English). Santiago.

————. *Recursos Naturales y Planificación Económica en América Latina, Parte II,* by Estevam Strauss (November 1965), mimeo. Santiago.

————. "Los Recursos Naturales en la Integración Latinoamericana," by Carlos Plaza V. October 1966. Mimeo.

IREN (Instituto de Investigación de Recursos Naturales, formerly Proyecto Aerofotogramétrico-Chile). *Final Report of the Proyecto Aerofotogramétrico, OEA/Chile.* (Submitted to the OAS, April 2, 1964.) Washington: Organization of American States.

————. *Información Básica para el Desarrollo Económico y la Planificación Regional.* Santiago, December 1964.

————. *Informaciones Meteorológicas y Climáticas para la Determinación de la Capacidad de Uso de la Tierra.* Santiago, 1964.

————. *Inventario de Dunas en Chile, zona 29°48'–41°50' Latitud Sur.* Santiago, 1964.

————. *Evaluación de la Erosión.* Santiago, August 1965.

————. "Encuestas Instituciones Que Investigan en Recursos Naturales" (preliminary version). Santiago, 1966.

————. *Potencialidad Agrícola de Tarapacá a Llanquihue Según Estraficicación de Predios por Avalúo y Superficie.* Santiago, 1967.

Kelly, Sherwin F. "The Pillars of Our Prosperity and the Impending Drain on Mineral Resources." Reprinted from *Western Miner and Oil Review.* Vancouver, B.C.: Western Miner Press, October 1960.

Laitman, Leon. "El Desarrollo de Datos Sobre Recursos Naturales para la Planificación Económica. Un Método Integral," in *Temas Geográficos-Económicos.* (Proceedings of Unión Geográfica Internacional, Conferencia Regional Latinoamericana, Vol. II.) Mexico City: Sociedad Mexicana de Geografía y Estadística, 1966.

Leicester, P. "Organization of Exploration," in *Techniques of Petroleum Development.* New York: United Nations, 1964.

Lliboutry, Luis. *Nieves y Glaciares de Chile.* Santiago: Ediciones de la Universidad de Chile, 1956.

Lowman, Paul D., Jr. *A Review of Photography of the Earth from Sounding Rockets and Satellites.* Greenbelt, Md.: National Aeronautics and Space Administration, Goddard Space Flight Center, August 1964.

Marsh, George Perkins. *Man and Nature, or, Physical Geography as Modified by Human Action.* Cambridge: Harvard University Press, 1965.

National Academy of Sciences. *Space Applications, Summer Study 1967, Interim Report*, Vol. I. Washington: U.S. Government Printing Office, 1968.

ONERN (Oficina Nacional de Devaluación de Recursos Naturales). *Programa de Inventario y Evaluación de los Recursos Naturales del Departamento de Puno, Sector de Prioridad* I, Volumenes 1–6. Lima: ONERN and Corporación de Desarrollo y Promoción Social y Económica del Departamento de Puno, 1965.

————. *Inventario, Evaluación e Integración de los Recursos Naturales de la Zona del Río Pachitea.* Lima, 1966.

————. *La Cartografía en el Perú.* Lima, February 1966.

————. *Oficina Nacional de Evaluación de Recursos Naturales* (a bulletin of ONERN describing its activities). Lima, March 1967.

Paddock, William and Paul. *Hungry Nations.* Boston: Little, Brown, 1964.

Pan American Union. *Inventory of Information Basic to the Planning of Agricultural Development in Latin America.* Selected Bibliography (1964), Regional Report (1963), and volumes for the various countries. Washington.

————. *Agricultural Land Inventory Techniques*, by Luis Vera. Washington, 1964.

————. *Annotated Index of Aerial Photographic Coverage and Mapping of Topography and Natural Resources.* (Published for the various countries by OAS during or after 1964.) Washington: Organization of American States.

————. Department of Economic Affairs. *Survey for the Development of the Guayas River Basin of Ecuador, An Integrated Natural Resources Evaluation.* Washington, 1964.

Phillips, John. *The Development of Agriculture and Forestry in the Tropics.* London: Faber and Faber, 1961.

Stamp, L. Dudley. *Our Developing World.* London: Faber and Faber, 1960.

UNESCO. *Informe Sobre Clima y Meteorología de Sudamérica*, by Alberto Martinez. Conf. Doc. UNESCO/CASTALA/2.1.1. II.1. (n.d.)

————. *Forestry Requirements in Integrated Surveys*, by D. A. Stellingwerf. Paper given at Toulouse Conference on Principles and Methods of Integrating Aerial Survey Studies of Natural Resources for Potential Development. Paris, 1964.

————. *Aerial Photographs and Soil Sciences*, by A. P. A. Vink. Paper presented at Toulouse Conference. Paris, February 28, 1964. Doc. No. UNESCO/NS/90.

————. *Methodology of Integrated Surveys*, by C. S. Christian and G. A. Stewart. Paper given at Toulouse Conference. Paris, April 17, 1964. Doc. No. UNESCO/NS/NR/94.

————. *The Soil Resources of Latin America.* UNESCO and ECLA Conference on the Application of Science and Technology to the Development of Latin America. Paris, 1965, mimeo.

————. *La Experiencia Recogida en Las Actividades de Las Naciones Unidas en América Latina en Cuanto a Recursos Naturales por la División de Recursos Naturales y Transportes del Departamento de Asuntos Económicos y Sociales de las Naciones Unidas.* Paris, August 13, 1965. Doc. No. UNESCO/CASTALA/ 2.1.8.

———. *Recursos Florísticos Forestales y Forrajeros de Mexico y Centroamérica,* by Efraim Hernández Xolocotzi. Paris, 1965. Doc. No. UNESCO/CASTALA 2.1.2. VII, 3.

———. *Aspectos Principales del Tema Recursos Naturales y su Utilización.* Paris, September 8, 1965. Doc. No. UNESCO/CASTALA/2.1.1.

United Kingdom. Minister of Food. *A Plan for the Mechanized Production of Groundnuts in East and Central Africa.* (Presented to Parliament by Command of His Majesty, February 1947.) London: H.M.S.O., Cmd. 7030.

———. ———. *East African Groundnuts Scheme, Review of Progress to the End of November, 1947.* (Presented to Parliament by Command of His Majesty, January 1948.) London: H.M.S.O., Cmd. 7314.

United Nations. *Proceedings of the United Nations Seminar on Aerial Survey Methods and Equipment.* (Mineral Resources Development Series No. 12.) Bangkok, 1960.

———. *Hydrologic Networks and Methods.* Flood Control Series No. 15. Transactions of Interregional Seminar on Hydrologic Networks and Methods, held at Bangkok, Thailand, July 14–27, 1959. Bangkok: ECAFE, World Meteorological Organization, 1960.

———. "Aerogeophysics and Its Role in Mineral Exploration," by L. W. Morley. UN Conference on the Application of Science and Technology for the benefit of the Less Developed Areas. New York, October 10, 1962. Doc. No. E/CONF. 39/A/100.

———. *Proceedings of the Seminar on Geochemical Prospecting Methods and Techniques* (Mineral Resources Development Series No. 21). New York, 1963.

———. *U.S. Papers Prepared for the UN Conference on the Application of Science and Technology for the Benefit of the Less Developed Areas. Natural Resources,* Vol. II. Washington: U.S. Government Printing Office, 1963.

———. *Techniques of Petroleum Development.* New York, 1964.

———. *Manual of Standards and Criteria for Planning Water Resource Projects.* New York, 1964.

———. *Los Recursos Hidraúlicos de América Latina: III, Bolivia y Colombia.* New York, 1964.

U.S. Army. *Survey of Data Needs of User Agencies.* (Study prepared for the Oficina de Planificación de Nicaragua and the USAID Mission to Nicaragua.) Fort Clayton, Canal Zone: Inter American Geodetic Survey, Natural Resources Division, April 1966.

U.S. Department of Agriculture. *Contracting for Forest Aerial Photography in the United States,* by Gene Avery and Merle P. Meyer. Station Paper No. 96. St. Paul, Minn.: Lake States Forest Experiment Station, March 1962.

————. Soil Survey Staff. *Soil Survey Manual.* Agricultural Handbook No. 18. Washington: U.S. Government Printing Office, 1962.

U.S. Department of the Interior, Geological Survey. *Aerial Photographs in Geologic Interpretation and Mapping.* Professional Paper 373. Washington: U.S. Government Printing Office, 1960.

————. *Botanical Evidence of Floods and Flood-Plain Deposition.* Professional Paper 485–A. Washington: U.S. Government Printing Office, 1964.

U.S. Department of State. *Aspects of Frontier Settlement in Northern Brazil,* Supplement I. (Report of Interagency Reconnaissance Team.) Washington: Agency for International Development, June 1964, mimeo.

————. *Feasibility Studies, Economic and Technical Soundness Analysis, Capital Projects.* Washington: Agency for International Development, Office of Engineering, October 1, 1964.

Villarroel, René, and Heinrich Horn. *Rentabilidad de las Obras de Regadío en Explotación Construidas por el Estado.* Santiago: Dirección de Planeamiento del Ministerio de Obras Públicas, 1963.

Willow Run Laboratories, Infrared and Optical Sensor Laboratory. *Peaceful Uses of Earth-Observation Spacecraft.* Vol. I: *Introduction and Summary,* Vol. II: *Survey of Applications and Benefits,* and Vol. III: *Sensor Requirements and Experiments.* Ann Arbor: University of Michigan, 1966.

JOURNAL ARTICLES

Allais, M. "Method of Appraising Economic Prospects of Mining Exploration Over Large Territories," *Management Science,* Vol. 3, No. 4 (July 1957).

Barraclough, Solon, and Arthur L. Domike. "La Estructura Agraria en Siete Países de América Latina," *El Trimestre Económico* (Mexico City), Vol. 33 (2), No. 130 (April–June 1966).

Christodoulou, D. "La Colonización de Tierras: Algunos Aspectos Fundamentales que Suelen Descuidarse," *Boletín Mensual de Economía y Estadística Agrícolas* (FAO), Vol. 14, No. 10 (October 1965).

Engineering and Mining Journal, Vol. 157, No. 6a (Mid-June 1956).

Goodman, Marjorie Smith. "Criteria for the Identification of Types of Farming on Aerial Photographs," *Photogrammetric Engineering,* Vol. 30. No. 6 (November 1964).

Griffiths, John C. "Exploration for Natural Resources," *Operations Research,* Vol. 14, No. 2 (March–April 1966).

Pemberton, Roger H. "Airborne Electromagnetics in Review," *Geophysics,* Vol. 27, No. 5 (October 1962).

Penrose, Edith Tilton. "A Great African Project," *Scientific Monthly,* Vol. 66, No. 4 (April 1948).

Peters, William C. "Cost of Exploration for Mineral Raw Materials," *Cost Engineering* (July 1959).

Pryor, William T. "Evaluation of Aerial Photography and Mapping in Highway Development," *Photogrammetric Engineering*, Vol. 30, No. 1 (January 1964).

Stewart, R. A. "Aerotriangulation Procedures for National Mapping of Canada," *Photogrammetric Engineering*, Vol. 30, No. 1 (January 1964).

Wright, Marshall S., Jr. "What Does Photogrammetric Mapping Really Cost?", *Photogrammetric Engineering*, Vol. 26, No. 3 (June 1960).

Index

Aerial photography, 23–26, 29, 133, 173; accuracy, 23, 27n; Andes, 56; Latin America, 76, 77; soil surveys, 38, 40, 41; stereoscopic coverage, 25, 57, 58, 59, 189. *See also* Chile; Forest surveys; Geological maps; Photographic interpretation

Africa, 78. *See also* East African Groundnuts Scheme

Agocs, W. B., 34n, 70, 71n

Agrarian Reform Act (Chile), 179

Agricultural surveys: aerial mapping, 28; UN Special Fund surveys, 85, 90, 92, 93; vegetation surveys, 35. *See also* Soil surveys

Allais, M., 49n, 54

Argentina: hydrologic gauges, 80, 81; per cent already mapped, 76; UN Special Fund surveys, 87, 90, 91, 92, 93

Arriagada, Andrés, 169n

Australia: integrated survey, 73, 74, 195; topographic map coverage, 78

Avery, Gene, 56n, 59n

Barraclough, Solon, 129

Beard, Leo R., 113n

Benelux, 78

Bolivia: Beni River project, 131; coverage by hydrologic gauges, 80, 81; mineral surveys, 87, 88; per cent already mapped, 76

Boon, D. A., 44n, 45n

Börgel O., Reynaldo, 83n

Bouvier, Leon, 33n

Brazil: hydrologic gauges, 80, 81; per cent already mapped, 76; settlement possibilities, 39–40, 44, 163; UN Special Fund surveys, 89, 90, 91, 92

Brown, Leslie H., 163n

Buck, W. Keith: aerial mapping costs, 58, 59n, 63n, 69n

Budget authority. *See* Resource agencies

Buringh, P.: soil surveys, 38, 41, 43, 64, 65, 68

Cadastral surveys, 43

Canada: aerial mapping costs, 58, 189; geochemical survey, 69; geological surveys, 34, 62, 127, costs of, 61, 189–190; topographic map coverage, 78

Caribbean area: UN Special Fund survey, 89. *See also* under names of individual countries

Carretera Marginal de la Selva (Andes), 163, 200

Casanegra, Milka, 178n

Central America: topographic map coverage, 78; UN Special Fund surveys, 88, 89. *See also* under names of individual countries

Ceylon, 130, 195

Chile: aerophotogrammetric project, 42, 43, 134, 144, 148, 173–80, 186, costs of, 72, 190, 195; colonization areas, 132n; hydrologic gauges, 80, 81; IREN, 155, 180–81; per cent surface already mapped, 76; soil surveys, 89, 145; streamflow data, 112, 142, 144, 168–69; UN Special Fund surveys, 85, 86, 87, 90, 93

Chow, Ven Te, 113, 120n, 140n

Christian, C. S., 73, 159

Christodoulou, D., 128

Clawson, Marion, 146n

Climatological information, 94, 98

Colombia: hydrologic gauges, 80, 81; per cent already mapped, 76; UN Special Fund surveys, 86, 88, 89

Colonization: evaluation of possibilities, 39, 129, 199; health problems, 129–30; new regions, 128, 150; Peru, 93, 183

Columbia River basin (U.S.), 80n

Designed by James C. Wageman

Composed in Times Roman and Optima Semibold by
Monotype Composition Company

Printed offset by Universal Lithographers, Inc.,
on 60 lb. P & S, R

Bound by L. H. Jenkins, Inc., in Holliston Roxite Fabriqué